STARTLINE

MORAL EDUCATION IN THE MIDDLE YEARS

Startline is the published material of the Schools Council Moral Education 8–13 Project which was set up at the University of Cambridge in 1972.

Project Director: Peter McPhail

Project team: Jasper Ungoed-Thomas 1972–75
David Ingram 1973–76
David Middleton 1973–76
Caroline Rennie 1973–75
Charlotte Bird 1973–76
Peter Hudson 1975–76

The *Startline* material includes:
Photoplay 1
Photoplay 2
Choosing Books 1–6
Growing
How it happens
Making it happen
Setting the scene
Moral education in the middle years (Teacher's book)

STARTLINE
Schools Council Moral Education 8–13 Project

Peter McPhail
David Middleton
David Ingram

Moral education in the middle years

Published by Longman for the Schools Council

Although this book is the work of the whole Project team, various sections were the responsibility of one author as follows:

Peter McPhail: Introduction, Chapters 1, 2, 8, the Postscript and Appendices E and K.

David Middleton: Chapters 3 and 4 and Appendices F, G, H and I.

David Ingram: Chapter 5 and Appendix J.

Other chapters were written cooperatively; thanks are due to John Sutcliffe for his contribution to Chapter 9.

LONGMAN GROUP LIMITED
London
*Associated companies, branches and representatives
throughout the world*

© Schools Council Publications 1978

First published 1978
ISBN 0 582 21486 6

*Printed in Great Britain by
Whitstable Litho Ltd., Whitstable, Kent*

Contents

Introduction

Schools have moral influence. They can instil attitudes, standards and principles which influence for life individuals' treatment of themselves, others, and their whole environment. Furthermore these attitudes, standards and principles are not always the ones which the members of a school staff intend to establish if they have a conscious moral purpose.

We know that the school's moral influence, like that of the home, can be destructive. Dickens, in *Nicholas Nickleby*, introduced the sadism and cynicism of Dotheboys Hall with this sanctimonious dialogue:

'I should wish their morals to be particularly attended to,' said Mr Snawley.

'I am glad of that, sir,' replied the schoolmaster, drawing himself up. 'They have come to the right shop for morals, sir.'

'You are a moral man yourself,' said Mr Snawley.

'I rather believe I am, sir,' replied Squeers.

'I have the satisfaction to know you are, sir,' said Mr Snawley. 'I asked one of your references, and he said you were pious.'

'Well, sir, I hope I am a little in that line,' replied Squeers.

The message is clear. What is said about moral education and what is practised may have little in common, and the practice is everything for the children. How can we resolve this contradiction? The belief that teachers can concentrate on teaching their subjects and avoid the moral dimension is an illusion. The impartial school, which represents an ideal for some, is unobtainable in practice. All communications, verbal and non-verbal, are value-laden and even the voluntary absence of communication expresses a value position – tells

I

people how you value them. In the 'just' school, an ideal for others, children may need love and care more than justice.

Those who care look for greater understanding of our influence on one another and more honesty about it. But we can only understand and be honest if we recognise the process by which moral learning takes place. We must understand the 'how' as well as the 'why' if we are to be morally effective. This is our reason for concentrating research on the identification of children's needs and what happens when they are, or are not, met. The work has been concerned with clarifying the way in which children learn to behave, i.e. to treat themselves, others and their total environment – the way in which individuals are moved, disposed or inclined to act.

We identify moral learning process in two principal ways. First, we relate children's descriptions of the experiences which are important to them to observations of their behaviour in, and subsequent to, those experiences. Secondly, we refine our understanding by considering the children's answers to specific questions about what they did subsequent to the significant situations.

This is exciting work because, if you are able to identify moral learning process, you have the means to improve every facet of life.

We believe in the validity of the picture of pre-adolescent and adolescent social learning which has emerged from this work. However, we are aware that we have not been funded to undertake the longitudinal study which could continuously increase our grasp on what happens and why. This makes the extensive presentation of the 8–13 Project's research method and data of first importance. The Project's research report,[1] materials and parts of this book include descriptions of children's experiences in their own words and pictures and offer a base on which to build. Our continuing concern is to encourage others to extend their understanding by investigating the experiences and behaviour of the children with whom they live and work and to respond positively to the human needs they discover.

We all bear the responsibility of applying whatever learning understanding we have to increase consideration and responsibility in the home, in the street and in the school. As well as writing this book the team has prepared and presented curriculum materials approaches and techniques. However, whereas valid curriculum approaches may have lasting value, the long-term outcome will depend on whether individuals apply their own understanding of social learning to their day-to-day relations with the young, as well as to the production and development of teaching materials and techniques. Long-term effect will depend on long-term commitment. We need to exchange the current preoccupation with statements about goodness (which are apparently so prestigious) and uncommitted criticism (which is so safe) for a commitment to action.

This book is for all those who live and work with children between the ages of eight and thirteen. In it we have attempted to avoid the use of jargon and the discussion of theory of doubtful relevance. Where there is theory it is derived from work with almost 4,000 children.

As our interest is practical we are sympathetic to William James when he encouraged people to turn

away from abstraction and insufficiency, from verbal solutions, from bad *a priori* reasons, from fixed principles, closed systems, and pretended absolutes and origins . . . towards concreteness and adequacy towards facts, towards action and towards power.[2]

Theory is for use, and the best test of moral learning theory is what happens when you apply it. When we have an affirmative answer to the question 'Is our proposed action as good as we can make it?', we have to look at the answer to the question 'What happens when we try it?'. We recognise the interest and value of work on the verbal analysis of moral statements and on the logical nature of moral decision, while being not in the least hostile to attempts to establish a developmental progression in stages of moral reasoning, whatever we may think individually of specific theories of this kind. However, our work, with its emphasis on motivation and individuals' actual treatment of one another, has a very different focus. Our concern is the practical one that people shall express in action their concern for others' needs, feelings and interests. We know that, whatever moral principles or procedures people advocate, and whatever stage of moral reasoning they may lay claim to, in the final analysis, to act morally, everyone has to be concerned with (and sensitive to) real-life situations. To implement, at a specific time and in a

3

particular place, decisions which represent the best of which we are capable means that we may have to abandon the unreal 'absolute right answer' which can survive only in the sterility of theory. What we offer is not a closed prescriptive system but an approach for people to try, to develop and to improve.

It is not easy for any of us to accept and apply an increased understanding of moral learning. Such understanding leads us all to question our own behaviour and even to doubt the validity of approaches we have used for years. The emotional impact and consequently our resistance to change are very powerful and the attractions of concentrating on a theoretical concern are obvious: We understand better why Christ was abandoned by his friends. Nevertheless, if we are able to review our practice with humanity, humour and the support of others who care, the rewards will be far greater than the effort we have made.

References

1. Ungoed-Thomas, J. R., 1978. *The Moral Situation of Children,* Schools Council.
2. James, W., 1917. 'What pragmatism means', in *Selected Papers on Philosophy*, p. 202, para 3, Dent Everyman.

1 8–13: The age of dependence and play

In the Introduction we committed ourselves to action rather than theory, but what does this mean in practice? It means that our central concern is behaviour and more specifically individuals' treatment of others. Our aim is not to develop a theory of moral behaviour, nor to increase children's capacity to argue morally, nor to improve their ability to say 'good things'. It is the practice of doing good things, of actually taking another's needs, feelings and interests into consideration as well as one's own, which concerns us first and foremost. Our purpose is to help children not only to know what 'love in action' is, but also to act in love, in affection – to act warmly and caringly. To those in teaching and other walks of life who have committed their lives to this practical aim we dedicate our work in the hope that it will be a support to them. To those who say that the primacy of 'love in action' is obvious and needs no research or argument to support it we can only point to what remains to be done in education and life generally to increase understanding of these things, to identify 'love in action', and to create the climate for concern.

The importance of understanding how children learn their behaviour

It is essential for a moral education approach which works through the whole life of home, school and community, as well as by the use of curriculum, materials and techniques, that it be based on a clear understanding of how moral behaviour is learned. To act effectively and understand the moral implications of your own actions as a parent, teacher or other involved adult you must know what it is that moves the child to treat others with affection and care, and what the effects of such action are on the interests of that child, i.e. on his quality of life.

Direct learning of behaviour from the way in which you are treated

The evidence of all our work is unequivocal. Children take pleasure in being treated with care and warmth; their prime source of happiness is being treated in this way. Further, when children are supported by such treatment they enjoy treating people, animals and even inanimate objects in the same way. Such a style enhances their quality of life more than anything else. We sometimes do not recognise this because man in his insecurity – a product of the misidentification of human need, competitiveness and lack of love – loses sight of the fact that morality is basically about respecting and caring for all things. Fearful, he is side-tracked in an obsession with formal moral structure expressed in rules, in law, in the 'thou shalts' and, less creatively, the 'thou shalt nots', evolved by particular societies to protect the rights and contain the dominant insecurities of individuals in those societies at specific periods in their history. He substitutes a seige mentality for faith in humanity and with it growth becomes impossible.

We know that the moral challenge in our complex interdependent society is how to help an individual show consideration for one person's needs without denying another. The law and 'the rule of law' may seem at first to provide an easy solution to this dilemma. However, the rule of law only guarantees a stage in human progress because the very impersonal quality of law which at first seems to guarantee its impartiality, its fairness, always grants the word and established practice priority over individual need. For the legalistic person, the fear is of losing what we have, what we have built up, when we should be progressing to new, fuller, more sophisticated ways of developing our love and concern.

The question is whether faith in man and optimism or fear and anxiety are to triumph. 'Faith', in this context, means believing that individuals have sufficient need of each other and concern for each other to make it possible for us, if we do the right things, to build a more caring and happier society than we have at present. 'Faith' does not mean a bland belief in inevitable improvement any more than 'caring', as applied here to society, means encouraging dependence by doing everything for people.

We can have faith while believing that some social changes, for example growth in population beyond a certain point, may make the positive development of relations so difficult that they call for responsible action. Indeed we only believe in man if we believe in his capacity to make decisions and to act for change.

However, we must be realistic in admitting that, although we have natural support in working for greater consideration, it is possible to 'educate' young children through fear, anxiety and a sense of threat to individual and collective inconsiderate and destructive behaviour. We also know that children will not be saved from being 'educated' in such a destructive style by any inevitable or schooled progression in their moral understanding or reason alone. It is only partially true that individuals can break away from a destructive life-style. The possibility may be very little more than theoretical. They need support and encouragement. They need love to do so as well as reason. Sometimes we, as parents, teachers or friends, work very hard for small returns in concern, and may fail to make any choice real if the emotional pressures on a child are great enough. Nevertheless, apart from the fact that we have a moral obligation always to do what we can to help children to a fuller and more responsible life, it is our experience that in the vast majority of cases we can do a great deal to increase the individual's expressed respect for others and for himself.

How do children between the ages of eight and thirteen learn their behaviour, i.e. their treatment of people, animals, and their total environment? The basic, most eloquent, most enduring form of education is the treatment we receive rather than information, reasoning, argument or appeal. At every age the way in which we are treated has an effect on our treatment of others, but this is especially true in childhood before a style of behaviour towards others is established. The fundamental social, moral, learning process is that in childhood we learn our behaviour towards others from their behaviour towards us. We learn particularly from treatment at the hands of those closest to us, those most important to our survival, security and wellbeing, generally our parents or their substitutes. To say this is not to relapse into fatalism because we can learn what good treatment of children is and we are able to treat them better. Rather it is to admit honestly what we all know from experience – that we are moved to love and care for others by being loved and cared for. A powerful though secondary influence is the treatment we observe being meted out to other members of the family or group and how this compares with what is happening to us.

The difficulty of accepting the direct influence of treatment

As was suggested in the Introduction, to accept this situation demands a maturity which we do not always possess, and when we inherit the legacy of bad relations or, even more disturbing, realise that we have not treated others well, we may reject the theory of direct influence. It is too much for us. The responsibility is too great and we prefer to argue for moral maturation or the development of moral reason independent of interpersonal influence. It is generally not difficult to reject the direct influence of treatment on behaviour when we know so little of the effect on individuals' lives. We can demonstrate the different moral survival rates between those who we imagine have had identical treatment, for example as a result of being brought up in the same home.

The emotional basis of attempts to limit moral education

Likewise under emotional pressure we can argue that the concern of moral education is properly confined to 'free' decisions 'freely arrived at' and concentrate our attention on assuming choice rather than trying to increase it. Another

8

ploy used to reduce the acceptance of responsibility – the feeling of guilt – is to argue that moral development depends on the use of a 'moral vocabulary' which few children possess. Teaching children to use a 'moral vocabulary' may be easier than treating them well! One of the saddest aspects of these evasions is that the greatest support for the declared objectives of the evaders [i.e. the clarification of situations and issues using appropriate symbols (words) and the development of reasoning power using those symbols] comes from the direct experience of reasonable and articulate people who demonstrates their care, and who are therefore liked and admired.

A common adult anxiety about putting the stress on the adult's relationship responsibilities is that it does not adequately emphasise the importance of teaching children to respect and treat others, including adults, well. These are not of course alternatives. The best way of teaching respect for others is to demonstrate respect and caring, and the discipline they impose. This discipline will only be accepted and enjoyed if there is strong positive motivation which most surely comes from being treated well. Effective moral education centred on the needs of those being educated can increasingly give way to such education centred on the needs of others who have and are seen to have so much in common with us.

The second salient fact about moral learning process between the ages of eight and thirteen is that children before puberty are dependent for their survival on the goodwill, or at least the tolerance of significant adults, principally their parents. They must learn what is accepted and what is not accepted by adults. To do this they have to find out, at present without lessons, how to interpret accurately from the non-verbal and verbal cues which adults give what those adults welcome, tolerate and disapprove of in their behaviour. Children then must moderate that behaviour to incorporate mainly what is accepted and to abandon what is strongly disapproved of. This is a form of moral education which begins immediately after birth and we usually describe it as 'social conditioning'.

From the answers to the questions we asked in the National Survey, evidence of the central status of social conditioning emerged in two ways. First, it stood out in the pattern of events described: for example 'I spent 10p I found on the floor of my sister's room. Mum found out and was very angry. I was unhappy.' Second was from specific answers to the question 'What did you do as a result?' [to continue with our example] 'I gave my sister 10p from my pocket money and (later) 'when I found more money at school I gave it to Miss Smith our teacher.' Even more basic evidence of the importance and effectiveness of social conditioning is that so many adults realise that in certain circumstances it is an effective way of teaching children to do some things and not to do others and so use approval and disapproval, rewards and punishments to change behaviour.

Social conditioning and learning moral behaviour

The process of social conditioning is basically very simple. A, in this case the child, does something (x); B, the adult, experiences (x) approves it or disapproves it, rewards or punishes, and, depending on the rewards or punishment, the child, after a number of similar experiences, repeats or does not repeat the behaviour. The child has learned socially.

However, there are a number of important points about social conditioning. The first is that, for learning to take place, the adult has to be significant to the child, and 'significant' in this context means important to his survival or wellbeing. Chance encounters are relatively less influential than established relationships. Teachers therefore vary in their significance depending on the time they are with the children, how long they stay in a particular job and how they interpret their role.

The first in the hierarchy of influence is generally the parent (and the younger the child the more true this is) followed by other relations, intimates of the family and teachers. However, teachers are often very influential, especially when parents are passive in the face of their children's behaviour. They can spend a great deal of time with particular children, and children are not easy to escape from! (Young ones cannot usually walk out of lessons or school, though some become sick and a few play truant.) Further, teachers practise consciously or unconsciously a moral

10

education function. Schools have traditionally used reward–punishment and approval–disapproval as a *modus operandi*. They are habituated to it and it is only gradually since the 1940s that a significant proportion of teachers in this country have come to consider the moral implications of their approval and disapproval of various kinds of child behaviour. Even today the majority of adults probably give little or no consideration to the significance of their social conditioning activity.

A prime responsibility is therefore to help individual adults give more constructive attention to their moral education function generally, and to their social conditioning function in particular. To be truly responsible we must consider what goes on, what the learning process is, and what our part is in that process. To confine ourselves to educational theory only delays the honest acceptance of life as it is and will not help us to improve our society.

A second point is that it is important to know whether the conditioning process is initiated by the child doing something or by the adult leading with some demonstration of what to do, or advice on what to do in a particular situation. It is more straightforward to discuss this later in the chapter when we consider the importance of 'social experiment'. Suffice to say at the moment, that the first move can be made by child or adult and it is significant which is the case.

A third point about the social conditioning of moral behaviour is that rewards and punishments, albeit not generally in the formal sense, are awarded and inflicted by a child's peers as well as by adults. The general position is that as children grow older the peer group becomes progressively more important as a frame of reference. Its rewards are more sought: its punishments are more feared. It is probably best to consider the conditioning influence of friends and other contemporaries separately, especially with the eight to thirteen age group, as this influence applies in play.

There are important general points to consider about the relative conditioning influence of individuals. How do we decide how dependent the child is on an individual for survival and support? This is important because the greater the dependence the greater the adult's influence, i.e. the greater his or her potential efficiency in socially conditioning

the child to behave in certain ways. Gesell[1] has pointed out
that the child of eleven is often a well-adjusted individual, but
dependent. As already suggested, it is too easy to conclude
that mothers and fathers are the only important social
conditioning agents. There are a number of important factors
which affect the issue.

One influence is the closeness of an individual adult. How
available is he or she? Is the parent around? When the parent
is there does he respond to the child's needs, to the child's
behaviour or is he remote and unresponsive? Does he regard
it as his responsibility to approve and disapprove – to support
some behaviour and inhibit other behaviour? If the parent is
physically or emotionally unavailable the child has to learn
elsewhere or not at all. At one time our greatest concern might
have been that parents controlled too much, i.e. were too
dominant. Some are still too dominant to allow their children
to grow into adults who might lead rich, creative and
independent lives. However, our evidence is that the general
tendency nowadays is for parents to be too remote, physically
and emotionally. General observations about parental
behaviour are, of course, of very limited practical value. To
work effectively with individuals you need to know about their
individual circumstances. You cannot even depend on
sociological findings about age, class, locality and so on.
Indeed these findings in their greater particularity [for
example by demonstrating that working-class parents tend to
be powerful social conditioners of their children in certain
areas of their lives while not responding to behaviour in other
areas] indicate to us that, to help individual children develop
positively socially and morally, teachers must know about
their children's lives – a level of professional involvement
which society often deems inappropriate. Nevertheless we
have to accept that many parents are simply not generally
available, and when they are physically available they do not
respond. They practise a *laissez-faire* style which is a function
of work concerns, career concerns, materialism introspection
and the spurious argument that they do not believe in
influencing their children.

We are not making these comments censoriously. It is easy
to recognise the social conditions which have helped to create
the situation. Nevertheless the facts are clear. Self-concern is

the assassin of 'love in action' and separates us from life and the living of it, as Tolstoy, in *War and Peace*, had Pierre the intellectual learn from the peasant Palaton. Care for the child can only be expressed through response to the child. Furthermore, our view of social conditioning and what it means here does not preclude our choosing between alternatives, nor absolve us from making decisions about the society we want and carrying them out. Our responsibility is to be available and to respond with our best judgement.

A further factor which determines the value of an adult, and particularly the parent, to a child during social conditioning is that adult's emotional acceptability to the child: being liked is important.

The adults the child likes are the most influential, and being liked is a function of the adult's manifest attitude towards the child. Learning theorists interested primarily in the establishment of a particular piece of behaviour, and with their understanding based on the behaviour of rats or pigeons in laboratory conditions, have sometimes regarded it as unimportant whether the behaviour was learned as a result of positive or negative reinforcement. The same can be said of some traditional educationalists, particularly those who have stressed the importance of punishment in the development of discipline. We cannot afford to take this view because, as those with a moral interest, we are concerned with the child's overall disposition and inclination towards others, his creativity and ability to adapt to new situations. The evidence of our work is unequivocal in this respect. If you want children to develop creative, positive, loving behaviour you have to ensure that support for doing things at least balances the inclination not to do certain things. In a mass society with, inevitably, a highly developed law and rules structure the danger is clearly to overstress the pressure to conform at the expense of creativity and of a positive approach to others.

It would be misleading to suggest that any of us has a precise knowledge of how much 'yes' and how much 'no' to introduce into a particular child's life. 'Noes' are important to survival and the preservation of a positive affectionate attitude to others is a function of a number of things: for example, the love and security the child receives and the contribution adults make by giving intellectual and informational leads about how to affect things, i.e. about how to build. Nevertheless, we believe that the greatest influences for social and intellectual growth come through positive reinforcement. In adolescence, when adult norms face their greatest challenge it is the adolescents whose early social training was most dependent on negative conditioning who are most inclined to reject outright the more valuable and constructive features of adult society together with the negative and restrictive.

An important feature of the social conditioning process is the degree of consistency in response which individual adults achieve. It is to be expected, and evidence confirms, that inconsistent and unpredictable adult reaction to the same social behaviour on the part of a child inhibits that child's social learning. Learning from social conditioning always takes time. Behaviour is not generally modified or developed as a result of a single adult response, be it simple reaction, argument or appeal to reason. Things do not happen all at once, though many adults seem to expect that they will. 'Once should be enough and I don't expect to repeat myself!' When adult responses to the same or even an apparently similar situation are contradictory then confusion results. Knowing what to expect and having it happen are very important to moral and social learning.

It is difficult for children to learn behaviour when the reactions of different significant adults to the same behaviour are contradictory. It is not simply a matter of 'you pays your money and you takes your choice'. The child may be equally emotionally attached to two adults, typically its parents, in which case their contradictory responses threaten and generate stress. It is not so much that a child between the ages of eight and thirteen cannot itself respond differently to two individuals, but much more that having to do this with those who matter most raises problems about how to treat others it knows less well and has not the opportunity, or time, to discover. In any case, resolving contradictions of this kind is a wearing business which does not encourage social facility or willingness to face new situations. In adolescence the individual's ability to cope with different responses, to act and to 'choose' between alternatives increases, provided there has been a secure base in childhood. Difference can then be challenging, enriching, and creative of new understanding, attitudes and behaviour, but before adolescence consistence of response from significant adults is, in varying degrees, essential to moral and social learning.

Another consideration which has a great influence on the child's learning is the timing of response to its actions. In much animal work we find that if learning, in terms of modified behaviour, is to take place the response to the move made by the animal has to be immediate. For example, if I wish to prevent my puppy from going through a garden gate which cannot be kept closed the ideal learning situation would be one in which something inhibiting inevitably happened to the puppy each time his nose crossed the line of the gate posts. All too often dog-owners give their animals a bad time when they return from an excursion, so that punishment is associated with coming back and on the subsequent occasions when the dog goes out he learns to stay away longer. In such a case the attempt at social conditioning has been counter-productive and, if the dog is consistently and severely punished often enough on his return, he is likely to stay away indefinitely. Some hands may be raised in horror at citing a well-known fact about animal learning to introduce a point about human learning. Nevertheless, allowing for the greater sophistication of human thought, together with the power of human memory and the ability to associate events, immediacy or near immediacy of response greatly increases the effectiveness of that response in influencing human learning. The closer events are in time the easier it is for the child to associate them. The easier it is to learn. Adults who store up their reactions until they are 'good and ready' to produce them are confusing and the agents of anxiety. They are resented and the best thing may be to keep out of their way. Nor is this only true when the response is of a negative punishing kind. Positive reinforcement is most effective when it immediately follows the rewarded behaviour. Children often say 'It didn't mean much then' or 'I'd really forgotten what he was on about' when a response intended to be supportive is too late after the event to which it is supposedly related.

Although learning through social conditioning is considered in this chapter as an interpersonal process, it would be mistaken not to point out the connection with the way in which children in the eight to thirteen age range learn from animals and even inanimate objects. Animals, particularly the domestic variety, react positively and negatively to overtures by children. They are generally consistent and they react at once. Their reactions to affection are frequently less reserved than human reactions and their responses to cruelty more effective in inhibiting the behaviour than human low-key protest. Above all, like that of people, animals' quality of life is enhanced by considerate treatment, i.e. by tolerance. At the basic level there is no conflict between the morality which children learn through their encounters with animals and that which we would like them to apply to people. Inanimate objects do not react but their nature, imposes limits on what can be done with them, and in that sense they 'tolerate' or even support certain treatment, while resisting other overtures. They provide a framework of possibility – a context for action, a discipline.

Moral education through social conditioning goes on inevitably at a basic level in every society. Individuals naturally positively reinforce the considerate treatment which they like and which makes them happy, while they inhibit the inconsiderate treatment which they do not like and which makes them unhappy. In both cases they do so as far as the conventions of a society will allow them. However, the limitations of society and so the child's frame of reference mean that the school has a prime responsibility not only to use social conditioning to encourage the considerate treatment of self and 'accepted' others, but also to extend that consideration to individuals not generally regarded in that society as entitled to it for example, Capitalists during the Russian Revolution. The sad fact is that prejudiced, limited parents or teachers have, in the first instance, to exert a considerable social conditioning effort to make young children's treatment of others more selectively friendly. The natural tendency is positive, i.e. affectionate, and it will continue to develop as long as it is not inhibited either by the individual approached or by a significant adult bent on changing the child's behaviour towards an individual or group. The least happy and most destructive societies are those which impose, through social conditioning, the greatest limitations on the natural expression of friendliness and support. 'Unless you become as a little child. . . .'

Objections to accepting the fact of social conditioning

There are theorists who do not accept that there is a human social conditioning process which influences behaviour in our society. They are rare and typically have great difficulty in explaining human learning without reference to human interaction. They generally fall back on presenting a theory of human nature as being innate in origin which, in an extreme form, makes moral and social education impossible.

More common is the argument, based on a stages theory of rational development (generally today that of Lawrence Kohlberg) that man becomes, or may become, the autonomous choice-maker at some point in his growth, typically during adolescence. Therefore, whereas the relevance of social conditioning to early social learning is recognised, as well as its importance in the case of those who do not develop, or employ, the capacity for autonomous action, the main concern in moral education after childhood is to help individuals make moral choices of the 'highest order' of which they are capable.

There is nothing about the procedure we adopt in our programme which conflicts with the interest of those who believe they can identify stages of moral development, and that individuals pass through them. However, the position outlined in the previous paragraph envisages an over-organised approach. One which is less effective than it might be because it undersubscribes the importance of feeling and positive motivation in adolescent and adult life and is concerned with verbal subscription rather than behaviour.

A position which has little to do with reality, and is therefore of limited educational value, is that of some educational philosophers who define education so as to exclude any form of social conditioning, and who make an absolute distinction by definition between moral education and socialisation. In the context of logical philosophy it is, of course, perfectly proper to do this provided you realise that the absolute distinction is purely conceptual and does not describe the educational situation, as it is, or as it can be. The school of English educational philosophy responsible for the development of this position has had the virtue of concentrating our attention on what we are saying when we make educational statements, and also on what we may be doing when we make certain educational moves. However the school has shown little observational interest. It is no coincidence that it has sired disappointingly little practical work and the movement has generally preferred to remain aloof from the application of its own position.

Since Wittgenstein, some philosophers have tried to force a number of false dichotomies on us. One which we must reject in moral education is that individuals are either free, or not free, to choose. Experience continuously affirms that freedom is always relative. We can work for greater freedom but we can only do so effectively if we look at human behaviour and identify its motivation.

Social conditioning and choice

Social conditioning as described here does not make irrelevant what is approved or disapproved, any more than it denies the importance of reason. What is 'good' is increasingly understood in relation to its effect on people's lives. Reason commends itself because it accords with experience, and because we make its importance self-evident.

Further, the process of social conditioning can be employed to support choice, and hence to support creativity. It is all a matter of what we reinforce and how we reinforce it. We should give up complaining about the influence of approval and disapproval and substitute greater concern with what is approved and disapproved. One way in which we can increase the capacity for choice is by helping children to recognise and evaluate the influences on them – including emotional pressure. We can consider whether it would be 'good' to dehumanise man by pushing him as close as we can to the exercise of 'pure reason' when we have destroyed the shackles of the more blatant and extreme form of destructive irrationality, which will not happen in our time!

Emotion and reason

All experiences are tinged with emotion, as Sir Frederic
Bartlett pointed out in his classic work *Remembering*.[2] We feel
them and respond to them through feeling, often unconscious
of our own motivation, though we are seldom short of an
explanation of our behaviour when we take pride in our
rationality! It is the subliminal nature of much social
conditioning which makes a nonsense of the more superficial
advocacy of impartiality or neutrality as a simple stance which
we should adopt in our relationship with young children. To
support rational development it may be good on occasions to
work for impartiality through the adoption of certain techniques (though our evidence is that children need emotional
response), but we had better believe that, while we live and
breathe, we always impart some emotional tone. Emotion
is contagious, and no emotion more so than love. The loving,
caring teacher may be a good, though unaware, moral
educator. The danger is that we may assume our influence is
good because we feel well disposed. Empiricism is a harder
task master than this. We have to observe what we do and we
need the observations of others on what we do and the effects
of what we have done. Data, analysis and the drawing of
conclusions are essential to improving moral education and
relationships in school. The limitation is that day-to-day
concentration on process by practising teachers can encourage
a neurotic preoccupation with self and performance, and
destroy positive relationships with children. Balance is
difficult to achieve. We can work towards it but there is no
magic formula which will ensure that we achieve it.
Fortunately young children can cope with, and even
positively use, a considerable range of adult behaviour
provided they have basic security. The realisation that some
kind of moral education is going on the whole time through
social conditioning in the home, in the street and in the school
is the breakthrough for adults.

In our programme we begin with verbal and non-verbal
cue recognition (see *Photoplay*, Chapter 6) because an
increased understanding of what individuals are saying
through their behaviour is a first step towards increased
understanding and consideration. The same should apply in

teacher education and in the primary education of the child. Sensitivity work encourages curiosity about people and curiosity is the gateway to learning and action. Einstein once said that whereas he had no particular talent he had great curiosity. To assume we know all about people and how to treat them is to close the door on learning. What we hope to have to offer is a way of moving forward rather than a guarantee of arriving.

The morality of communication

For social learning through social conditioning to develop beyond the crudest 'hit and miss', 'stop and start', 'no–yes' level the young child has to develop a number of abilities, the first and most basic of which is reception ability.

Reception ability means the practised capacity both to recognise that another individual is passing a message to you, i.e. is communicating with you, and to be switched on to receive that communication. It is so essential to learning that we make no excuse for the emphasis we put on it, and for rewarding its development in the early part of our programme. Ironically it is one of the capacities which most frequently atrophies in adult life and which limits the ability of children to communicate their needs to older people. In the crowded, busy, depersonalised society in which many of us live, dominated by impersonal official messages, it is a common defence mechanism to reduce demands on ourselves by not looking and not listening. We must work to create a society and an educational system which has time for people and their communications or we will progressively limit the contagion of considerate treatment in favour of more unused information and unemployed theory.

The second basic capacity is *interpretation ability*. The child needs to understand what another individual is saying, verbally and non-verbally, to appreciate what the message is. We sometimes flatter ourselves that there is no need to be concerned on this score because so much of education is about understanding communications, about knowing the meaning of words, appreciating the importance of definition, respecting the integrity of words, recognising and using the structure

20

of language, and about understanding and employing verbal argument. But our approach to teaching communication has generally been confined to words and their use so that those generally regarded as educational successes are often non-verbal 'illiterates' with little sensitivity to man or concern for his feelings. Such people are 'just plain bad' at understanding the non-verbal messages which others pass to them. Again, no excuse is required for putting so much emphasis on the interpretation of all communication in the early part of our approach. Understanding non-verbal as well as verbal communication is a *sine qua non* for later clarification and argument. We would do well to remember that when there is a contradiction between an individual's verbal and non-verbal message it is frequently the latter, which has not been prepared for public consumption, that gives a truer indication of that individual's needs, feelings and interests.

It is essential to stress both that developing the child's reception and interpretation abilities is a matter of verbal and non-verbal education and that they are intimately related. There is no necessary conflict of interest here any more than there is a conflict of interest between accepting and using responsibly the fact of social conditioning and doing your best to encourage the growing rational capacity and application of reason to the solution of problems. In both cases the approaches should be complementary.

In sociological terms we are keen to reduce 'alienation' in the sense in which the term was first used by Karl Marx and has been developed by the existentialists and individuals such as R. D. Laing. We would like to see the gap reduced between individuals' explanations of their behaviour and the true understanding of that behaviour. We want to see rational-isation reduced and reasonableness increased. Although behaviour alone does not provide explanations, it is only through the more careful observation of behaviour and its context that we shall attain greater honesty and realism.

'Learning' describes the long-term modification of behaviour, and for behaviour to be modified the child needs to possess the ability to express himself, to communicate his reaction through verbal and non-verbal behaviour. This *'expression'* or *'message' ability* (to employ the rather more limited description we used with reference to adolescent

21

learning in *Moral Education in the Secondary School*) itself only develops as a result of encouraging response and rewarding it. It follows that a programme of moral or social education must provide the context and emotional backing for the parent and the teacher to encourage this. Reference 4 provides this context and backing. Perhaps more important we hope that our total approach will encourage parents and teachers to develop their confidence in, and techniques for, encouraging children to express themselves positively.

I hope that no readers will at this stage assume that, because there has so far been only a brief reference to *decision-making* on p. 18, we propose to say no more about choice and reason. As we have already argued, choice, reason and decision-making should be positively reinforced and encouraged as soon as the capacity for them begins to emerge. Here, we are concerned with the groundwork, in most cases up to about the tenth year. In the consideration of trial and error and adolescent social and moral learning, *'response ability'*, which involves decision-making, will be considered at some length.

The prominence given in this chapter to the influence of treatment and of a form of social conditioning underlines our conviction that these are the basic processes through which eight to thirteen year olds learn their treatment of others. There are further observations to be made about behaviour and learning process in this age range, however, and the first concerns imitation.

Imitation

All children imitate, and they most frequently imitate the behaviour of those significant or impressive to them. Imitation is a facet of the learning process, a starter but not itself a separate way of learning. What is imitated is then resolved through the process of social conditioning, to become, or not to become, a repeated piece of behaviour – part of the child's repertoire. For example, the imitation of an impressive, admired, adult figure, perhaps a violent hero, who exercises the kind of power, the kind of control, a 'subject' child would like to exercise, may conflict with the imitation of the parents' behaviour. Such a conflict can, in behavioural terms, be resolved by conditioning on the part of the parent. It is important to realise that the emotional effects of suppressing the violent behaviour (even when the child is capable of appreciating the argument in support of the conditioning) may be destructive of the child's wellbeing if some form of positive self-expression is not encouraged and substituted. As Niko Tinbergen has pointed out[3] the education of the human young often lacks biological balance. Its emphasis is cerebral and restrictive, while it is weak in physical expression and creativity. As we argue later in this chapter, there should be a positive emphasis on learning through play up to and into adolescence, because much of the human learning process takes place most naturally in play.

In Western society children are small and dependent in the adult world, and so, whereas before puberty children do not want, and could not handle, complete independence, anything which attracts attention, enhances their image and increases their control over others tends to be attractive to them, and so to be imitated. Association with the big and powerful ('My father, Gort Smothers, is the biggest man in this town') is usually not enough. It is even better to be big yourself – to make a big impact, to make a big noise, to make big threats, even to make big trouble! Often such behaviour is rewarded by the admiration of your friends and the amusement of adults (all too soon to change to displeasure). Imitative behaviour is positively reinforced when others in turn imitate you, even when it is only in some physical expression such as jumping up and down. Recruits show their approval, and to be accepted and approved is to be happy.

Derivative though imitation is, the function of imitation is frequently underestimated as a preliminary to the development of imagination and the ability to create something new. In adult life we find it very difficult to decide what we owe to others ('I don't know where I got the idea'), but the indication is that those who in adulthood have the greatest experience of variety and difference stand the best chance of making the new observation, of creating the new ideas or of developing the new position. It is scarcely surprising when so much that is new results from relating what already exists, in the field of behaviour, as in the case of the field of ideas. Having variety to imitate encourages comparative evaluation later, which is one of our reasons for using imitation as a starting point in some of the work with children. A disposition to observe is illustrated in imitation, and observation is preliminary to the exercise of the imagination, which is a great instrument of moral good. Imitation is a form of affiliation which only fails to be morally positive in its influence when boys and girls are denied the possibility of comparing individual styles of life and their effects.

Some child behaviour, particularly that of the younger children in the age range which we are considering (those of eight, nine or ten), is described by adults as imitative because it duplicates, or almost duplicates, adult behaviour which the child has experienced. But the child's responses are not necessarily ones of conscious imitation even when, if asked what he did, a boy or girl replies 'I did what Mum did' or, even more assertively, responds to the question 'Why did you do it?' with the statement 'I did it because Mum had done it.' The explanation is requested and the response in the terms imposed by the question is accepted, or approved, so that explanation has been reinforced and may be established. Obviously we must expect imitation, or more realistically duplication, of parental behaviour often to be approved by parents, i.e. to be positively reinforced. What we should not assume is that the imitation 'explanation' describes a mental process which took place prior to the behaviour. Not surprisingly human young behave in ways common to the human race, and the possibilities are limited, which makes such behaviour look like imitation. Again, as we have maintained, behaviour is contagious and the general truth is that kind, considerate behaviour, to take the most powerful example, is responded to with kindness, i.e. with consideration. The kindly disposition is built up by the experiences and attractions of kindness. It just happens that way without the individual 'imitating' kindness.

Trial and error learning

Trial and error is a feature of social and moral learning process between the ages of eight and thirteen, although there are, during that time, significant changes in its sophistication and the way in which it is employed. In a basic sense when any behaviour changes take place as a consequence of social conditioning they do so as a result of trial and error learning, although it may take few or many consistent responses to a piece of behaviour for any individual to learn. When a child acts, another responds and the child modifies his behaviour, we can describe the process as one of 'trial and error' provided we do not assume that it is necessarily a conscious process. [This process uses the argument 'I tried "x": it didn't produce the result I wanted so I'll do something different in future.'] With a growing vocabulary and increasing ability consciously to relate events and handle ideas, the great majority of children will come to advance such an argument before puberty, but simple trial and error learning which is practised by all adaptive creatures does not imply the ability to express any argument at all. It is all a matter of learning to produce the behaviour that works.

Dependence – a sure base

The ends served by trial and error learning vary and change during the growth of the child. Trial and error learning is a natural process for the infant, a process through which security, boundaries and control over the environment are first established. The security of the mother's love and support is surrounded by space into which to move, space bounded by a growing frame of reference animate and inanimate. The early 'reaching out' of the young child by making noises, facial expression and movement develops a style dependent on response, i.e. feedback. As we argued on p. 16, objects do not 'respond' but their nature and position make some action or control possible, other action or control impossible. This control, or lack of it, in turn affects the child's interests and becomes a facet of his world. If the young are allowed to learn in part by trial and error, the potential and limitations of action, for control, force operational reality on them.

Whether a child becomes more confident and exploratory or more uncertain and confined is a function of the experience which follows 'reaching out'. The child's needs are both for

25

security and for room in which to increase control over his environment, but there is no simple general formula which we can use to decide on the best proportions of containment and freedom in an individual case. However, if we are sensitive to feedback from our babies and young children the extent of need for limitation and space are demonstrated. We can learn to 'read' them and respond to them. Here is the very basis of morality in expressed need and what we do to meet it. Moral behaviour is about identifying and responding to need as best we can in the context of others' needs, feelings and interests. It has its origins in the trial and error social learning of the very young; the wants and by interpretation the needs are revealed. We respond and the child learns first survival, later more than mere survival. The style of meeting need is contagious.

In those cases where a child initially enjoys little love or security, shown, for example, by a warm expression and physical contact, we have no reason to assume that he will in turn be able to love and show consideration. It would be comforting to know that reason, and education in reason, can always later provide a corrective to inappropriate or destructive behaviour, but there is no evidence that it is so. Similarly, when there is a virtual ban on a child's exploration through early trial and error learning, we have no right to expect that healthy, considerate, interpersonal relations will be possible for that child. Rather we can expect the development of a remote, disturbed, unhappy, frightened and possibly destructive child.

The young child then, in trial and error learning, is reaching out and starting to understand the nature of things from the framework with which he comes into contact and the responses he evokes. Initially the strongest positive motivation is being sustained and warmly supported. When the baby is thus treated, the behaviour which achieves that end is positively reinforced and the child in turn behaves affectionately. The first learning about others' needs results from having his own needs met. At the same time, in maturation, the development of the baby's sensory equipment produces a natural curiosity which results in a progressive farther reaching out. The searching disposition is rewarded at some points and penalised at others. This natural curiosity is often

26

expressed in what we call play. As we argue on pp. 23 *et seq.* freedom to play is essential to moral growth. Unfortunately adults are increasingly forced by the development of the crowded, technological society to inhibit trial and error learning, because so much of it can be fatal for the child. This underlines the importance of guaranteeing, and if necessary contriving, play situations, which are bounded and secure but which invite exploration. Our programme begins by doing this for the eight year olds, though such provision is of course a responsibility of parents from the earliest days and for the teachers from the beginning of collective education in nursery or school.

Another form of strong positive motivation for reaching out which develops from the earliest years is the attraction of manipulating (of excercising) control, already referred to on p. 11. Essentially the young child is contained (controlled), but from birth the gradual development of a sense of identity depends on the individual becoming instrumental, acting on things and being able to predict the effects of his actions on others.

Between the ages of eight and puberty, trial and error social learning progressively embraces more of the concerns of the larger world into which the child is moving. A boy or girl becomes increasingly aware of the importance of the context in which action takes place. The pace of social growth is, in the individual's case, principally controlled by a balance between the need for security, love, and a safe retreat, and the need to extend experience, to move out, and to learn to handle new situations. The circumstances which the children quote as happy, unhappy or puzzling illustrate this. Individual and group needs vary and so it is not possible to define the 'right' amount of social contact or dependence for children at any age.

Institutionalised education is governed by economic and political forces, i.e. by statements about what is economically possible and generally desirable. This places a very heavy burden on parents and teachers to adapt the system as far as possible to meet the needs of individuals. The adults who are lazy in this respect are satisfied with trying to cater for the 'norm' which, it is statistically obvious, will suit very few. The very lazy do not even attempt that. The black Senator Julian

27

Bond in a recent speech to American teachers in Atlanta, Georgia, rightly stressed that 'the art of the possible' is a phrase frequently used in the attempt to justify not giving children what they need. There are no political or organisational solutions to the problems of meeting the needs which we are discussing, because such 'solutions' can only create the general conditions in which things may happen. Whether anything useful takes place at the individual level depends on that person's active concern for other individuals.

As well as increasing scale, trial and error social learning between eight and puberty demonstrates steadily increasing sophistication. Children of eight and nine still exhibit traces of an earlier animism in which there is little distinction between their attitudes to, and treatment of, objects and people. Imaginary friends and make-believe roles (for example, of being fully-fledged adults) still flourish but there is gradual increase in realism in that the child becomes much better at identifying effective action and at learning how much innovation is possible. Independence grows and is demonstrated by enthusiasm for a room of your own, den-building and the treasuring of secrets. A healthy hedonism develops and the assumption is that life ought to be enjoyable. Children in this age range expect to be positively motivated and so have had a very healthy influence on education. The growth of self-knowledge through trial and error learning, and the feedback on which it depends, strengthens the feelings of identity and gradually decreases the attraction of playing a part in favour of being oneself. Individuals become more aware of what they want and how to get it. The materialistic social conditioning which most children go through in this country means that great pleasure is taken in acquiring things. Presents bring happiness but create more wants.

These changes take place against a social background in which individual children between nine and thirteen tend to become progressively less the family centre of attraction. There may be younger more 'affection-inviting' children in the family circle, more dependant children, children with fewer 'edges' who are making less of a bid for independence. Even if there are no more children in the family, those in this age group are less a focus for attention. They become, by the nature of things, more competent, more independent and more enthusiastic about spending time and playing games with other children. Success at school is made more important and the criteria for success are already established in the intellectual and physical spheres. The idea of education as progression to a better state is implicit in the school experience.

These changes, combined with the great individual variations in size, strength and maturity amongst children, particularly in the middle of this age range, temporarily create insecurity which affects trial and error social learning. Often for a year or two around nine, ten and eleven there is a less experimental attitude. Children identify with the statements and behaviour of their parents. They are moralistic, censorious and 'report on' their friends. They need the approval of significant adults and act out parables with which they closely identify, so one cannot describe the performance as only 'role-playing'. Girls identify strongly with their mothers, boys only slightly less strongly with their fathers. Sex roles are being established prior to puberty and children may give the impression of being quite well-adjusted small adults who are 'pleasant' (easy) to teach because they do not pose a strong challenge. Nevertheless children do reveal increasing personality differences during this period before puberty and call for sensitive and individual attention. They move in the direction in which they find their strengths lie. Some are more reflective and dream, while others are all action. When parents or teachers establish a standard approach to children between eight or nine and puberty they create educational problems which will be forced on their attention during the adolescent stage which follows.

Adolescence – the age of social experiment

Trial and error learning continues to be used to a varying degree by individuals throughout their lives, but the Oxford work[4] on adolescents for the Schools Council demonstrated that trial and error social and moral learning reaches a peak during adolescence – that adolescence is the age of social experiment. The work of the Schools Council Moral Education 8–13 Project in Cambridge has suggested that trial and error social and moral learning increases between the age of eleven and thirteen when children imitate more, which is in line with the earlier findings.

Adolescence is the period which begins with puberty and ends when the individual is accepted as an adult by adults – ideally, from the individual's point of view, on terms of equality. The adolescent is faced with only two possibilities: first, to remain in a permanent state of dependence (though this is generally regarded as pathological), or, secondly, to establish his equal status as an adult. Not surprisingly most adolescents pursue the latter alternative, and they do so with general support from society, though from established adults there is always some resentment of the challenge and questioning which are inevitable. Specific resentment and opposition, when they come from more insecure adults, can be very strong and bitter.

Social experiment is a trial and error process. It takes place whenever an individual adopts a course of action, whether or not as the outcome of a conscious decision. As a result of the response to his course of action on the part of a person or persons who matter to him, the individual is either confirmed in that action so that it becomes part of his adult repertoire, or he modifies or abandons it. The process is illustrated diagrammatically.

Social experiment as the most advanced, sophisticated form of trial and error learning has a number of characteristics which distinguish it from the earlier forms of such learning.

1 The initial move is more frequently consciously prepared.

2 It shows much greater variety of approach.

3 It more often shows a concern over how to live with people.

4 The reading of feedback and its interpretation shows increased sophistication, for example in interpreting non-verbal cues.

5 Adolescents using social experiment are increasingly concerned with what makes people tick.

6 Social experiment more often assumes choices, alternatives and it is comparative.

7 Such experiment is concerned with reason, with the arguments and evidence on which response is based. The

30

reaction of someone who matters to you is always influential, but it is usually especially so when it is reasonable.

8 It often demonstrates a concern with increasing complexity in time, space and human scale. It is more related to behaviour which is capable of generalisation. [This is a positive feature which can be developed negatively by those who learn to abstract all issues, to stereotype and no longer to look at situations with detailed reference to those involved – unfortunately a common adult intellectual fault.]

9 Initiation is more commonly by speech and non-verbal cues than through overt action.

The development of reason

Between eight and thirteen the value placed on reasons for action and argument as demonstrated in *response ability* increases steadily, provided vocabulary is expanded. Reasons are offered by significant adults and arguments are advanced. What the child is exposed to and what is rewarded are crucial. There is no genetic endowment or maturational progression which guarantees that reasoning power will increase and be employed to solve moral problems. We have to prepare the soil and create the conditions in which reason and its use develop. It is not difficult to demonstrate a rational progression among those growing up in a given society, but the progression is not necessarily contingent on growing up. Like other social development it depends on social conditioning and trial and error learning. The key question is what do adults reward and how effectively do they reward it? Only the potential is present in varying degrees in children. It is the responsibility of education to realise that potential.

The basic motivation for appreciating rationality and applying reason comes from the realisation that:

1 Some questions do not have an immediate proven answer. (Habit does not necessarily provide an appropriate solution.)

2 Responses to situations vary in their results.

3 It is not necessary to try all the possible courses of action by the process of trial and error. In other words it is possible to move some distance down the road by arguing the likely or probable effects of actions.

Theoretical discussion and generalisation can in themselves become attractive activities for the growing child, but whether the arguments are applied in behaviour depends on the disposition of the child towards others, i.e. on his inclination. In moral education we work for sympathy, the caring attitude, an appreciation of reality, rationality, curiosity and the confidence to act.

Theoretical discussion, though it may be attractive in itself (particularly if you are good at it and rewarded for being so) only maintains its attraction for most young people if it is an effective instrument – if it works and is seen to work to achieve the end of a better quality of life. Arguments are instruments, their use has to be demonstrated in the real world to motivate further reasoning and action based on them. Instrumental morality comes from experiencing and observing what is good for people and from applying reason to the insight. Abstraction must always be related to actual experiences to encourage action. Furthermore, it is a universal limitation of linguistic–logical analysis that as a means of finding practical solutions it can never get you to the point of achieving the best action unless it is allied to the reception and accurate interpretation of the messages which others pass to us. Each situation must remain an object for study if we are to decide what others' interests are and how best to serve them. Fortunately, if we build our moral education on the development of a considerate life-style, we can avoid encouraging children on the one hand to abstract all issues, and on the other hand to observe and analyse empirically (to the point of distraction) every situation calling for action. Given such a style and active moral education, it is our experience that anxiety about individuals' rational or observational potential and grading is generally misplaced.

The importance of play

It is the social context which supports or does not support social and moral learning process. Before puberty play provides a natural context for social and moral learning process to work. In play children identify their own and others' needs and respond to them. They clarify issues and

32

test solutions. When they are playing, children choose their own agenda and substitute practice for theory. All their senses are involved. They move and expend energy. They enjoy themselves. They are motivated and they learn. Then the children are involved in what Niko Tinbergen[5] calls 'a biologically balanced form of education'. They are liberated from the constraints of putative learning evolved by adults – which often produces low levels of involvement.

The games children play together are social and in them we can see at work reciprocal treatment, social conditioning, imitation, trial and error (including more sophisticated social experiment) the exercise of reason in the discussion of what to do, a self-conditioning through the ego ideal and the building of a relationship with the total environment from feedback. In short, a complete style of life is evolved, and yet some still persist in contrasting play with work in favour of the supposed productivity of work. Fortunately this is less true than it used to be and there are many splendid examples in English primary and middle school education of teachers encouraging children to play, and helping them to learn through play. Nevertheless still playful adults are often guilty about their playfulness and try to hurry children on from play to work as early as possible as if they were stages in the ascent to heaven. Man's seriousness and intellectualisation of all his experience are probably the greatest barriers to children's social and moral learning, social flexibility and creativity.

Adjustment, innovation and play

As students of animal behaviour have reminded us, man is 'a culture producing as well as a culturally constrained species'. We impose steadily increasing demands for adjustment on our children because we create a society of steadily increasing complexity. Mere competence in our society makes great demands and yet we hope our children will be able to initiate changes for the better, as well as adjusting. Indeed adolescent boys and girls need to feel that they can, and do, initiate change in order to experience a sense of individuality, to accept that they have identity and to know what that identity is. Not only are other animals more gene-constrained than man, they do not have to adjust to, or create, change anything like so rapidly. The result is, as Tinbergen[6] has pointed out, that young animals, already maturationally more advanced at birth, play largely in order to discover their parents' way of life, and that, helped in their play by their parents, they do not need to play for as long as human children. The message is clear. If we do not encourage and respect children's play we shall make it difficult if not impossible for them to be mentally healthy in the face of the demands made on them.

A feature of increasing complexity is that education is becoming more and more specialised, which in turn means that it is becoming increasingly institutionalised (see Chapter 5). Schools are usually large, housing many activities and possibilities and with progressively greater demands on their time. Too often, in spite of the work of teachers in the face of education cuts, they reflect the impersonal society which creates them, with its limited and limiting criteria of success. Some, like the author of *Watership Down*, even apply these criteria of rightness and success to the animal world. The increasing institutionalisation of education combined with the adult work and living patterns developing in our society steadily decrease the amount of uncommitted, unstructured and unplanned time which children have with their peers and with adults – time for playing. There is most play when the pressures are off, and the pressures are just never off!

Play provides unique opportunities for social learning because of its unordered nature. The combinations and permutations of circumstances and behaviour which play embraces provide an ideal school for the growing personal adaptiveness which, we have argued, is essential to social living and the practical expression of concern for others. The part of adults in play is certainly important for their own health and wellbeing, as well as encouraging the social and moral development of their children. If, as we have argued, play is most valuable because of the exploration, the creation and adaptation which it makes possible, adults should guard against insisting on the establishment of rules and conventions to the exclusion of improvisation. They should resist the temptation always to organise play, to institutionalise it, or to put the emphasis on the 'do nots'. If there is this kind of control, play becomes serious and ceases to provide an

34

extension to the task-dominated world. Children in fact always try to introduce structure (i.e. rules) into their games when the freedom and unpredictability of those games becomes threatening. This natural evolution of rules is used to limit the dominance of powerful individuals and subgroups, so that adult intervention very rarely becomes necessary.

Professional football is, in one sense, a game which allows some improvisation within its rule structure, but its primary emphasis is on winning, the development of skills and the entertainment of others. It provides a job for the players who are rewarded with money rather than through opportunities for pleasure in their work. Children invite adults, directly or indirectly, to play with them and enjoy their involvement, provided the grown ups do not take over. However, often, they only want to be left to their own devices with the encouragement to 'do their own thing'. In play all things may not be possible but many things are. If we put individual's needs before tasks, we are bound to support it.

There are of course no precise universal prescriptions about the right balance between an individual's adjustment and initiation of change. Identifying the needs of individuals, groups and whole societies will always involve reading the evidence and interpreting it. However, if we educate for a growing consciousness of, and sensitivity towards, the messages people send and their interpretation in terms of need, and if we encourage the development of the 'best', most appropriate responses to need and their clear expression, we can steadily improve the quality of life – which is what moral education is about. Furthermore, those who can take and interpret feedback (response) have a built-in means of improving their treatment of others and thus of the whole environment. The pleasure of responding and being responded to in this way provides the basic motivation which keeps the moral learning process going. It grows in play.

Physical activity

Our traditional tendency to consider moral and social learning in cerebral terms often blinds us to the importance and significance of physical activity in moral learning.

Health contributes directly to the considerate treatment of others and of the self. It facilitates moral learning process. By being healthy we mean enjoying that sense of wellbeing which depends on operating as fully as possible as a person. It is much easier for physically involved children to be happy and thus well disposed. They need physical achievement. They need to do rather than only to identify with others' doings. The positive motivation for good treatment comes more powerfully from the experience of action than from the contemplation of action.

Physical activity provides a rhythm to living, a beginning and an end to the day. Energy leads to activity and achievement. Activity tires and gives us relaxation and rest. Anxiety and destructive tendencies are reduced. To relate well, children and adults need to produce adrenalin and glucose and to use them. If we do not recognise this and cater for it much more effectively in school education, our children will increasingly indulge in destructive activity in their spare time – an unconscious protest against the unnaturalness of their lives.

Many conditions and trends in the mass society militate against physical expression. Sheer lack of available physical space is the most obvious limitation. It is not our purpose to go into detail here, tempting though it is to include a chapter on the moral effects of living in a high-rise block of flats. Suffice it to say that we must look much more honestly at the behaviour which our crowded and inflationary society encourages, and do something about it, if we are to discourage the development of an impersonal and indifferent style of life. In the Postscript (p. 168) to this book, it is argued that our contemporary national problems are largely the result of ignoring motivation and that we can do something positive to change the situation.

Although they are related to the interpersonal benefits we discussed in connection with play, there are three most important ways in which physical activity specifically encourages children to treat others, and indeed their whole environment, with consideration.

First, physical work and particularly movement through space is a source of bodily sensation, i.e. of pleasant, satisfying feelings which support an even temper and friendly disposition. Joy, tolerance and patience can be born of physical movement, as well as promoting a sensitive realistic appreciation of others' feelings. It acquaints the individual with success and failure, happiness, fatigue and fear, and makes it easier to feel with and for others.

Secondly, physical expression is a form of creation. It helps the individual develop an identity, helps him to know what he can do and so, indirectly, who he is. This is vitally important because the non-exploitive relationship with others depends so much on the individual's confidence; which in turn is a function of operational, instrumental experience. When you feel that you are an effective person your inclination to control, to manipulate others is reduced. In particular the need for self-expression, and so of potential aggression is healthily channelled into challenges to the self through physical activity and achievement.

Thirdly, and finally, moral and social action (unlike ethical consideration) involves commitment, and this can be developed as a habit through physical action – through doing things rather than just thinking about them. Commitment is only threatening, only amoral, when it is not allied to the sensitivity, empathy and consideration of courses of action with which we are concerned in the moral education of children, and which, as we have already pointed out, can also be in part derived from physical activity and experience. It is the body–mind dichotomy which has encouraged the intellectualist fallacy that our moral concern is properly only with what Gilbert Ryle[7] referred to in the *Concept of Mind* as the 'internal operation of planning what to do'.

There are also many particular moral education purposes to be served by incorporating more physical activity in education, too many to discuss here. However, two are worth a mention. First, if we value the development of self-control and self-discipline we should encourage physical work undertaken together with another person. Secondly, much work involving both boys and girls destroys the myth of female physical weakness while increasing the realistic understanding of an individual's physical potential and limitations. The stereotypes die in action.

It is our opinion that much of the nastiness and spitefulness at present so prevalent in the adult world would disappear if more people had enough physical activity to make them physically tired every day. The most general influence on the context in which moral learning process takes place is school organisation. Once we accept that some kind of moral education is going on continuously in all schools, it is obvious that organisation is a key influence on what happens and what does not happen. In brief, a type of school organisation provides a context for growth and can make positive 'moral' education relatively easy or exceedingly difficult.

It is, however, a mistake to assume, and no part of the function of this book to suggest (see Chapter 5), that a definitive form of school organisation is alone appropriate to positive moral education. Every society and each area has its own need priorities and so ideally should have its own changing organisational variations. What we can say with confidence is that whatever form a school's organisation takes it should be one which encourages the development of the following supports of good moral education:

1 Warmth: the morality of better communication between young people, their peers, younger and older children; between teachers and children; and between parents, teachers and children – which all add up to respect for individuals in action.

2 More curriculum and school activity based on the identification of the needs of those growing up in our society, i.e. more relevance to life.

3 The opportunity for teachers and students to be operational and instrumental, and to make decisions and choices for change.

4 A high level of individual recognition and positive encouragement for boys, girls and teachers.

5 Anxiety levels which individuals can resolve positively without recourse to neurotic or psychotic avoidance or anti-social activity. This implies many, rather than few, ways in which you can succeed in school.

6 Support for reasonable behaviour allied to a positive attitude to human emotion.

7 A climate of belonging and security without complete dependence, and with the ability to move out confidently when the time comes.

38

This list of conditions for positive moral education is not exhaustive and readers will add to it, but it emphasises some basics. First, the 'just school' in the legalistic sense is not enough to provide the climate for moral growth. Secondly, the traditional hierarchical school organisation, though it has a positive side, must be capable of modification, of establishing greater respect for the individual, greater relevance to those individual needs which tend to be submerged in contemporary society. Thirdly, where large schools have been dictated by economic, political and even some educational considerations, we must, as a matter of urgency, find ways of supporting and developing the emerging identities of our young people through individual contacts, corporate tasks and work in small groups.

The discussion of moral learning process in this chapter, under the headings of reciprocal behaviour, imitation, simple trial and error and social experiment, does not represent a progression of stages. Sophisticated adults reciprocate behaviour. However, there is a growth in the complexity of the learning processes and in the variety of them which children use as they grow up and social experiment reaches a peak in adolescence.

References

1. Gesell, A. and Ilg, F. L., 1946. *Child from Five to Ten*, Hamish Hamilton.
2. Bartlett, F. C., 1932. *Remembering: A Study in Experimental and Social Psychology*, C.U.P.
3. Tinbergen, N., 1977. 'The importance of being playful.' *Times Educational Supplement*, 10 January.
4. McPhail, P., 1972. *Moral Education in the Secondary School*, Longman, Chap. 3, p. 50.
5. Tinbergen, N., *op. cit.*
6. Tinbergen, N., *op. cit.*
7. Ryle, G., 1967. *Concept of Mind*, Hutchinson.

2 Honesty and its central role in moral learning process

It would be wrong and misleading in this book either to offer a panacea for all the difficulties which eight to thirteen year olds have in learning consideration, or to attempt to spell out detailed answers to specific problems, without personal involvement in the real situations. Rather, we hope that the understanding of moral learning process offered here, allied to the study of the children's happy, unhappy and uncertain situations and reactions in the Project's research report, materials and writing will help adults to develop the understanding, communication ability and practical responsibility which are morally contagious and constructive.

Nevertheless it would be dishonest not to state quite unequivocally some conclusions about the effects of adult treatment on young people, and consequently some adult responsibilities. These conclusions are given later in the chapter, in the knowledge that whether understanding them helps an individual to behave differently will depend on that individual's attitudes and motivation and the social climate which helps to form and sustain them. Changing social climate is never a once and for all activity. You have to break into the cycle and affect it where and when you can. Social and moral learning process allows, and indeed requires, the concerned person to do this.

There are a number of adult attitudes which, for those who hold them, make it difficult or impossible to stimulate moral growth. For example, as long as an adult maintains that children's moral learning is independent of experience, there is little that can be done directly to influence that individual's

Figure 1 The Child's World   The Unknown

The unknown outside world is the area for discovery. It provides limitations, a framework, and at the same time a potential context for the exercise of freedom and of control. Above all, it imposes reality, the situation 'as it is', with which all individuals have to come to terms.

When the unknown outside world is too threatening, too daunting for trial and error exploration by the child, a context for trial and error learning can still to some extent be provided by the adult through play within safe boundaries, in a protected inside world.

41

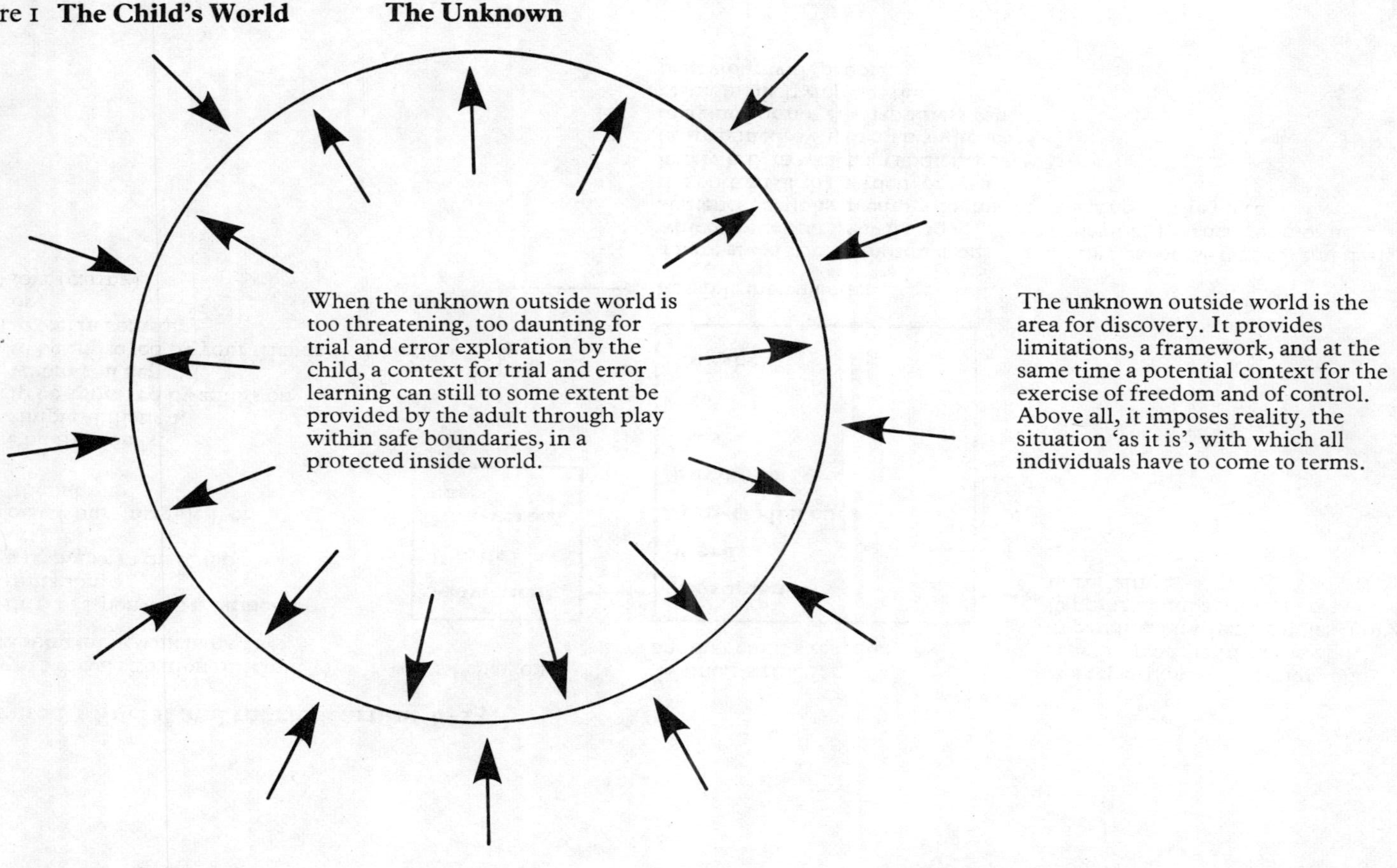

Figure 2 Social and moral learning 8–13

Given a social situation the child 'A' does something which may be:

(1) direct response to treatment,
(2) imitation,
(3) a response to direction,
or
(4) behaviour 'imagined' or 'thought up'.

The motivation is:
(a) simple affiliation,
(b) to be approved by adults on whom you depend,
(c) to be approved by your friends,
(d) to feel in control,
or
(e) love (caring).

A's behaviour

| Movement |
| Words |
| Non-verbal cues |

Possible intermediate stage

There are of course those actions which are rehearsals with no audience, actions in empty rooms, at the bottom of the garden, or on a lonely hill, in which an audience may be imagined. Whether an audience is imagined or not A's happiness can result in his trying out the behaviour with people.

'B' adult's reaction or another child's reaction

| Movement |
| Words |
| Non-verbal cues |
| Saying to |
| 'Yes' |
| 'No' |
| 'Maybe' |

A's repetition of the action, non-repetition or modification of it, depending on whether it has brought happiness, unhappiness or uncertainty.

It may of course take several trials of behaviour for social or moral learning to take place.

behaviour, whether it be based on cynicism, perversity or rational conviction. Of course anyone holding such a view may in practice be morally constructive or destructive in his behaviour. He simply believes that his treatment of other people is irrelevant to their moral growth. When such a person is destructive, we have a real problem about how to encourage growth without limiting his freedom.

Honesty about personal influence is the sole long-term hope, and this is only possible when we progressively reduce the penalties attaching to honesty. Honesty is opposed on the grounds that we must 'cool' things because those involved are behaving emotionally, not rationally, and yet long-term immoral and destructive behaviour is sustained on the basis of argued set positions which feed hate but do not admit love or compassion. The rationale for political action provides a dynamo when it in turn is based on dissatisfaction and indignation about the historical treatment people have received. The truth is that neither 'cover-up' nor political action can resolve the kind of conflict which is going on in Northern Ireland. Our only hope lies in bringing as much honesty about underlying need, argued position, motivation and behaviour to the problem as we can, and to stress, as the Ulster Peace Movement has initially done so bravely, the here-and-now human need and emotional rejection of what is being done. This is as true of resolving any institutional or political problem as it is of effecting constructive change in Northern Ireland. Abstraction can dehumanise and if others are to admit their rationalisation and abandon it we must admit and abandon our own.

The morally lazy or indifferent adult poses special problems. He may argue, if he takes the trouble to do so at all, that we cannot identify the needs of children or, less assertively, that we cannot be absolutely sure that we are distinguishing between wants, expectations and needs. Being 'absolutely sure' is, of course, generally to be removed from the human condition, which nevertheless demands commitment for survival. We are obliged to state our grounds for talking about a 'need'. We must offer evidence that something is necessary or important to the individual's survival, growth or wellbeing, but the results of doing so to anyone who rationalises his disinclination to accept responsibility and to admit obligations is bound to be disappointing. In the last analysis, rational persuasion alone will not guarantee the acceptance of a statement as fundamental as 'children need love'. Those who will not accept their moral influence often argue that children's bad, unhappy experiences are not only inevitable, but also beneficial because they toughen the children, who learn from them how to cope with the world as it is and 'as it will always be'.

Not only does such an attitude absolve us from doing anything, it also discounts the fact that learning only to cope is a desensitising and demotivating experience which, in accepting the status quo, perpetuates it.

Our obligation is to help children to grow, to choose and create a better quality of life for themselves and, in turn, their children. They should be persuaded not to accept uncritically either society as it is or the fashionable contemporary blueprint of society as it might be. They should always be helped to refer to the identification of their own and others' needs when acting or deciding what to do. It is true that living well always depends on learning to live with what we cannot change, as well as changing what we can for the better; but in the foreseeable future even a maximum effort to improve the human condition will leave enough that we cannot change to demand toughness, adaptability and endurance. The idea that stressing consideration will threaten the development of the virtues such as bravery is the reverse of true. It takes determination and bravery even to advocate an honest attempt to identify human need in the face of the personal anxiety, bitterness and political insecurity generated by asking radical questions.

In the end, whatever help is given, and whatever social climate we create, we all have to find our own answer to Hamlet's dilemma. No-one can act for the individual when he is challenged.

If we adults accept the obligation to support and generate the constructive influences in children's lives, and to weaken, and where we can eradicate, the destructive influences, what are the inescapable facts? First, some experiences, some forms of treatment always increase happiness and wellbeing, i.e. always help children grow in their ability to relate, in their recognition of interdependence and their capacity for considerate autonomy. We know this from children's descriptions not only of the events significant to them but also of the actions they took as a result of their experiences. The only qualification is that recognising the 'when' and the 'how' is always as important, and often more difficult than knowing what to do. Without timing and technique, basically sound behaviour can have very disappointing results. This is our reason for continually stressing the importance of non-verbal as well as verbal communication. In particular it is the reason for giving a central role to the *Photoplay* work (see pp. 119–25). The basic question 'What does he or she need at this time?' always has to be asked and answered. Without the ability to interpret communication you cannot expect a valid answer. It is as fundamental as that.

Given a concern for 'when' and 'how', children respond positively to, and often imitate, the following behaviour:
the expression of love, affection, warmth and good humour; being approachable and available, listening, showing understanding, responding with suggestions or advice, giving help when it is asked for; expressed enthusiasm for life and what it has to offer, sharing interests and introducing new things and new experiences; offering physical and intellectual challenge; positive response by non-comparative praise and disapproval; offering reasons and arguments; the rich use of language, verbal and non-verbal; providing a retreat and support against the world; encouraging experiment and moving out to greater independence; pleasant surprises against a background of general predictability; and finally any realistic expressed confidence in the future.

You can be even more emphatic about the bad, destructive behaviour and treatment. In many cases (we leave the reader to decide which) it is impossible to think of a time or situation in which behaviour in the following list would aid moral growth:
the expression of coldness, remoteness, bitterness and personal hostility, including insults, sarcasm and destructive remarks and comments; mental, physical and sexual threat including pre-meditated physical punishment; forcing competition and the making of interpersonal comparisons which erode confidence; abandoning, crowding or confining the child, particularly in a strange place or a locked dark

room; dwelling on sickness or the fear of death; invading privacy – which includes searching a child's room, listening-in to phone calls, opening and reading others' letters; passing on fear and hostility generally including the expression of personal, sexual and racial antagonism (not criticism); the attempt to alienate the child particularly from someone close (for example, the attempt of a father to alienate the child from its mother or vice versa); prolonged hostility between parents; containing the child emotionally and denying it the opportunity to play and to experiment; and finally the generation of uncertainty and anxiety about the future.

A book of this length precludes the detailed discussion of these morally constructive and destructive situations, and the behaviour sequences they initiate. Fascinating as such a discussion is, this may be good because our aim is to encourage personal consideration and growth from personal experience, not to suggest universal answers. The general conclusion – that the conditions for learning to care are expressed concern and optimism – only becomes operational in the terms in which the concern and optimism are expressed in a specific situation.

We do not outline here the range of situations which create uncertainty because anything new or relatively rare can do so. The uncertainty is natural; it is a prelude to learning. The destructive force is adult unwillingness to help or, worse still, the generation of too great an anxiety not to 'get it wrong'. Commitment is essential to social and moral learning and trial and error learning requires children to play and make mistakes. We only owe them protection when mistakes would be 'too destructive'. What is meant by 'too destructive' must remain a matter of judgement.

There is no mention of presents, holidays and specific activities in this chapter except by implication. The reason is that, although they undoubtedly figured prominently when children were happy, they included and expressed a variety of elements which have been referred to: for example, consideration, affection, pleasant surprise, togetherness and freedom. The nature and value of the present, the luxury of a hotel, or the status of an individual vehicle or place are determined and sustained in a particular society and subculture (for example, by advertising), and are primarily of

46

commercial importance and certainly inherently less significant. It is in this area that the distinction between want and need is most important in the establishment of educational priorities. Present wants rather than basic needs can, if they are emphasised, support the increasing materialism of individuals faced with anonymity in the poor communication of the mass society. From children's descriptions we know that great concern with things and specific status experiences generates more unhappiness than satisfaction in the medium term because of the inevitable failure to obtain things and keep them. The form in which concern is expressed could come to dominate expectations and the very concern itself if we do not identify the basic needs.

When deciding on the pace at which to introduce children to new experiences, fresh stimuli, greater freedom and more sophisticated arguments, there is no substitute for working from response, i.e. feedback. 'Stages' or 'maturational' theories, and writing based on the study of child development may provide useful initial insights into where to start and what to expect but in the final analysis it is what children say and do in response to the moves we make which decides how far and how fast we can go. We hope that the use of our materials and techniques will help by providing a stimulus to respond from which adults as well as children can learn what is appropriate and how to move on.

It would be pleasant to end this chapter with the statement that the great majority of children's experiences, especially of adults, are good and supportive and encourage them to treat all creation with consideration. Most adults do care to some extent and yet our children suffer far too much indifference and too many destructive experiences. For example, it is obvious from our research survey that many fathers 'humorously' frighten their children and that many teachers generate too much competitive anxiety. In both cases the outcome is destructive of the child's health and morality. Allotting blame is not a useful way to approach the problem. We are an anxious, frustrated society, much threatened by the forces of depersonalisation and by the nature and pace of change. Few live as they would like to live. We are, as a result, inclined to preoccupation with self and passing on to others what were once assumed to be our responsibilities. We need a radical approach which neither accepts things as they are nor simply condemns those caught up in the situation. It is possible to encourage constructive change by becoming, and helping others to become, involved. Judgement achieves little and may only result in hardening attitudes and hence more aggressive behaviour. Natural inclination is on our side: children have to be taught to hate and not to care.

3 Creativity in moral learning

We know that social conditioning can inhibit or encourage individual choice. We also know that the individual has to achieve a balance between his personal adjustment and capacity for innovation. Our responsibility as parents, teachers or other concerned adults is to help individual children establish this balance so that they can live in society as it is, and at the same time make a positive contribution to change for the better. Institutionalised education almost invariably stresses the need to adjust more than the capacity to change, which leads to the misconception that most people are not capable of initiating improvement and this is a prime cause of our contemporary world difficulties. Innovation and creativity are undersold. Individuals are forced into accepting it, or revolting. Human need is too often not seen as the criterion for change.

Moral education should develop children's abilities to make moral decisions and implement change, i.e. should help them to be operational – aware of the many possibilities in a situation. They can learn to take other people's needs, feelings and interests into consideration as well as their own. Their ideas of right and wrong can be developed by experimenting socially with others. From others' reactions, children can gain ideas about themselves and the type of people they are and in so doing develop an operational, moral life-style based on consideration of others' viewpoints as well as their own.

How far a child can become operational in this manner depends on the nature of the authority that he or she encounters. Authority at home, in school, or in society generally may only demand that the child conforms. In conforming, the child is denied the opportunity to treat individuals differently and so appropriately. In this case the child requires little input. Set solutions become unrealistic, stereotyped and unproductive. The child is uncreative in his or her personal relationships and in interaction with others. This, especially in adolescence, leads to frustration and boredom with the status quo, rules, regulations and authority generally. The boy or girl cannot affect change except by aggression; behaviour becomes increasingly insensitive and destructive.

Through this type of social conditioning the child is not encouraged to formulate needs and beliefs that call for changes in behaviour. Indeed, children's sensitivity to others is actively reduced by some child rearing and educational practices, and any natural ability to solve moral problems creatively is inhibited. Social and institutional authority pressures often prevent a sympathic relationship emerging between different groups; for example, between teachers and children. It seems to be that the bureaucratic elements in our society exert pressures on children that deny them opportunities to identify situations that need to be changed. They are encouraged by such elements to produce stereotyped performances most unconducive to creative thinking or the consideration of others' personal needs. Depersonalisation is the contemporary threat.

Society has never been in quite the same state of rapid change as it is now. Education itself is finding difficulty in keeping pace with changing attitudes, beliefs and values. We must try, by teaching children to be more flexible and adaptive in developing their life-styles, to favour construction rather than destruction. Children need to be positive about, and active in, change. This is not to say that they ought to favour any particular change or pace of change; indeed there are good arguments for rejecting many proposed changes and for slowing down the pace. The key question is do we help children to cope and contribute? It is difficult to overstress the importance of the answer. In the Appendices of this book some of the situations which call out for creative solutions are specifically mentioned.

Flexibility, imagination, clarity of thought and positive

commitment are the educational priorities. Moral creativity depends on our success in relating them.

Creativity is often discouraged in family life. Within many families, clothes, food, books, ideas, behaviour, attitudes and trends are all conformist. To be original or different is often felt to be dangerous. Yet children are expected to cope with the different social and moral priorities of the family and school. They may be asked to grow up with dual standards of morality in home and school, with different motivational emphasis on rewards and punishments. The degree to which a child can adapt to two versions of morality and be imaginative in his moral behaviour depends on his degree of moral creativity. Within each society the individual needs to become acquainted with the practices and rituals of social life, yet at the same time be prepared to make changes and grow out of them. This gain in social maturity within widening social horizons is helped by being 'open' to other courses of action and being willing to learn from previous experience. Those whose creative abilities lie dormant will be less inclined to bother, being content with the existing social and moral norms, and be less willing to guess at, or consider, other outcomes. As was emphasised in the first chapter, we are all afraid of sudden change and the temporary insecurity and anxiety it can bring. But if we are emotionally prepared to abandon the practice of always applying set solutions, then to initiate change is not so formidable.

A child's moral, social and intellectual make-up is closely related to the specific society and culture he or she inhabits. Practical morality is bound by context. If contexts are restrictive then so will be the nature of the thinking and moral action. Children can be encouraged through mutual trust and understanding to evolve their own forms of moral thinking and inner control, but only when this is positively rewarded in interaction with others. Verbal encouragement is not enough. When the contrast between what is said and what is done is sufficiently masked, the child is encouraged to withdraw and adopt a schizoid style.

Opening up the situation for discussion between those involved, combined with the possibilities of creative expression of solutions, can help to build up a healthier, less controlled relationship, based on interdependence. Children become able to modify their own viewpoints in the light of group reactions and offer different solutions or alternatives for action from those with which they were originally presented. The creative process has been defined[1] as the capacity within the individual to find new and sometimes unexpected connections. Applied in this context it would mean that the child can see more possibilities when making moral decisions or merely acting, and can therefore contribute positive and constructive ideas to putting morality into action.

Recent work on the way children understand[2] problems has suggested that they proceed in contrasting ways. One way of thinking is that often supported by traditional educational curriculum and teaching processes, in which children are questioned to give or recall the right answers previously learnt or worked out. In addition, they may learn rules, sometimes together with logical and deductive methods of thought. This type of thinking has been called alternately 'closed'[3] 'vertical'[4] or 'convergent'.[5] If employed in moral education, this thinking approach encourages pupils to adopt a subservient role and attitude to their teachers. The right moral 'facts' are learnt and general statements and intentions of good behaviour produced. Children learn to know what teacher expects in the form of good answers and become very able at giving them when required. The resulting change in actual behaviour can be negligible, even when arguments are offered for the agreed ways of doing things.

However, we prefer a different approach to moral learning, as we wish children (with active help) to think and act for themselves whenever possible and so be in a much better position to absorb what is learned. This approach to teaching, enables children to perceive the possibilities of modifying their behaviour to be more considerate. It is an approach that emphasises a range of mental faculties including fluency of thought, flexibility in moral behaviour, thinking and action, together with a certain degree or originality and sensitivity to feedback. This sort of thinking has been called lateral,[6] open,[7] creative[8] and divergent.[9] It encourages children to consider as many possibilities for moral action in situations of concern as they can. It also provides the opportunity for children and teachers to discuss and express as many relevant courses of action as possible.

Being creative in developing a considerate life-style demands certain abilities and skills which are encouraged throughout our programme. These skills are initially learnt by children in specific, personal, moral situations. Obviously the greater the range, the greater the chance of acquiring a greater number of skills. Competence in the skills involving perception and expression increase with practice. The basic positive motivation for this learning depends on need of concern for and identification with others.

Skills learnt in specific contexts build up confidence and give children the base for further experiment. The involvement of peers and adults can provide situations of joint reference where 'how to act' is established. Cooperation will help to provide the reasons for particular actions and why some are supported and others not. This joint process conditions not only the type of moral relationship of those involved, but also the degree of creativity allowed. The child learns the functions of skills in particular contexts but needs to be given the opportunity to modify them to personal needs.

Initially, rudimentary communication skills allow children to express their basic moral view, idea or action. But as complexity increases children may find they have the intention of expressing considerate behaviour but not the full skills to express it. Children generally enjoy communication practice though the degree of flexibility and competence it generates will, with the best education system possible, vary from very limited to first rate. It is possible to be unrealistic about the possible outcome and to be counter-productive, as a result of ignoring the feedback from the children.

Children may be able to express their initial moral view but not be able to predict the consequences of their own actions. This leads to unforeseen situations in which the child feels particularly vulnerable or insecure and is likely to follow peer-group leads to regain confidence. Moral creativity depends on the ability to predict and understand consequences. There is no substitute for practice, and it is easy enough to give through the use of the *Startline* materials. Guessing is supplemented by understanding.

It cannot be overemphasised that greater personal autonomy is gained through communion with and attachment to others, rather than by constraint or compulsion. This closeness of interaction between individuals has been called 'envelopment'[10] and it suggests a joint creation of a continuing morality in which individuals educate and re-educate each other in the light of the failures and successes of each other's demands. We suggest that encouraging individuals to be creative in their relationships will help them handle both compulsion and cooperation in a positive way in their own lives.

Personal autonomy is inhibited in an atmosphere or system unconducive to sympathetic personal relationships. The educational atmosphere and social structure surrounding children needs to be sufficiently open and democratic to allow them opportunities to think and express creatively. This atmosphere depends crucially on the nature of the personal relationship that exists between parents, adults and teachers and the children they care for. The question of how this supportive atmosphere is to be built up remains.

From *Lifeline*'s[11] survey of staff and pupils, and research carried out as part of this project's work, it emerges that close personal relationships between children and teachers are encouraged by smallness of schools, classes, groups or units. Schools in close communities are often able to foster closer adult–child relationships as meetings between them occur in a variety of ways and on many occasions. The depersonalising effect of large schools was noted in the previous Oxford adolescent work for the Schools Council. Both staff and pupils mentioned the depersonalising influences in school, and reported that large size was the most significant factor. In short, the larger the school unit the greater the lack of personal communication and education to meet personal need. The rationale of the large school (apart from its economic attractions) is that it caters better for individual need by offering a wider selection of options – a narrow understanding of need. However, this is not to suggest that large school units cannot be organised to promote closer personal relationships between staff and pupils, and indeed, some large schools make great efforts.

Social organisation to promote considerate behaviour, whether it be in the classroom, school generally or outside society, will only be successful through the joint action of individuals of like mind and with similar aims. The school

54

curriculum is of great significance because it is the medium through which moral and social relationships are perpetuated and moral norms established. These norms, produced through interaction, establish a common moral base which may be a resting place from which individuals can create new understandings and different expectations. It is possible then for children and teachers to generate different hypotheses and alternative courses of considerate action in the context of the class and the school.

Once a moral basis has been established in this way it influences and guides but does not fully determine group action. It provides a point of reference in school life, personal expectations and expectations in moral and social situations. These expectations tend to become the social and moral norms and they in turn influence interaction in the school: the degree of change and flexibility within this system is affected by the degree to which members are willing to become experimental. Classroom organisation can allow the integration of individual personal goals that are reflected in the moral education curriculum. As a result, moral and social actions are affected by the moral norms and at the same time leave room for choice. This makes possible a social and moral life within the classroom and school generally which can influence the social community outside.

Recent work[12] suggests that informal schools provide an environment which develops qualities of personality that result in a high level of creative thinking ability whereas formal schools do not. Informal schools are those that emphasise self-initiated learning and creative activities generally. Formal schools are those run on traditional lines, placing emphasis on authoritative learning and convergent thinking. Behind the emphasis on self-initiated learning, and fundamental to the informal schools' success, is the pattern of interpersonal relationships within the school. Children can mix fairly freely in a relaxed, friendly atmosphere. The informal atmosphere therefore is closely related to the teaching approach that allows the development of creative thinking. The relationship between teachers and children is based on the teacher's confidence in the child's ability to think adventurously and in new directions. This in turn, raises the child's estimate of him or herself and correspondingly the development of his or her abilities.　55

If the teacher can enter into the child's thinking, if he/she is prepared to let work develop in unexpected directions according to the child's needs and interest, if he/she can find and express genuine pleasure in the child's effort, then self-initiated learning can be developed. It is in this climate that divergent thinking abilities are seen to flourish.[13]

There is much support also for the idea that teaching styles create particular kinds of atmosphere and result in particular classroom organisation. Two main teaching styles have been identified as either 'open' and democratic or authoritarian and 'closed'. In authoritarian classrooms teachers tend to dominate through formal teaching methods and an emphasis on competitiveness, positiveness, and the encouragement of convergent thinking. Children in such classrooms are allowed little creative activity or physical movement. Democratic teaching methods on the other hand are represented by child-centred learning and less teacher dominance. Here the individual needs of children are considered through group work involving teacher–child and child–child interactions. In this process creative problem solving is introduced and children are guided to solve moral problems with solutions and ideas they generate themselves. Complex moral dilemmas that demand guessing, insight and cooperative behaviour are often solved more easily by this process.

Although the educational atmosphere may offer children the opportunities to think creatively about moral situations and problems, success in the last analysis depends on the individual child's capabilities. If the child has insufficient experience, knowledge or ability he or she can hardly be expected to combine or play with these assets to produce new or original solutions.

It has been suggested[14] that an individual cannot create or diverge from nothing. In any realm of creative thinking a core or base of knowledge, techniques and abilities must be built up in order that new combinations can be made and new patterns of meaning produced. Similarly, the greater the number of associations which a child constructs, the greater the probability of discovering new combinations and moral solutions. It is possible, however, that informal schools might fail to teach the basic abilities, techniques and knowledge that are essential to the solution of moral problems in creative ways. Beyond a certain point it could be argued that an unstructured teaching style fails to provide the essential prerequisites for creative thinking. It is therefore necessary to consider what the basis for creative moral problem solving may be and build up children's expertise and experience in those areas. This in fact is one major aim of the Project's publication programme.

The creative process and decision-making

Many definitions of the creative thought process have been attempted and some common agreement has been reached on its four main stages.[15-19] An idea of how this works is useful if creativity is to be practically fostered by relating thinking to action in moral education.

The first stage is that of preparation, where a particular moral-situation problem may be investigated from many sides. The child is often conscious of a feeling of uncertainty that may last some time or only a few seconds.

The second stage is often one of frustration in which other activities may be substituted for the realisation of, or thoughts about, a solution. The child is possibly not consciously thinking about the problem at all and may seem oblivious to it.

A period of confusion typifies the second stage and is followed by a moment of insight. This is unpredictable. It is accompanied by a flood of ideas and alternative suggestions often arising in quick succession. Max Ernst, the Dadaist painter, said of this third stage, 'I had only to reproduce obediently what made itself visible to me'.

The final stage of the creative process is seen as one of verification, elaboration or modification. Here the ideas gained are checked against external realities and modified by reactions to them. This is achieved through social interaction where moral solutions are tried out.

From our work[20] with children, it seems they rely on their memory to retrieve information previously experienced and stored. The child notes and remembers earlier steps or experiences that aid later thinking and action.

Thus, in the initial stages of preparation where the child has a moral problem, he or she can retrieve information from memory storage. The child's ability to do this depends on his individual production operations and abilities. A child is able either to diverge, by bringing a variety of ideas forth, or to converge on a single idea and use that. The divergent boy or girl can be highly flexible in the use of ideas and concepts and therefore able to generate several alternative ideas, behaviours or courses of moral action. These several solutions may be seen as the result of insight or illumination, where connections and new relationships are made with the aid of remembered previous experience.

Conversely, children who think convergently are often typified by a limited perspective on a moral problem that results in just one solution being recognised and suggested. The processes through which this solution is achieved can be seen as conformist in style. The convergent thinker considers the solution to be the right one and is often not open to further possibilities or suggestions. Support for this attitude arises from the sequential nature of this thinking where each step forward is taken, one at a time, with firm connections between each step. The divergent thinker may, however, 'jump' several steps and arrive at a solution or idea more quickly, though perhaps not being able to say how he or she got there. This ability to leap, to have sudden ideas, may be related to guessing, in that, when a solution does not suddenly 'appear', it is guessed. This 'leaping' also accelerates the process of moral decision-making and action. Poor or irrelevant guessed solutions can be monitored by the techniques used in the *Startline* programme.

Creative thinking, typified by divergent abilities in children, is particularly relevant to moral experimental situations. It offers the opportunity to change values, attitudes and behaviours. When social interactions occur, the creative thinker may actively seek to adapt his moral view or standpoint. This wish to be available and relevant enables the individual to question standard processes of social conditioning by looking for other factors that may affect the situation, and emphasising reasonableness in response; he or she operates and plays with ideas sometimes not obviously relevant to the situation. This can change the social conditioning pattern. This reorganising of elements makes different approaches and solutions possible. In this way, overt

58

conditioning of children to accept single, 'right' answers is avoided. The child often does not look at ideas seen as relevant only by adults. This can result in 'inappropriate' behaviour or awkward questions, as children tend to question factors 'taken for granted' by adults.

Similarly, the child thinking creatively does not feel he or she has to be right at every step to reach a satisfactory decision eventually. He or she is willing to experiment in different social and moral contexts and therefore is prepared to make moves that may be wrong at least in situations in which there is not likely to be serious damage. The hope is that a 'right' solution will be found in the end. The child is not therefore put off completely by following unpromising leads and is capable of coping with the negative reactions of others in a constructive way. If he or she is 'wrong', however, then very often the criteria for judgement may be questioned or steps taken to change the frame of reference or social context. Obviously a healthy moral style is developed through children being willing to reconsider their criteria for moral decisions and behaviour in the light of others' reactions. This may result in a need to change factors within the situation, by making various sorts of response or enabling interaction to take on other directions, possibly by including ideas from 'outside'. For example, a consideration of the future long-term consequences of a particular action on others may help to change the frame of meaning or the individual criteria for decision. The frame of reference tends to grow as the child who is thinking creatively is not selecting the right course of action by exclusion, but rather by inclusion.

The ability to be 'open' to modification in moral life-style is aided by a willingness to keep labels or categories open to change and to use them cautiously. The child thinking creatively uses initial categorisation, or stereotyping, as a temporary guide to understand particular situations. In the light of further experiments and experience he/she is willing to adapt, re-categorise or abandon them. This is a necessary prerequisite if children are going to progress from the known to the unknown. It enables the present limits and factors in moral and social behaviour to be questioned, adapted if appropriate, or given up.

Adults seen as significant by children, i.e. who have been

accepted in one particular role or as a particular type, may react differently and be recategorised as something or somebody else. Children begin to develop new ideas about the security and love provided by adults as they meet a wider variety of adults. Not all adults are like mum and dad. A creative aptitude helps children experiment with the depth and nature of this adult love and security. They are willing to consider adults not as stereotypes but individuals from whom different personal styles in dress, vocabulary, attitude and behaviour can be learnt. Often adult and individual reactions to children can change within different situations. Children have to cope with these transitions in people and contexts. Being willing and able to operate with temporary categories greatly helps the child with his ability to cope. This is linked to the previously mentioned ability of the child to move in what can be unfruitful directions but not be put off, or lose motivation by not finding a solution. The child can try different approaches, not necessarily to find a definite solution in the end, but to maximise the possibilities of finding a solution, however temporary this may be. In other words, he or she tends to keep his or her categories and moral options open rather than foreclosing them. This is an essential quality of children if they are to survive in a society of changing relationships and values, and develop a considerate life-style.

Crucial is the degree to which an individual is willing or allowed to become divergent. This affects the degree to which particular children are willing to live with uncertainty, and are able to adopt and modify their positions and generally experiment successfully in, and with, patterns of social and moral conditioning that surround them. Children are in a world of changing relationships, where their best friend one day may be their worst enemy the next.

These surrounding patterns often involve children in interaction with their peers, where the security of the group may give them courage to experiment. If a child is sensitive to the reactions of the group, then he or she may be conditioned through peer-group pressure to conform to their demands. However, the child who uses creative abilities is less likely to conform meekly, preferring to question the consensus of views and supply alternatives. This may be particularly useful if the group is considering action that may be seen as immoral.

If exclusion from the group is the result of this decision, the child who utilises creative abilities will tend to be less worried by this negative behaviour as he is basically less dependent on limited groups and situations. Alternative ideas of self are often built by changing from group to group whereas those children that remain permanently in the same groups have less opportunity of finding new self-images or gaining different sorts of feedback about their behaviour.

Children who tend to infringe social and moral rules are often liked by their peers as long as the infringement does not have dire moral consequences or break the limits of social tolerance. This ability to question moral parameters demands fine judgement and sensitivity to others' reactions in deciding just 'how far to go'. This sensitivity is often acquired through a heightened perception to the communication signals of others and is combined with an agility in personal expression. Although all those involved with the situation may, by their condoning presence, be partly responsible for the resulting behaviour, they may not acknowledge it. 'He told me to do it' or 'I didn't want to do it', are indications that the individual does not regard himself as totally responsible for particular actions.

In solving a moral problem children have to develop an understanding of its nature in order to begin to formulate an active solution or solutions. If there is not enough relevant information stored, particularly in entirely new moral situations, or the child forgets, then he or she may turn to search the environment. The search may take the form of social experiment purely to see what will happen – 'I will treat Susan better this time' – or it may be directed to adults, peers and animals for further guidance and information. If children feel restricted, insecure or rejected it is highly unlikely that they will want to experiment or express reactions other than those that are apparently safe and conformist in nature.

Creativity

Attempts to define a creative person have a limited value for those concerned with the everyday practical aspects of children's moral learning. Unfortunately, to be detached, neutral, and objective in looking at the world (not only the moral and social world of children) is seen by some as the only way that will reveal 'true' meaning. In moral education both the terms creativity and morality take on more relevant meaning when applied specifically to treatment of others in interpersonal contexts. As these are widespread, they suggest an understanding of what is meant by creativity and morality which is based on an adaptation and flexibility in thinking and approach. To develop a life-style based on consideration for others that does not become static and entrenched demands of the individual the abilities to imagine, modify, create and sustain an empathetic working relationship with others.

Creativity is a basic facet of being human. Its development is dependent on stimuli. Creativity as used here is not restricted to the Einsteins, Galtons[21] or Newtons of this world, but as it presents itself in all of us to greater or lesser degrees. If the right conditions are there, then some degree of creativity will emerge.

Creativity in moral learning can be nurtured and brought out in all children to some extent. Our aim is to encourage creativity in moral learning, not in an abstracted way but in specific individual qualities and situations of moral concern. We realise that this viewpoint demands a personal commitment to action which suggests that an external 'objective' approach to morality and creativity will reveal little understanding or benefit for those concerned.

Part of moral education, part of being creative, is being aware and sensitive to the communications of others, whatever the media, whether it be a painting, a piece of sculpture, a particular bodily movement or behaviour. To what extent verbal success relates to the formation of a considerate life-style is difficult to assess, but it is unlikely to be impressive.

It is important then to understand by what means children 'think' in interpersonal situations and how they utilise verbal, visual, aural or kinetic communication signals in behaviour. Certainly there is much evidence[22] to suggest that different people use different signs and symbols to think with. Some think mainly with visual and tactile images without words. Others[23] operate mainly with words, symbols and mathematical signs. The media of thought is closely related to

62

the practical activity the individual is engaged in. The more remote the individual is from the actual task, the more abstract and remote his media of thinking may become. Morality is a practical activity. The closer the medium with which we encourage children to 'think' is to the media in which they behave, then the greater the chances of an effective and practical morality emerging. Most interpersonal communication involves thinking and action with some visual, verbal, aural and kinetic signals and the use of them in different combinations. A view of education (and particularly moral education) may be that it 'is the fostering of growth which is only made apparent in expression'.[24]

The creative social interaction model (on p. 65) has eight main stages and represents a sophisticated development of the moral learning process discussed in this chapter and the preceding chapters on moral learning.

Stage one: Sensory perception

The child perceives signals from others, indicating how they feel, and how they see the moral situation they are in. 'Others' here may include animals or objects as they too have been frequently reported by children as significant in interaction. This stage relates to reception ability and the preparatory stage of the creative process, where the problem is viewed from all sides with initial intrigue or even bafflement.

Stage two: Interlude

Here the child is unconsciously working on the information from sensory perception received within the context of the situation. He or she may seem to give up or momentarily lose interest. This relates to the second stage of the creative process.

Stage three: Interpretation

The child interprets the perceptual data aided by memory storage to understand the messages of others.

Stage four: Experimental hypothesis forming

Here a boy or girl is considering alternative courses of action. The degree of creativity is determined by the degree of divergent ability to recall and manipulate stored information and relate it to the present experience.

Stage five: Insight

Where the child 'knows' what to do: awareness of the 'right' action to take. Deciding what his response will be entails response ability, including on occasions 'thinking out' a course of action, as well as insight or even guessing.

Stage six: Action

The child's action or behaviour. Response ability is expressed through message ability here.

Stage seven: Personal reaction

How the child's action makes him or her feel.

Stage eight: Reaction of others

How the child's action affects others. Judging their reaction involves reception ability and can initiate a whole modification of behaviour.

It is useful to be able to spot children who are already creative in their personal relationships because they can be encouraged both to help others become more creative, imaginative and socially fluent by working with them and to develop mutual understanding and cooperation.

In the Project's Yorkshire research,[25] some children reported guessing at the moods and future actions of others involved in moral situations. From the quality of their responses it was felt that these children might on occasions be operating with insight in that they had a 'sudden idea' or a 'brainwave', in which case 'guessing' is not necessarily a good description of a process followed by a 'flash of insight'.

64

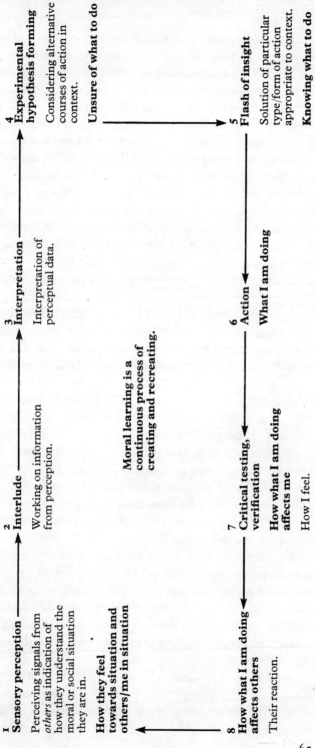

Figure 3   Towards a creative social interactional model

1
Sensory perception

Perceiving signals from *others* as indication of how they understand the moral or social situation they are in.

How they feel towards situation and others/me in situation

2
Interlude

Working on information from perception.

3
Interpretation

Interpretation of perceptual data.

4
Experimental hypothesis forming

Considering alternative courses of action in context.

Unsure of what to do

5
Flash of insight

Solution of particular type/form of action appropriate to context.

Knowing what to do

6
Action

What I am doing

7
Critical testing, verification

How what I am doing affects me

How I feel.

8
How what I am doing affects others

Their reaction.

Moral learning is a continuous process of creating and recreating.

65

One of the most interesting findings of the Yorkshire survey was that the children were best able to understand the needs, feelings and interests of others through perceiving a wider than average range of communication signals and their significance, though they could not always explain how they understood. They were also able to generate a larger than average number of possible courses of considerate action.

However, it was also apparent that children in the sample put the emphasis on the variety of different groups of cues when describing an interpersonal situation. Some reported features of facial expressions in great detail and at great length. Other children reported the bodily actions accurately and at length. If they were still unsure of what was going on after reviewing expression and action, they connected non-verbal sounds to actions to obtain a fuller and deeper understanding of others' feelings. Many children resorted to asking how others were feeling if they could not tell by other means. This suggests that moral education should use simulation which involves kinetic and visual forms of communication. Also that work with children involving non-verbal sounds in interpersonal communication would enable many to understand these sorts of signals a little better. The aim is always to increase the amount and quality of the sensory evidence which enables children to understand and act.

Children whose natural curiosity in interpersonal situations is keen can help to generate a general class interest in other people. If this natural curiosity is tempered with sensitivity and consideration then the learning encounters children have with adults, peers and animals will cement the formation of a considerate style of life.

Keen observers appear to possess an openness of mind and to be helpful and supportive; indeed recent[26] work has shown that children who are observant and creative are often most liked by others. As behaviour is contagious it follows that if children are allowed to develop and utilise observation and creative response along the lines suggested, then the caring school becomes a strong possibility.

Considerate behaviour can be stimulated through moral education curriculum process in much the same way as an artist produces a piece of work. Both rely on the individual experiencing particular problems and through interaction with others, including objects, reaching solutions. With both artist and individual there is a certain tension between the idea of what to do, what is wanted, and what is actually happening. Once the artist has achieved completion, the work becomes 'right', it 'fits'. Similarly each child constructs and projects an image of him or herself onto others. If the individual is open to reactions of others and can modify what he does, his behaviour becomes 'right'. It feels 'right'. To produce a good work of art and a good or considerate behaviour are for artist and individual very similar. Both are creative processes but operating through different media. All children can be artists in personal relations.

The finished product can be seen as a complete and static expression. At the same time it may be seen as part of a continuum of either behaviours or works of art. Preceding actions and forms have affected what is produced. Particular behaviour or an art object will affect what is produced in the future. Both represent a view, a comment in the contemporary context that expresses a personal understanding. Others' reactions may be immediate and at once change the emerging forms of art or behaviour, or they may take months or years gradually to modify the general course of the individual's or societies' progress in morality or art.

The teacher may support this process by initially suggesting moral significance and putting it in communicable form. The meanings are then 're-created' by the listener, the observer, or the pupil to make them personally valid. In this way, appreciation and understanding become creation and re-creation: morality has meaning for the individual.

Creative growth in interpersonal relationships is not just restricted to a particular moral education curriculum slot. Indeed it is our contention that both teaching and learning across the whole curriculum are based on social process. The nature and extent of such teaching and learning are dependent on the nature and extent of the personal relationships established between those concerned in the process. If personal relationships are seen as fundamental to children's learning and development, any adaptability and flexibility that can be encouraged will extend and deepen the nature of this learning. Creative abilities are fundamental in encouraging and extending children's commitment to life.

Creativity, atmosphere and attitude

Some recent studies[27] of how children are divided into particular groups or classes have suggested how such divisions may affect teacher–pupil relationships and subsequently creative growth. When children are segregated by achievement into permanent groups, pressures develop that can be detrimental to the development of a sympathetic and supportive relationship between teacher and child. Such pressures often act as barriers to personal communication and generate attitudes unsympathetic to creative work or the growth of consideration. As children become more aware of the nature of the differentiation between groups and classes their relationships with other groups become more strained. They see themselves selected as either better or worse than others. In such circumstances the content of the curriculum is often chosen as being tailored to suit particular groups. But this tailoring is often a bad indicator of true need. Intellectually advanced children, for example, are often assumed not to need emotional support or interpersonal ability. The processes through which the selection is made known to children militate against their feeling willing and confident enough to commit themselves to new forms of thinking or activity. Similarly staff begin to expect less from the 'less able' and to use routine classroom activities and methods unrelated to pupils' personal needs. In short, the gap between what children should or could do, and what they actually do, widens. The more able are often selected to represent the group or school in social activities, therefore depriving the less able of visits, outings and holiday ventures. This prevents relationships developing between groups of 'dissimilar' children and their teachers. It has been suggested[28] that discipline and some delinquency problems are reactions to this hierarchy of credibility fostered by the school, in which the 'less able', the under-achievers, can only express their frustration in a destructive manner, having no legitimate access to the world of the more able, the achievers.

One of the particular problems in encouraging children to use creative abilities and generate a variety of solutions to moral problems is that they can express and develop attitudes which conflict with those of their teacher. This may mean in

68

some cases that the creative problem-solver is discriminated against, because he or she performs in a way which is not to teacher's expectations. A 'good' moral child may be seen as one who is traditionally academic or accords with some other school stereotype. Those children who conform to the teacher's moral and social expectations increase their chances of 'doing well' at school. Those that do not conform in thinking and behaviour can reduce their educational opportunities.[29]

References

1. Kubie, L. S., 1961. *Neurotic Distortion of the Creative Process*, Farrar, Straus and Giroux.
2. Middleton, D., 1975. Creativity in Children's Social and Moral Learning, unpublished M.A. thesis, London University Institute Library.
3. Bartlett, F. C., 1925. 'Feeling, imagining and thinking', *British Journal of Psychology*, XVI.
4. De Bono, E., 1972. *Lateral Thinking*, Ward Lock Educational.
5. Guilford, J. P., 1959. 'Traits of creativity' in *Creativity and Culture*, Harper, New York.
6. De Bono, E., *op. cit.*
7. Bartlett, F. C., *op. cit.*
8. Cropley, A. J., 1967. *Creativity*, Longman.
9. Guilford, J. P., *op. cit.*
10. Buber, M., 1937. *I and Thou*, T. T. Clarke, Edinburgh.
11. Schools Council, 1972. Moral Education Project for Adolescence (*Lifeline* Series), Longman.
12. Haddon, F. A. and Lytton, H., 1968. 'Teaching approach and the development of divergent thinking abilities in primary schools', *British Journal of Educational Psychology*, Vol. 38, 171–80.
13. Haddon, F. A. and Lytton, H., *op. cit.*
14. Cropley, A. J., *op. cit.*
15. Wallas, G., 1926. *The Art of Thought*, Harcourt Brace, New York.
16. Patrick, C., 1937. 'Creative thoughts in artists', *Journal of Psychology*, IV.
17. Vinacke, W. E., 1952. *Creative Thinking in the Psychology of Thinking*, McGraw Hill, New York.
18. Hutchinson, E., 1949. *How to Think Creatively*, Abingdon, New York.
19. Koestler, A., 1964. *Act of Creation*, Hutchinson.
20. Middleton, D., *op. cit.*
21. Terman, L. M., 1947. *Psychological Approaches to the Biography of Genius*, Eugenics Society.
22. Hadamard, J., 1945. *An Essay on the Psychology of Invention in the Mathematical Field*, Princetown University Press.
23. Dewey, J., 1958. *Art as Experience*, Capricorn, New York.
24. Read, H., 1958. *Education through Art*, Faber.

25. Middleton, D., *op. cit*.
26. Vernon, 'Spotting the creative', *New Society*.
27. Lacey, C., 1970. *Hightown Grammar*, Manchester University Press.
28 Becker, H. S., 'Social class variations in teacher–pupil relationships', in *School and Society*, University of Chicago.
29. Parsons, T., 1961. 'The school class as a social system', in *Education Economy and Society*, eds. Halsey and Anderson, chap. 31, Freud Press.

4 Children's drawings and moral learning

In this chapter we consider the evidence of social learning and how it takes place, from drawings of happy, unhappy and uncertain situations by children between the ages of eight and thirteen. The conclusions are mainly general, but specific drawings are used to illustrate particular points about social learning.

Some basic evidence is only available if you actually watch a child draw when you have a direct indication of emotional state as it attaches to the experience he or she is representing. His or her expression, body posture, the way the pencil is held, the attack on, or overture to, the paper speak volumes. All human experiences are tinged with emotion and there is no better way of appreciating this, than by watching a child draw.

However, the evidence of what has been drawn on paper tells us a great deal about the children's social learning. We can see the visual aspects of situations in which children experience happiness, unhappiness and uncertainty. The people who are most significant to children are portrayed. We can learn what they look like, where they are in relation to the child and how they act. More importantly, we can often see how the child reacts to the different sorts of treatment he or she receives as both his or her feelings and actions may be clearly drawn. It is obvious from the children's drawings in the national survey that they are motivated to treat others well after they themselves have received good treatment.

By looking at children's drawings we find that the most important personal messages may be conveyed non-verbally.

Drawing 5 for example, effectively expresses interpersonal attitudes and feelings. The girl on the stool aggressively rocking her baby sister in the pram is grimacing and sticking her tongue out. The baby's reaction is clear, as its face is drawn looking away from her sister. The non-verbal aspects of this situation are illustrated clearly and simply and yet they were not recorded in the girl's written responses. By looking at the facial gestures and body gestures drawn here we can begin to understand the nature of the relationship between these sisters.

Other visual aspects of the situations drawn are indicative of both interpersonal attitude and relationships. In *Drawing 1* we can see the boy's enjoyment and involvement with his model Dalek from the size he has drawn it in relation to himself. The Dalek is larger, coloured and patterned, and stands close to him indicating the closeness of the relationship. It was very difficult for this boy to articulate his emotional attachment to his toy, but he was able to indicate it by what he drew and how he organised his picture. We tend to forget that visual language has a logic and function all of its own which can only partially be expressed in words. There is a shortage of words, in any case, in most languages to describe nuances of feeling and details of personality. Furthermore, it is difficult, especially for young children, to select the most appropriate words to convey their feelings and understanding of others' emotions. It is simpler to draw emotional states and facets of personality in a direct and unembarrassing way than to attempt to write about them. In children's drawing and social behaviour, many attitudes, values and emotions are communicated non-verbally. Further, words can mislead in interpersonal communication. They can actually inhibit action, as we often find it easier to say what should be done than to do it! Just as important, we often do what we prophesy we would not do and describe verbally what we have not done! Drawing directly represents the action and makes it clear what is going on.

From the results of a follow-up study to the national survey completed in Yorkshire schools[1], it is evident that children are more affected by visual stimulation when identifying interpersonal attitudes and feelings than even tone of voice. It is also clear from children's reports that, in preference to talking about it, they respond directly to the visual signals which others use in expressing their feelings and intentions.

When the children were asked to report which personal forms of communication were most helpful to them in understanding other people's feelings and behaviour and which they used most in expressing themselves, we found that 146 different types of facial expression and body gesture were suggested. This compared with the 78 separate types of sound and verbal forms which were reported.

Drawing personal encounters from their own experience is for children a way of achieving sensitivity to what is communicated. So that, by looking closely at the drawings and social behaviour they portray, we can begin to understand both the children's feelings and the nature of the emerging personal relationships they form. From further work in classrooms with children and teachers, whilst developing *Photoplay* and during trials, it became apparent from the children's drawings that much success in classroom interaction is dependent on unambiguous non-verbal communication between teachers and children: an increased all-round awareness of personal communication styles clearly leads to better interpersonal relationships in this case. The children show in their drawings that they are aware of many of the attitudes and values we attach to others that are implicit in what we say and do and how we do it. They acknowledge our basic social conditioning function and call on us to improve our contribution. If we do this, we become more capable professional communicators and also more available to children who need our understanding.

Some relationship problems illustrated by children are the result of contradictory communication when a principle is advocated in speech but contradicted in action. The idea, for example, that God is love is not advanced by forcing children to write out hymns as a punishment! Nor are verbal statements about being good to one another effective if the accompanying treatment of children is threatening. If children do not see the connections between what is said to them and what is done then they are unable to perceive meaning and intention clearly. They will be confused over what is expected and what is communicated. One eight year old boy reported that he did not know if his teacher liked him because she confused him by smiling whilst saying nasty things. This kind of situation is only rarely reported in writing but is more frequent in conversation, drawing or the child's description of its drawing. The form of the communication is important because only when clear and honest communication is achieved does morality become a practical possibility.

Through drawings, we are able to observe the non-verbal elements of children's behaviour, and to understand why they acted as they did. From their drawings, it seems that many of children's problems in relating to others result from their inability to observe (1) the general context of what is happening and (2) how others are feeling. We can get an indication of the degree of interpersonal sensitivity a child possesses by the inclusion or lack of interpersonal details in his drawings. *Drawing 13* suggests a fair degree of interpersonal perception. The girl has drawn each family member in detail to show how they are feeling towards her. She has also drawn herself to show frustrated annoyance on her face when she is leaving the family table. It is also clear from the family's faces that she knows they are relatively unsympathetic to her attitude and behaviour.

Failure to observe others closely creates stress and may lead to breakdown. If a child notices that someone is tense or nervous, for example, then it can modify its approach and adopt a more sympathetic way of relating to that person – unlike the nine year old girl, for example, who drew a strip cartoon of herself happily playing with her friend in the garden, when her parents were rowing in the house. She skipped into the kitchen where her mother was standing tensely by the sink, clattering plates and cutlery in anger, failed to notice what was going on and asked loudly and happily if her friend could stay to tea and spend the night. Her mother turned sharply on the girl and shouted at her to go away. The girl, surprised and hurt, appeared unable to account for her mother's bewildering behaviour. Perhaps the commonplace accusation that 'It's not fair' may, on occasion, be a substitute for 'I didn't realise how you were feeling' and 'I didn't expect you to do that!' To observe and consider another in a sensitive way is the first step to relating effectively to that person and treating him or her well.

When children's verbal and non-verbal communication is contradictory or does not synchronise, they often become isolated or even ill-treated by other children who fear or do not understand them.

Social drawings enable children to recall past social experience significant to them at that time and to convey their present feelings about the experience. Present and past feelings affect the content and how it is expressed. Facets of the child's personality are revealed in a drawing as well as the emotional state. For example, where a drawing is located on the paper may tell us something about personality and emotional state. Uncertainty gives rise to small hesitant drawings, (*Drawing 3*), sometimes in corners, whereas confidence is demonstrated by large drawings, often badly executed, which cover most of the paper (*Drawings 2, 11 and 15*). The amount of freedom to act that a particular child feels is demonstrated by the ideas and solutions it represents. Some children, a number of whom appeared confident in the interview, were able to draw up to six different courses of action to solve particular social dilemmas. Others, limited by conventional thinking, had difficulty in offering any other possibilities.

The work suggested that the generation of many ideas for social actions was linked to the child's ability to predict interpersonal behaviour, mood and intention. Using the Project's materials in a supportive atmosphere, many such children's ability to predict personal behaviour and initiate change increased. This attitude and behaviour became progressively more evident as the cartoons developed. The cartoon style, using bubbles (*Drawings 15 and 16*), encourages children to add detail of thoughts, sounds, smells, impressions and what was said in the bubbles or the drawing; detail which does not usually appear elsewhere. This additional information is often crucial to understanding the nuances and subtleties of behaviour and the whole social context in which the child is learning.

As we talk with children about their drawings, it is easy to become more concerned with aesthetic rather than social content. It is tempting, for example, to become enthusiastic over the use of colour or high quality drawings, in preference to considering the child's needs and how to meet them as

75

revealed in the drawing. In this work, children's accounts of their experiences should stem from why they drew what they did, rather than the focus being put on the aesthetic impact of colour or method of representation chosen. In practice, aesthetic impact and social message are intimately related, but if the discussion of the work with the child is too artistically critical the expression of need will be inhibited.

We found working with children that listening to them talking whilst working is one very good way of increasing your understanding of what their attitudes are to what they are drawing. Regular teachers and the child's parents are particularly fortunate in being able to place their understandings of a child's drawings and behaviour in the context of prolonged interaction with that child. This allows the development of a particular child to be understood as a progression, something a single drawing or piece of research can never do.

At different ages children attach different meanings to events they encounter and this is evident in their drawings. We can see them progress from the use of 'compulsive' strokes at eight years (*Drawing 2*), indicating the determined world, to a more controlled form of expression (*Drawing 8*), suggesting the capacity to change things. As their social world widens, so does their repertoire of behaviour and image. Both are modified and applied in attempts to understand more clearly the increasing complexity of social encounters. *Drawing 13* is, again, a good example of how this girl has drawn the essential features to show the nature of her interaction with the family. The drawing is indicative of how well she managed the situation and how others in it reacted to her behaviour. Very often, the developing ideas of self and the ability to draw oneself grow side by side. Self is externalised and observed (*Drawing 3*). Learning to look at your own drawings is learning to look at yourself, and to consider your own emotions and views can be the first step in sensitively relating to others.

Conversely, looking at other people's drawings with care is learning about them and their needs. If we look again at *Drawing 1*, for example, we can see the happy relationship this eight year old boy has with his Christmas Dalek. He has established his own identity and mood by drawing himself separately and smiling. The Dalek, the main subject, is drawn

76

larger than the boy, centrally placed and coloured in detail for emphasis. It seems that the Dalek is placed near the boy and facing in his direction to establish the nature of the relationship between them. The boy can control, manipulate, disregard or love his Dalek as he so chooses. He can establish his own personal identity in relation to the toy through trial and error. If he treats it well, then it will continue to operate successfully and please him. His happiness is based on the harmonious balance he has established between his freedom of action related to the Dalek and the limitations imposed by its physical properties. The boy's written account of this happy situation, however, loses the emotional quality of the drawing, and so gives a much more limited indication of his needs, feelings and interests. 'I can remember that once at Christmas I got a Dalek and it could talk. It also had a button on it and when you pressed it it sent some little pelts [*sic*] at you and that made me pleased very much.'

As it is feelings that provide the main stimulus for expression, children tend to draw those objects, animals or people that are most significant to them emotionally. The intense emotional feeling a child may have for a best friend, for example, is more clearly shown by this eight year old girl's drawing than in her limited written description (*Drawing 2*). Both are skipping happily together against a background devoid of detail apart from the happy sun shining down on them. Their personal feelings are shown as reciprocal with the two figures balancing and complementing each other compositionally. There is a feeling of harmony and joint identity. Both are wearing similar clothes and have similar facial expressions and gestures. Their complementary relationship is confirmed by the feet pointing toward each other and the skipping ropes linking and balancing the two of them. The differences between them, their hairstyles and dress colours are also drawn, but they do not split the friendship. Rather, they demonstrate respect for identity. Through playing, the children have learnt to establish a balanced relationship that acknowledges their individual differences. We can feel and see the pleasure they both take in being affectionate towards each other, both by what is drawn and by the way in which the composition is organised.

We can see an even closer personal relationship drawn in

Drawing 3. The writing that accompanies the drawing is simple and unemotional and it does not convey the intensity suggested by the subject or the method of drawing. The close smiling faces and the twining arms of the two figures indicate the intimacy of the relationship. This drawing is an excellent example of the importance of dependence and security for the eight year old girl who drew it. We know her mother had been in hospital for a month, and the girl shows herself cuddling Auntie Vera with whom she is staying. Auntie Vera understands and meets the girl's need for love and security. The girl's happiness at her aunt's goodwill and sympathy is emphasised by the symbolic sun placed near the two figures to add to their enclosed warmth.

Not all children, however, in similar circumstances find a caring and supportive aunt. The ten year old boy in *Drawing 4*, for example, has drawn himself telephoning his mother in hospital. This, he writes, is the action that allays his anxieties about his mother's illness. Dad, however, is drawn leaving the room at this crucial moment, making himself emotionally unavailable. It may be that he is unable to provide the love and security the boy needs and so keeps himself remote. The boy's only possibility, it seems, is to be dependent on his mother for the reassurance and understanding he needs.

As is apparent from *Drawings 1 and 2*, children emphasise, with detail, pattern and colour, the most important figures in their drawings. Conversely, they often omit or partly obscure those that constitute a threat in some way. A main cause of such anxiety is often the behaviour of a brother or sister. In drawing the family, a child troubled by siblings may omit them and draw a depleted family group. It is only by talking with the children and comparing several family drawings that such omissions become evident. Two drawings from the same nine year old girl (*Drawings 5 and 6*) provide an example of sibling anxiety. *Drawing 5* shows the girl in her pram as a baby. Her elder sister is able to rock the pram by standing on a stool. All is not well. The baby's head is in fact turned away from her sister who is grimacing at the baby and sticking her tongue out. The girl's writing confirms the older sister's antagonism. Her smallness and weakness as a baby may well add to her feelings of insecurity and anxiety at her sister's threatening behaviour. Early feelings towards her sister are

78

not forgotten, as *Drawing 6* shows. It is Christmas and the family are opening their presents. She has placed herself centrally under the warmth of the light, with her presents, symbols of family love. Her mother and father, who have been unable to create a loving family relationship, have been omitted. So, too, has the elder sister. In her writing, the girl describes in detail the presents her parents, her brother and she herself have received. Her elder sister's presents are not mentioned, nor does she appear in the drawing. The girl's feelings of anxiety towards her younger brother prevent her drawing him completely. He is half drawn, leaving the picture with his back to his sister, clutching a ball which obscures most of him. The most appropriate method of coping with interpersonal anxiety, it seems, is by exclusion. This is evident in social behaviour, writing and drawing where exclusion by omission and spatial isolation are often obvious. It is very difficult for this young girl to write down the complexities of her family's emotional life and her involvement in it. Yet, through her drawings, she is able to convey the essence of how she feels and reacts, particularly as the most significant interpersonal communication in this situation is non-verbal. To attempt a verbal description of how she felt in *Drawing 5 and 6* would be difficult and embarrassing. What she cannot, or will not, say or admit to feeling is expressed in what she has drawn and how she has drawn it.

During our work with children of eight to thirteen, it became apparent that, through the age range, there is an increasing concern with the physical properties of things related to their own size. To many children, being tall is a form of status. It enables adults to look down on children, either positively, with a kind expression and relaxed posture, or negatively, in a threatening way, to produce insecurity. *Drawing 7* illustrates a form of positive adult behaviour in a social situation of uncertainty for the child. It shows a number of features that are not included in the child's writing. Brown Owl is recognised by her beret 'status symbol'. She is tall, large, and centrally positioned. The Brownies in the background are small. The nine year old girl who drew this picture is seen emerging from the contained security of her peer group, shown as made up of identical and overlapping figures. She is crossing the space to the unknown adult to ask what the

79

group should do in the competition. She has indicated her social purpose in the drawing by her size and position. She shows courage in experimenting to find a solution to the group's dilemma and being able to adapt to the unknown situation. Her written account told us that her act of reaching out for guidance to an adult was later rewarded by Brown Owl's positive behaviour. She simply stated that Brown Owl told her what to do. From her writing, we do not feel the significance of her leaving the group's close-knit identity and of her tentative journey to Brown Owl. Both appear as key features in her drawing and are fundamental in helping us to understand the nature of her social learning and why she was successful.

To many children, social success seems a rare occurrence in a world dominated by adult standards and demands. All too often, they feel unable to be effective in the situations in which they find themselves. Yet many are experimenting within adult frames of reference, often in minor or less obvious ways than this Brownie. Social confidence comes from mastering the ability to relate to a variety of people in different social contexts without embarrassment or loss of face. The next drawing (8) is drawn by a ten year old boy to demonstrate his happiness in mastering the business of buying something in a shop. He knows what to do. We can clearly see the details of the toy he is buying, its price on the box, the correct money, carefully coloured, on the eye-level counter. The social competence of this small boy is supported by the tolerance and goodwill of the two adults within the situation, his mother and the shopkeeper. From their reactions to his behaviour, he is able to negotiate his purchase and predict some of the possibilities that may attend his next shopping excursion – both the limitations and the potentialities.

Not all children, of course, supply us with such rich examples of finished work, or of their social growth, but much of the scribbling, doodling, day-dreaming, mumbling and general playing-around which can go on when children are invited to represent their experiences give us valuable indications of their priorities – their hopes and their fears. It can be a source of learning for parent or teacher and an opportunity to increase relevance, motivation and moral growth. Such behaviour has an experimental side. It is a challenge, but also an opportunity. For example, we can learn a great deal from the behaviour of children who habitually want help or draw attention to themselves. Similarly, the child's offer of help is a growth point. We see the immense pleasure children get from the friendly reaction of an adult to their offer of help, particularly as this is expressed in their drawings. From the national survey, we found children greatly enjoy the mutual support to be gained when they join an adult in doing an adult job. They highly value being treated as a responsible individual whose abilities and personality are in demand. They may have to exercise some control over their natural tendencies or reactions to complete the job satisfactorily. They may enjoy exerting control over another person – in a situation with obvious negative, as well as positive, possibilities.

A typical controlling situation, shown in *Drawing 9*, is that of riding a horse, which is much larger and stronger than the rider. Riding one horse regularly, enables the rider to learn its moods and behaviour and generally get to know its personality. When something unpredictable or inconsistent happens, as in this case, the challenge is direct and cannot be avoided. Two main reactions observable in the drawing seem typical of many children. Either they initiate a new course of action to resolve the problem or they retreat to adult or peer-group security of one form or another. The details of this girl's reaction is shown in her drawing. The telephone is the girl's link with her parents. From the written account it appears that whilst riding, away from their home area, the girl and her companion had both fallen off and the horses had run away. The girls found a telephone and rang their parents to come and take them home.

The way the horses are drawn reflects the girls' feeling of dependence on their behaving as predicted. In the case of the drawing we have been considering, horses are drawn in identical single positions in flat profile with the riders, well seated and in absolute control. We find stereotypes in drawing; so do we in behaviour.

Children's illustrations of objects, animals and people may become increasingly stereotyped and this is usually paralleled by imitation and stereotyping in social behaviour. Knowing how to behave like everyone else, or knowing how to draw imitatively, 'gets you by' socially: whether it is encouraged and becomes a way of life is decided by the reaction of others most significant to the child. The drawings young adolescent girls produce of themselves and their peers are often unimaginative stereotypes of the latest in fashion. Behaviour, too, is concerned with the fashionable thing to do rather than with developing effective individual courses of action. The stereotypes fulfil an immediate purpose and may only work for a limited time in restricted contexts. Growing out of the stereotypes demands a questioning and evaluating of them and the development through social experience of individual attitudes and courses of action. Being independent of stereotypes raises the individual's self-confidence and supports a positive individual identity.

Drawing 10 shows some experiment within the stereotyped representation of the figures. All the figures show feeling, particularly through facial expression, but they have fashionable eye make-up, eyelashes, lips, hairstyles and clothes. The body stances show attempts to draw it 'like it is', but the experiment generally fails. The written report states that the girl on the right is walking away after being teased by the other girls. The writer's sister with the hat is incapable of doing anything to improve her own situation. This inability to act often results from being unable to modify earlier behaviour to suit changing contexts. From the National Survey findings, it appears that most children become increasingly realistic and are able to identify the possible effects of their actions and how much innovation is practical in particular situations, but whether they do so is a function of the support they receive. If a child finds it impossible to change his or her behaviour, this is reflected in a drawing and repeated drawings which will be of a very limited and stereotyped kind.

As drawing reflects aspects of the individual's personality, it is possible to identify particular children by how they draw. Individuality influences the values and attitudes a child is willing to express and his ways of expressing them. Peer-group pressure may prevent some children attempting new ideas or original action of any kind, and this is common where living conditions are duplicated. The children may then draw rows of houses or a series of tower-blocks.

Expressing yourself can become a dull routine task if others' negative criticism is dominant. Dark-coloured drawings often illustrate this situation. As they grow older, children inevitably experience tension between their individuality and what is acceptable to others. This tension is often expressed in very clear, neat, controlled drawings of people, each with a marked, separate identity. The relationships between people in the composition are indicated through a use of space in which individuals are performing specific actions that give them social meaning.

The need for cooperative action is frequently most clearly expressed in drawings. The girls in *Drawing 11*, for example, are deciding what to do following the accidental collapse of a toy pram. The drawing is realistic: we can see details of the pram, its mechanical parts and the girls on each side of it have clear identities. They are jointly registering their response to what has just happened and the onus on them to do something.

Children consistently show concern over the range of personal decisions they have to make, their isolation in different situations, and the effect of what has happened on others as well as themselves. A nine year old girl, in *Drawing 12*, for example, has drawn herself alone in the kitchen, separated from her mother by a wall in the foreground. She has apparently accidentally broken a cup and saucer whilst 'helping' with the washing up. She doesn't know what to do. Mum, drawn in isolation, has not seen or heard what has happened.

Many parents and families are relatively insensitive to each other's needs and generally unsupportive. The girl who drew *Drawing 13*, for example, has drawn the complete family around the meal table, each labelled to show who they are. They are drawn to show how they relate to her. She shows herself facing out, isolated in the foreground and labelled 'me'. She is obviously extremely angry with her brother, Mark (who has eaten her doughnut which she saved from a previous meal). Both her mother and brother are significantly drawn as larger than her father. Her mother appears amused and unsupportive. The sister, Ruth, seems indifferent, being drawn with her back to us. All the family appears to be smiling except the artist who is cross at their attitude to the unfair treatment she is receiving. From her writing, we learn what happens next. She leaves the room. She wrote 'I was really angry, but I didn't hit him because he nearly always hits me back. So I went into a temper. I banged my feet on the floor. I went out of the kitchen door and slammed it behind me. I opened another door and slammed that behind me as well. I had started to cry when I found out Mark had eaten my doughnut.'

Children often feel they want to be on their own and isolate themselves. Competition can be destructive, particularly in school when it results in individual isolation of the type shown in *Drawing 14*. The boy has received encouragement from his teacher in the form of a silver star. The incident could well have established a style for that boy. Drawings showing children isolating themselves to get away from others' success and superiority are also common.

We all know that the need for security and happiness is fundamental for children if they are to grow up to be reasonable beings. Both can be provided by parents, 'close' adults, animals and sometimes, to a lesser degree, toys and other objects. When children draw their toys they frequently ascribe human characteristics to them. The Dalek and Action Men who complement many boys' lives, and the walking, talking dolls that are put through domestic and social routines by girls, are all well-known subjects for drawing. Each toy or object is shown in a way that allows the child to project its fears, fantasies and expectations. The reactions the toy or object 'makes' in the illustration to these play experiments may be children's own reactions to themselves. Children project the behaviour they see as a possibility. Many possibilities for different types of action can be played out and explored in children's drawings. The toys and objects shown are predictable in their reactions to particular treatment, more so than people or even animals. This sense of predictability can provide a form of security where children feel supported in the situations important to them. This is why the Project's publication programme incorporates a number of situations where toys and objects are the central concern. These are linked to a range of activities which enable children to work out a number of different ideas about themselves and to express the outcome. Both the form of expression and the

84

context of the classroom provide a degree of security that allows a child to experiment socially in a fairly stable, safe atmosphere. The consequences of possible actions can be explored and considered without the inevitable destructive effects of social failure in real life.

Drawings put people and problems safely on paper. A picture is produced that is played with and modified until it fulfils the requirements of the individual producing it. In *Drawing 15*, the toy has become the girl's favoured possession. The illustration shows through a series of events the saga of this ten year old's continuing affection for Bellie, her teddy bear. Her writing, simple and clear, does not convey the complexity of each situation. The drawings, with their colour and detail add much to our understanding of what she has tried to convey in her writing. We can see who the members of the family are, what they look like, and how they behave towards each other. The significant features of each drawing are coloured to emphasise their importance for the little girl. The first drawing uses colour to highlight the key event of her mother giving Bellie to the baby in her cot. It was her first toy. Bellie than becomes increasingly involved in her daily life. In the second illustration, speech bubbles are used to show her father reinforcing her mother's suggested name for the bear. The girl has placed herself centrally between her parents, facing her mother. She and the bear are obviously the focus of family attention. Her involvement and identification with Bellie becomes more clear in the third illustration where he provides her with comfort and security in her cot. In the fourth illustration, a reversed question mark over the girl's head indicates her uncertainty about Bellie's condition. The words 'missing fur' written on the drawing confirm the reason and illustrate a relatively common occurrence where a child uses words because it does not feel confident expressing everything important in drawing. Interestingly, the girl has drawn herself the same size as Bellie, which shows her deep level of personal identification.

The final sentence in her writing was 'Bellie is alive today'. It is not usually children who lack human support who identify so closely with dolls and animal toys in their drawings. Typically, this little girl's father and mother were supportive. They made love natural and love always needs a personal, intimate object.

As they grow older, children include more detail in their drawings of people to give them greater social significance and specific identification. The role and status of the two boys shown in the cartoon in *Drawing 16* are indicated by their actions and appearance. Bully Boy Banks has stubble on his chin, bovver boots, rolled-up jeans and patches. His actions (related to cigarettes and smoking) throughout the strip, are unmistakably bad. He is a stereotyped 'baddy' who is complemented by the other boy, a stereotyped 'goody'. Both stereotypes may be facets of the artist's personality. His use of stereotypes may enable him to show the observer how moralistic he is. Dealing in stereotypes may also actually prevent him identifying what he might do in the situation, or how near his own personality is to that of either boy drawn. Sometimes, the stereotyped idea of behaviour persists into adult life and forms a bulwark against reality.

The twelve year old boy drawing the strip warms to his stereotyping, and draws the hero, Edward, as good, fresh-complexioned, neatly dressed, with shorter hair. Edward is the one who thinks out the 'moral' thing to do. In the second picture, we see a sophisticated use of cartoon close-up technique, to focus attention on his appearance and thoughtful facial expression. However, it is the speech and actions that indicate the precise nature of the good–versus–bad confrontation. Bad Bully Boy Banks, drawn with larger-than-life cigarette and huge match, confronts Edward running home from school. 'Ave a fag, or I'll burn your hair off' is a threat not to be dismissed lightly. Edward, of course, refuses to smoke, so a huge cigarette is pushed into his mouth and his hair set on fire by Banks. Naturally, he dies from such ill treatment, the 'grievous bodily harm', and Banks is 'put behind the bars' in true, comic strip fashion.

It may be that the artist's fantasy world is projected onto a background of real events which make it difficult for him, and many children like him, to distinguish between fantasy and reality at times. Fantasy is not, of course, to be regarded as of less importance than factual reporting. It may be of even more significance.

Studying children's drawings during their social development makes it possible for us to help, particularly by providing support for imagination. Seeing someone else's point of view for the first time may be very similar to drawing a physical object, animal, or person from another perspective. It is even more closely paralleled by a child drawing a situation several times through the eyes of different parties to it.

There is also a parallel between children seeing and predicting the consequences of social behaviour and their seeing the effect of a particular line or shape on a picture. Both social situation and picture alter as the relationships and positions of their elements change. A drawing is a 'frozen' picture of their experience – social interaction stopped for a moment so that its complexity can be studied. Personal feelings are externalised, communicated and considered. The expression of these feelings becomes more effective as the child's social skill or ability to use a means of artistic expression develops. Both behaviour and drawing express what is seen, thought and felt. Our concern is to reduce ambiguity and encourage direct, clear communication which makes possible a life-style based on observation and consideration.

Different groups of children can, by looking at a selection of their drawings, begin to accept that there are different versions of the same situation. The idea that different people express different attitudes and values in their drawings, writing, speech and behaviour is accepted as a natural state of affairs. This dawning recognition of what it means to be an individual raises many moral questions. We can help provide some of the answers by increasing the level of sensitivity in observation, understanding, thought and action. We can provide vehicles for the expression of observation and reaction through creative activity. The basis for such work should always be the child's reaction to its world. Children's experiences and their relationships with others are the fundamental starting points for moral and social growth. To become more sensitive in perception and expression of personal understanding is the essence of learning to live well with others. We can support self-expression, and further our own understanding of what it is to be a child, by inviting children to draw.

References

1. Middleton, D., 1975. Creativity in Children's Social and Moral Learning, unpublished M.A. thesis, London University Institute Library.

Drawing 1

Drawing 2

Drawing 3

Drawing 4

Drawing 5

Drawing 6

Drawing 7

Drawing 8

Drawing 9

Drawing 10

Drawing 11

Drawing 12

brother
Mark

Maddy

mummy

sister
Ruth

me

Drawing 13

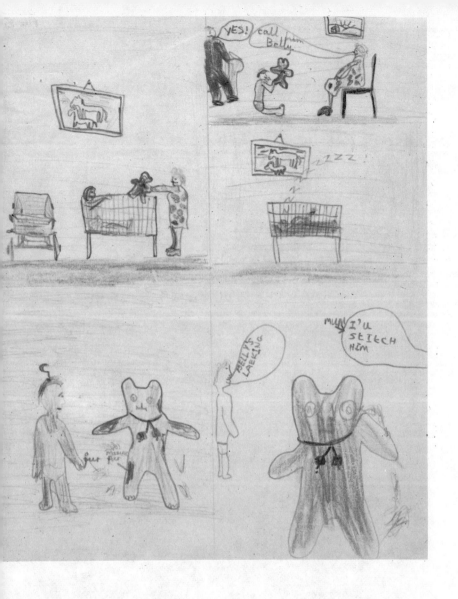

Drawing 15.

5 School organisation and moral education

Encounters, endeavours and cooperation

In the preceding chapters we have considered how children learn their moral behaviour. Later in this book attention will be paid to the materials and techniques developed by the Project for planned curriculum activities based on these learning processes. One unmistakable conclusion from our research is that the quality of relationships is fundamental to social learning and that relationships are integral to any community life. No adult who is a member of the school staff can claim to take no part in moral learning, whether or not his activities in this area are intentional or recognised. Furthermore, the ways in which schools are organised, and their physical conditions, can play a part in shaping the character of these relationships. This social learning through the interaction involved in teaching and community living is often described as the 'hidden curriculum'. One major concern of this chapter is to consider how this hidden moral curriculum, providing as it does many of the social experiences, may become the subject of deliberate planning. Through the experience of responsibility in the everyday life of the school, children may gain the self-confidence to act positively in those situations where they recognise a need, which may itself be the result of planned moral education activities.

No school can regard moral education as the responsibility of any one teacher or team of teachers. The most carefully planned, thoughtful and sensitive programme of moral education, in a school where the social climate is unfavourable, perhaps being excessively competitive or restrictive of individual action, is going to be hampered and unfortunately limited in its results. The two aspects are complementary and one would ideally hope for moral education activities in the classroom to take place in a positive school climate where the two aspects would be mutually supportive. In the same way the moral learning functions of home and school can be reinforcing.

The final section of this chapter examines the ways in which schools may relate to the value-learning patterns of the home. The research survey, discussed in Chapter 9, showed that many of the significant events reported by children took place out of school, and the people reported as important to them in these events are their parents, siblings, other relations and friends. These factors combined mean that, if schools are to become effective moral agencies and if they organise moral education curriculum activities around the situations reported by children, then they must recognise that they do so against a background of values learned elsewhere. Schools will have to work out their own individual relationships with parents, homes and the community; they must decide to what extent they can build on the base provided, so as to reinforce selectively some existing values or to attempt to change patterns of behaviour radically. There is little evidence to suggest that schools which have sought to turn their backs entirely on the local community have had much long-term success. Though if the society is unhappy and destructive then the school has no alternative but to work through honesty about the status quo towards radical change. If schools wish to build on existing foundations then good home –school links become a first priority and the key word will have to be cooperation.

Encounters

As was shown in Chapter 1, for children to develop as balanced, responsible and independent beings they require from adults security, trust and love; most particularly they

90

require these from their homes and ideally the school would offer a continuity of style of relationships. They need the security provided by their social world being organised for them, giving them the opportunity for as much independent action as they feel they can handle within a basic framework to which they can return; and safety too in a sense of confidence in the consistency of treatment and the permanence of the structure. They should have mutual trust, so that they are not belittled by feeling that they are cheated or used, and so that they can see themselves as people who are responsible and trustworthy. It should not be too difficult to see how schools might attempt to provide for these basic needs. Nevertheless influences outside schools are very strong indeed, children may actually not be trustworthy and may abuse opportunities provided for independent action; furthermore 'love' may seem too strong or too personal a word for schools and patterns of caring which involve hundreds of children, some of whom may be less than attractive in their behaviour. However, teaching remains one of the caring professions.

We all value our own individuality and there are many small ways in which schools can recognise the individuality of their pupils and in so doing show that they matter as people and thus establish a climate of respect. The most basic way is probably by the use of names. This is not a plea for teachers to encourage children to call them by their first names. This is a practice which many children might find embarrassing and in many ways confusing, as the teacher's role and respect for the teacher are reflected, for most children, in the form of address of 'Mr Smith' or 'Mrs MacArthur'. What is recommended is much simpler, the addressing of children by name, whether John, Elizabeth or Smith, according to the custom of the school, rather than as 'You boy, you know who I mean' or 'That boy at the end of the row, no, not you, him!' Some teachers with pastoral responsibility use photographs to help them learn children's names. A kindly use of personal knowledge, an interested enquiry after a pet, progress with a hobby or the events of a previous weekend, in all of which most children will take and share pleasure and reasonable pride, and conversations as held between friends may begin. Personal knowledge may emerge which a teacher might make good use of in promoting motivation or which may explain facets of the child's behaviour not previously understood. This is no more than saying talk to children, treat them as individual people and the school community will be better for it. This all raises two issues which will be returned to again: whether the size of the school or the class affects the social health of the community and whether the pressure of work can make real relationships impossible.

The phrase 'school community' has been used freely here without any clear discussion of whom it comprises besides teachers and pupils. When young children aged five or six are asked who there is at school the reply often follows the pattern of,

'Well there's Mrs Collins, she's our teacher and Mr Keast' (he's the headmaster) 'and Mr Barry, he owns the school' (he's the caretaker), 'and Mrs Browne and Mrs Hughes' (they are 'dinner ladies'), 'and then there's Mrs Molly' (she's the crossing attendant).'

There is very often no mention of the other class teachers who, when discussing the school community in the staff room, would include themselves in it but might not always include all the ancillary, auxiliary and service staff who may loom large in the child's perception of his day at school. The lady who controls the playground or the dining hall, the lady who serves the food, and the caretaker who locks away coats and bags left lying in the classroom at the end of the day – these can make a great impression on a child's day. The research survey provided many stories from children of clashes with authority at school, and about which teachers may know little; one of these stories has been included in the curriculum unit *Choosing* and additional references are made to this in the research report. It may be worth including these 'non-professional' members of the school community in staff meetings when relationships with the pupils are discussed and discipline and control are the subject of debate. It is very likely that they have insights into the problems or behaviour of children. Where clashes between adults and children occur within the school the headmaster who wishes to retain the loyalty of his staff must most often feel inclined to back his staff and support them, yet the situations reported by children to the project team revealed several instances where an injustice or unkindness appears to have occurred. One of the saddest comments made by a teacher is 'Of course I care but . . .' there is some other factor interfering, perhaps a lack of time and too much work or a feeling that the child is 'only attention seeking' and yet may need attention, or that the child is a nuisance or naughty so much of the time that it is difficult to be patient. It may be that the teacher has become so burdened by administration or concern about proper uniform or has so many problem children sent to her that she can no longer cope with the child as an individual and resorts to stereotyped reactions. This should be the moment to find the time to smile and an opportunity to show that, however it may seem from the pattern of everyday chasing-up and nagging, teachers do care about children. This is the moment when to see the situation from the child's point of view would be invaluable. Teachers who have administrative responsibilities can have their relationships with children warped by the demands made on them by their colleagues, who may even go so far as to use them as a scapegoat to avoid a personal confrontation themselves. Teachers locked into one dominating, authoritarian role and finding this souring their pleasure in school life have reported that seeking other settings for other roles has been particularly useful: joining, though not necessarily organising, a rambling group, a voluntary service team or a study group has provided the opportunity to see the children in a new light and be seen by the pupils as less menacing and quite human after all.

Large schools can have a bewildering complexity. No less difficult for a new member of staff than for a new pupil and there may be difficulty in forming relationships, teacher–pupil teacher–teacher teacher–head and head–pupil, and though many heads make enormous efforts the point can be reached where without enormous administrative skill the school fails to gel as a coherent body and teachers and pupils alike may feel themselves to be drifting in unknown seas. The opportunities available at large schools to participate in a glittering range of extracurricular activities may be most prestigious and appealing and yet the level of participation can fall as the school grows in size, and the opportunities to represent the school decrease. Where a school of 350 pupils may take a walking group youth hostelling in Wales, a school of 1,400 would need to send four groups and this is sometimes not possible. This problem facing large schools is not necessarily insuperable and there are notable successes in keeping large schools human in scale. Nevertheless in terms of human satisfaction villages can be more satisfying than cities; we may see fewer faces in the village but a much higher proportion of familiar faces.

Another of the decisions which has to be taken relates to the teacher's role in counselling, and may arise from moral education discussions or chance encounters around the school. The choice would seem to lie between two basic styles of operation, between a 'professional authority' model and a 'shared problem' model. The major difficulty presented by the former is that it is difficult for a genuine dialogue to take place: one person is saying 'I have a problem' or 'I don't understand this piece of social behaviour' and the other is saying 'I can give you some good advice' or 'I can tell you what you need to know', and, although the teacher may have a real concern to help, this approach may be seen by the child as an extension of the school's authority and concern for order. It can too easily maintain or create distance between the two parties. The 'shared problem' model would emphasise the personal dignity and independence of the child which is important if the aim is for ultimate autonomy; the teacher and the child would be sharing views on a situation of common concern: common because it may stem directly from the life of the school community, common because of a general concern the one has for the other, or common because they have both faced similar situations. There may be very good reasons for adopting the former model, it may be the only way an individual can cope with the very large number of demands made on him. It may be that the teacher feels that, because children require adults to provide a framework for their lives, as shown in Chapter 1, it would be better for them if he were to maintain this controlling position rather than confuse the child. Finally, it takes a great deal of confidence to be able to admit to a child that adults do not always know what to do in their own lives and admitting to human frailty in one context may lessen their credibility in another. The balance adopted by the individual teacher cannot be dictated but it should be a reasoned position, taken up after a consideration of the consequences.

94

It should be borne in mind that children can be perceptive interpreters of non-verbal cues and nuances of language and intonation and there are many ways in which the authority of the teacher can be conveyed.

A number of children's responses in the National Survey revealed that children resent overbearing authority and situations where they are controlled without reasons being given and where there is no opportunity for them to express their reactions. An example from the everyday life of a school might be where a teacher is organising the seating plan for a classroom. The children may have preferences for particular arrangements but the teacher may have his own criteria and, though the Project is not advocating that such arrangements should be the result of democratic decisions, the teacher might explain the principle on which he is acting, and even if that principle is to separate likely troublemakers some honest reasons could be given. This could provide a move towards children accepting more rather than less responsibility for their behaviour. To grow into rationality children need reasons not rationalisations, and Chapter 1 discussed the ways in which behaviour is contagious. During these middle years and the approach of adolescence, children are working out an image of themselves and we would hope it is one in which they are responsible and in which their teacher, who has a highly significant role in their lives, recognises them as responsible. There are opportunities for fostering this responsibility in the academic work of the school, as well as in social organisation, where the teacher's role as expert or guide leaves room for sharing the love of learning and of tackling problems. Learning rather than teaching is the major activity of the classroom. One way in which teachers have attempted to meet the learning needs of individual pupils is to provide them with separate tasks on workcards. Although this is intended as a response to the individuality of the learner, the amount of work created by writing the cards and maintaining the work done can too often turn a classroom into a 'battery' or 'deep litter' where in practice the individual is subjected to the system and without some additional assistance the teacher has less contact with the pupil than under a traditional class teaching system. Despite the fact that this method is adopted with genuine social learning aims, in mixed ability teaching it can produce feelings of isolation. All too often when this system is operated in large and complex schools the difficulties are compounded.

The care of a school should be for all its pupils and where the school sees its aims in narrow terms the opportunities for pupil success can be very limited. The question 'What is a good pupil?' might be asked of any school, and for many, organised on a model which involves restricted transmission of knowledge, the answer is all too often 'The one who achieves high standards in academic work.' The others who may be performing well against their individual pattern of abilities and hindrances are not so recognised. Perhaps it might be better if the good pupil were also identified by achievements other than academic ones. The narrow academic school can too often over-value passive compliance and foster a slightly neurotic anxiety which, though useful in achieving targets even in the case of self-regulating work, does so at the expense of individual choice, initiative and drive and creates a pattern of external dependence.

For many children selection, whether by type of schools, stream or set, can be taken as a form of rejection and the reaction may be one of rebellion or self-devaluation, and the social confidence important to social action may be damaged. In practice, remedial groups, classes or schools are most often organised so that relationships can develop and thus motivation to learn is improved; these relationships are facilitated by smaller work groups and longer periods of time with the same teacher. The link between relationships and motivation is so often mistaken and those who suggest that schools put 'the social cart before the academic horse' take too simple a view of the social factors which influence learning.

That teaching can be a stressful occupation is being increasingly recognised, and yet we may not be sufficiently aware of the effects of stress. A busy school day can provide occasions for shock, anger or fear, as in the story in *Choosing* where a girl comes close to drowning:

'I . . . panicked and went under . . . I was brought out of the water and my teacher hit me . . .'

Self-control exercised in fraught situations can be a most

96

useful model for children whose need for effective adult examples is discussed in Chapter 1.

Such encounters have been for the most part the chance occurrences of the school day. Against this informal pattern should be set those which are the result of the formal, planned life of the school.

Most schools provide 'pastoral' time when children are with their class teacher or tutor. This time is often used for administration, for handing out letters to parents, marking the attendance register, collecting dinner money and checking on progress. This time can be very important for children because, in schools which are academically oriented and subject-organised, it may be one of the few official, relaxed 'non-work' times of contact with the teacher. Sometimes the developing relationship may be strained by the pressure on the form teacher to pass on complaints, correctives and admonitions. These may be more significant for the child, when they come from the tutor, rather than the subject teacher or supervisor, because of the understood differences in the relationship. Sometimes sufficient time is allotted for this to be the case. This pastoral time may be a good opportunity for discussions which can have a beginning with the *Startline* materials.

Just as the form teacher can have his contact time with pupils overwhelmed by administration and disciplinary concerns this can be particularly so for heads, deputies, heads of sections of the school and year tutors. As has been pointed out, children may gain an entirely false view of the teacher's patterns of concerns and the teacher becomes stereotyped in the children's view and a scapegoat to the rest of the staff. This may be the point where the buck stops, but it can be passed on all too often.

Some occasions can assume a peculiar significance and shape the pattern of interpretation of subsequent experience. These may be unpredictable, but for example starting at a new school is a critical event in all children's lives. Some schools go to great lengths to reduce the anxiety and setback that the transfer might cause, and establish a pattern of visits by year tutors (or some other key figure) to contributory schools, visits by the children to their new school, visits by their parents, the issue of brochures with all the necessary information or even the opportunity for friendship groups to remain together wherever this is thought desirable. With this kind of careful preparation and concern for the individual, self-confidence can continue to grow. The change will provide a trigger to growth. For some children, however, the transfer seems to bring only problems. Homework can be a symbol of the new status and an interesting addition to the routine, but it can be distressing and some schools persist in the practice of 'piling it on' in order to set new standards which all too often has a negative effect.

The arrangements which are made for sick or injured children provide an opportunity to provide care at a time when the child feels vulnerable and in need of support. If the school is seeking to establish, as far as is possible in a large community, a familial type of relationship, this is an important opportunity and the arrangements warrant detailed attention.

Assembly can be a very useful time in the school day. It provides a reinforcement of the idea of community. The opportunities for moral education are wide and most schools have a rich pattern of activity, with opportunities for children to present plays and readings, to perform on musical instruments and to set up displays, all of which are valuable for the development of self-confidence and a feeling of being valued – issues which are discussed in a later section. The danger lies in assemblies where the pupils are marshalled, only to be harangued, given the orders for the day or subjected to the exhortations of authority. In some schools, minority groups may be excluded from assembly at the request of their parents. This can have a serious effect on the pupils' views of themselves within the context of the rest of the school community. In such cases it is important to give them a context in which their sense of belonging can be restored.

Finally in this section, it is worth looking at the organisation of sports activities. It is not proposed here that any new rule should be laid down but rather that certain issues are raised for contemplation or discussion in the light of their social effects. One fundamental question is the function of school sports: whether school teams are chosen which are most likely to win, and perhaps increase the confidence of the whole school, or whether they are formed to provide the pleasures of participation. Perhaps more than one team would be required. Two more basic questions are whether school games foster competition or cooperation and what are the social consequences of either. Too often school games are in the hands of those who are good at them, are accustomed to the satisfaction of striving and winning, and have too little insight into the feelings of the persistent loser. The pleasure and satisfaction which can be derived from physical activity is important to social growth, to health and balanced living and was emphasised in Chapter 1.

Endeavours

In this section we intend to discuss the ways in which schools might positively organise opportunities for pupils to demonstrate and develop the social behaviour which the school advocates. In general terms it is not reasonable to argue that young people should be responsible, independent and capable of making wise decisions, when the schools they attend do not provide them with opportunities for choosing, for taking any kind of initiative or for coping with the consequences of their own actions. The structure of the school is such that pupils are merely required to do as they are told.

The point has already been made that very large schools may diminish the likelihood of pupil involvement in activities. They also reduce the opportunities for the pupil to be significant, and this can reduce their confidence to take independent action. A sense of significance, achievement and self-esteem may be the result of public display or performance in a very wide range of academic and craft work, or through a musical or dramatic performance. The National Survey conducted by the Project provided many accounts from pupils of the pleasure they took in public recognition, in practising hard for some event and then in enjoying its success. School assembly may provide the opportunity, exhibitions of work offer another. Many such events are the vehicle for teacher–parent exchanges and for the parents to join in some school activity in support of their child, and a later section (p. 112) discusses the value of such contacts.

Many schools provide opportunities for pupils to take some

responsibility as monitors or prefects, and though this can be excellent it raises one difficult question: whether schools should select those pupils who already seem best fitted for such responsibility (perhaps as a result of their social learning in the home) and then use them, continuing their growth and widening the performance gap between them and their classmates. It is not advocated that some kind of levelling down should take place but that the opportunities for social development should be equitably distributed. It can be argued that using 'natural' monitors is closer to exploitation than education and that the school should help develop the social skills and competence of the pupils although that might result in less administrative efficiency within the school.

As the range of academic work widens, schools frequently look to their neighbouring environment as an object study. This may have many effects, intended or otherwise. It can raise the level of understanding of the environment; it can lead to a desire to improve that environment; but it cannot be a neutral, value-free exercise. The teacher is taking the pupil into a world which the latter knows well in many respects; the pupil may add several new dimensions to his understanding, but it is a topic where he has knowledge and access to knowledge which the teacher can use. The pupil can say, 'I have important things to say' or 'I can be your guide.' Such a change in roles and relationships can provide another opportunity to gain confidence.

Our adult society is governed through a system of councils and committees of representatives. The practices involved in their operation are important social knowledge. Giving children the opportunity to learn to operate in the same kind of way provides a valuable element of social education. If the experience is entirely simulated so that the exercise becomes a charade, a replication of adult activities without meaning, then only a formal knowledge of procedures is being provided. Committees and councils have meaning only when they have a focus for their activities, i.e. when the matters under discussion are matters of interest and concern to the members and to those whom they represent. There is widespread belief that pupils who take part in councils will inevitably seek to affect the pattern of government of their school and that the establishment of a school council is only one step towards pupil restiveness if not revolt. This is not necessarily so, even when senior pupils in secondary schools are involved. Chapter 1 on pupils' learning shows clearly that during these middle years children expect and require a firm structure for their social lives, yet one which allows them the opportunity to grow in independence and acquire the confidence to act according to their own decisions. The council needs to have a clear brief and one headmaster writing of his experience of pupil councils in junior schools writes, 'The skill required of the adult is to limit his/her observation to the parameters.' There is a story of a headmaster who, after arriving new at a secondary school, established a pupil council as one step towards building himself a liberal image. The council members were assured that they would be taken seriously and their decisions acted upon. They debated school uniform and passed a resolution asking for its abolition. Within hours the council had been banned and the head's image was in shreds. The topics which are discussed by the council need very careful consideration, not so much to inhibit the development of pupil power as to avoid confusion. They ought at best to be those in which pupils can play a major part in implementing their decisions and will obviously vary according to the ages of the children concerned. It is a matter for debate whether the age range of the council should be restricted so that the discussion is not dominated too much by the concerns and arguments of older pupils. It may require some skilful diplomacy on the part of the adult to set a pattern of balance. However, mixing the age groups does provide an opportunity for common discussion across the school and younger pupils may gain much from the older pupils' insights and capacities. One other issue which demands attention is how the involvement may be as widespread as possible. Some schools operate a whole school meeting or moot, but most rely on a pattern of class, tutor-group or year-group debates which can involve all pupils and from which the representatives can draw suggestions.

The head whose comments were quoted previously wrote,

To begin, its organisation will be frail. It is very difficult for a child to act as chairman without the initial help of an adult. The secretary's job is easier and it seems important to have a reminder at the beginning of each meeting of what was decided at the last. If the general intention of the council is to help the school and the community then ideas quickly come from the children. A coffee morning for mums with small children, a concert for old people, a sale to raise money for pictures for the school, an exhibition of hobbies and a lunch time football competition have all been proposed and carried through. The resulting events may not be as efficient and well run as some adults might wish but that is largely immaterial; the effectiveness of the council is in its attempts to discuss items sensibly, carry them through and see the results of their actions. (Mr C. Curtis, Bottisham Primary School, Cambridge.)

During the middle years many schools arrange trips and visits. Even day trips provide a significantly different social pattern, but in this section we intend to confine discussion to excursions which involve at least one night away from home. Such occasions provide an additional load of responsibility for the teacher but they can be very valuable for social learning. From the point of view of better understanding the children and the interaction between them, the surface consequences of which may have been apparent in the classroom, it can be very useful. However, the observation takes place both ways. Children are given an opportunity to get to know the teacher rather better, and this will extend the social repertoire of the child. During visits they will see how the teacher copes with a range of situations far wider than those which occur in the classrooom, and will be an important source of imitation and modelling (see Chapter 1), as he comes to this residential situation with the patterns already established in the school. They can observe an adult other than their parents and find out something more of his moral style and social skills, even at the level of 'What you say when ...' or 'What you do when ...'. It is almost inevitable that in this new context relationships will on occasions be less formal than they are in the classroom and this friendliness is likely to increase the teacher's social learning significance. At the same time, bearing in mind the example which is being provided, this increased friendliness should not be accompanied by any decline in standards of behaviour either given as an example or required from the group.

Often school journeys will include the opportunity for vigorous physical activity in which children can burn off excess energy (see p. 36) and have a new confidence in themselves and their ability to cope with a physical challenge.

Such journeys may require staying away from home for the first time and may appear threatening. The preparation needs to be carefully done, and the parents given plenty of notice so that they can decide whether their child should take part, without the additional problem of a nagging child, and so that they are able to play their part in preparing and reassuring the child. Lists of activities and suggested clothing should be provided in plenty of time. Once away from home, children may well be deciding what clothes to put on in the morning, independently, for the first time in their lives. They may be eating unaccustomed food without the same opportunities to have special attention paid to them. They may be walking when they are used to riding in a car. These experiences can go a long way towards creating independence.

School journey parties which go abroad provide another set of problems and possibilities. For children without a good command of the language of the country they are visiting, and without a practised grasp of the social conventions, there can be considerable insecurity so that encounters with the people of that country are emotionally charged. One way of reducing this difficulty would be to provide relevant learning material as a part of the preparation for the visit or as a part of language teaching. Another problem which is often faced by teachers taking parties of children abroad is the attitude of the children who feel an emotional release in being abroad. A feeling that they are free from observation, that no one knows them and that as a consequence they are free to do as they please. Nevertheless, foreign journeys, if adequately prepared and supervised, can be a valuable experience.

Schools can help children to become socially operational and take the initiative in the community in which they live. Over a few months, beginning in the autumn of 1976, a small-scale pilot investigation was carried out with the generous assistance of Mrs Jo Pelly. Attempts at beginning community service work with children are usually based on an adult perspective of what needs doing or what adults think that children might find satisfaction in doing. This work was an attempt to discover the child's perspective, in the hope that, if it is possible to identify those issues in their social and physical environment which matter to them, we would have a better base for deciding what action to take. The motivation for any action the children might take in the community would come from their own interest in the world, rather than from being told by adults.

The Project's National Survey gave an indication of what these issues were; their preoccupations with playing facilities, their families, with animals and with old people, for example. The survey also revealed an inhibition of action; many children also reported situations where they felt that something needed to be done but that the stimulus was lacking. In this pilot investigation the first intention was to extend the understanding of the child's view of the world and secondly to discover ways of providing support for their action. Children were interviewed in three schools. The interview was open and flexible but began with the questions 'What do children of your age enjoy doing most in this area?' and 'What sort of things annoy children in this area?'

Though it may seem rather strange for researchers with a concern for moral education to be apparently encouraging an interest in what children want for themselves and their friends, it was felt that , if the children's first steps in acting upon life, instead of letting life always act upon them, are motivated by the strengths of their own interests, this might be a way in which they can get a first taste of the confidence needed to develop into adults who initiate and perpetrate action in the community.

The main point is that children's community service might more effectively form a part of moral education if it lay clearly within the scope of children's concerns, decisions and abilities.

This route into community service might best begin with a discussion between teacher and pupils and proceed through a joint examination of desired action in the social and physical environment of the school.

In the last part of this section we will consider the formal support systems of the school. First, the uses of staff meetings, secondly, record-keeping procedures related to moral and social development, and lastly, the possible use of a self-scrutiny profile.

In many schools staff meetings are organised primarily for

administrative reasons; in others opportunities exist to discuss the progress and development of individual pupils.

The occasion for a discussion of the latter type may be some behaviour difficulty or some academic problem. These are often linked. While these matters may be the subject of informal consultations between teachers, the formal discussion in a meeting of all the staff, or perhaps the staff of a section of a school, provides an opportunity to share insights and observations. Some degree of consistency of treatment and support may be achieved (see p. 14). The first section of this chapter outlined some of the areas of a school's operation which affect the moral climate. Individual action is less effective than some concerted move. As the level of professionalism of teachers continually rises then the need for outside direction decreases and a programme of school development might be set in hand which draws on the individual strengths of staff members, one of whom may have a particular interest in moral education and can lead a discussion which may result in the conscious ordering of the life of the school in order to maximise the opportunities for moral learning. Such meetings seem to be most effective if there is some focus, and the two items which follow could provide a focus on the difficulties of monitoring moral development and the production of a school profile from which particular needs may stand out.

Pupil records can be a controversial issue and generate a great deal of emotional heat. The following extract is from a newspaper article[1] pointed out by one head who at that time was developing a new recording system for her school.

Ironically teachers, who have to assume the role of parents, may keep records on children which their real parents are not allowed to see. . . . They are often secret, anonymous and confidential; secret in the sense that parents are not told of their existence; anonymous in that the teachers writing the entries do not always have to sign them and cannot be held to account for anything they say no matter how unjust, prejudiced or quite simply mistaken; confidential in that neither pupils nor parents are allowed to see what has been said about them.

It would be a mistake if, because of this kind of comment teachers decided not to keep records of the social development of their pupils. What seems to be important is that such records are factual and are descriptions of events rather than merely the interpretation or judgement of events. In this way a 'case study' type of file is built up and the generalisations which are occasionally required are more grounded in events. If, for example, there is concern that a particular child seems to be having difficulty in making friends and seems to be unhappy and alone, observations can be jotted down on a day-to-day basis. A simple form such as that below may help in such record-keeping.

Setting	**Date**
Incident	
Comment	

The following account is from a middle school:

The moral education programme was undertaken as a result of team discussion, which led to the realisation of a need for work of this kind for our pupils' development. We had a well-developed pastoral care system whereby the pupil's registration group teacher and teaching group teacher met regularly to discuss individual progress and the academic programme. We had four teaching groups which were further divided into four different groupings for registration. This was to allow the widest possible pupil–teacher contact between members of the teaching team.

Each teacher had to keep an account of the development of each pupil in his care, whether in a registration or teaching situation. In this account was put down any observation about any aspect of the pupil that the teacher noticed or that was brought to his attention. These matters would be reported at the weekly unit meeting and a course of action (if necessary) decided upon. This action could include counselling or a gentle warning. The accounts were also used in compiling reports on the pupil that might be required at any time. (Mr D. Barnes, Blackwood Middle School, Streetly.)

Records are most suspect when they contain judgemental comments such as 'uncooperative', 'sullen' or 'aggressive', without any instances of such behaviour being cited. The behaviour might have been misinterpreted, particularly when motives are being ascribed. This may well be because the teacher-observer is seeing only part of a continuing pattern of action and people's intentions are never easy to judge.

However problematic the suggestion might be, one solution would be the discussion between teacher and pupil, of incidents which are recorded. The pupil may then be aware of the teacher's concern, can consider his behaviour as it is observed, and can provide some interpretation of it which can then be added to the record along with the teacher's comments, of which the pupil can be aware. Such a participatory form of record-keeping can be valuable in counselling and learning.

Many schools have worked hard to develop a comprehensive record-keeping system, and the sheet reproduced (p. 108) is from one of these. It relates to social factors and other sheets deal with: 1. General information. 2. Physiological factors. 3. Physical development. 4. Social factors. 5. Emotional factors. 6. Play. 7. Intellectual factors: 8. Attitudes to school work. 9. Reading. 10. Creative and Imaginative skills. 11. Special difficulties or special strengths. Such records can be useful as checklists or as summary sheets but need to be backed up by careful observation and a file of detailed information. Without this such a record system can encourage termly judgement without justification, with the pupil processed as an assessment unit rather than being treated as an individual.

Finally a self-scrutiny profile is provided so that heads and staffs of schools may have a clearer picture of how they stand with regard to the issues raised in this chapter. It could usefully be the starting point for an in-school professional in-service training programme, which could be handled by a staff, with minimal outside support. It provides a framework for considering those matters of internal school organisation which have been discussed so far. The profile also includes items on the ways in which the school relates to the community it serves, the discussion of which forms the last section of this chapter.

Social factors

	Year 1			Year 2			Year 3		
	1	2	3	4	5	6	7	8	9
Very sociable									
Gets on reasonably well with others									
Submissive									
Aggressive									
Withdrawn									
Cooperative									
Distant with all adults									
Distant with strange adults									
Friendly with trusted adults									
Teases other children									

Additional notes if required on social development.

Date	Notes	Initials

School profile

Questions to Heads

Name of school   Number of pupils
                                                  in roll

Type and age range   Sex

_____

1 **Timetable**

(e.g. integrated day – subject discipline – blocked time – mixture –
morning/afternoon – difference in departmental practice)

- -

Comment

_____

2 **Operational groupings**

(e.g. streaming – family grouping – friendship groups – mixed ability)

- -

Comment

_____

3 **Teacher organisation**

(e.g. team teaching, subject specialists – mostly form teaching)

- -

Comment

_____

4 **Staff meetings and pastoral care**

(a) How frequent per term are staff meetings?

(b) What proportion of staff meetings is spent on matters of pastoral care?

- -

Comment

_____

5 Record-keeping – pastoral care

(a) What records relevant to pastoral care are kept?

(b) What type of information is recorded? (e.g. home background, relationships, attitudes)

Comment

_____

6 Pupils and extra-curricular decision-taking

(a) If pupils take part in extracurricular decision-taking, what form does this take? (e.g. school councils, committees, informal consultation)

(b) Frequency of pupil participation – often – sometimes – seldom

----

Comment

_____

7 Discipline and punishment

	Often	Sometimes	Seldom
Detention or extra work			
Corporal punishment			
Talking to			

Comment

_____

8 Use of names

Staff use pupils' surnames or Christian names, or mixture

_____

Comment

_____

9 Assemblies

Frequency per week   Dominant form

Class

Year

School
Other
Nature and extent of pupil participation

Comment

10 **Parents**

Methods of contact	Frequency	Proportion involved	Groups not participating
Parent–Teacher Assoc.			
Parent Assoc.			
Informal contact			
Parental interview			
Visits to home			
Parents evening			
Parental help			
Other			

Comment

11 **Meal arrangements**

Serving
(e.g. self-service – pupils serve – assistants serve)

Seating (teachers)

Seating (pupils)

Comment

12 **Sickness arrangements**

Where does a sick child go?

To whom does a sick child go?

Who contacts parents and how?

Comment

---

13 **School lay-out**

(e.g. traditional – open plan)

Comment

---

14 **Games**

Comment

Cooperation

Parents and teachers are both actively involved in the social and moral development of children and the most fruitful working relationship would be a partnership. As schools are organised at present in the United Kingdom the responsibility for developing home–school links lies with the teachers as they are in command of the school, and home visiting on the scale which would be required as an alternative to school visiting would be practically impossible.

It is tempting to measure the success of a programme to develop home–school links in terms of the numbers of parents who have been contacted. This would be reasonable only if these contacts created avenues for communication, if they make for real exchanges and learning and if they build up some form of mutual respect.

Those teachers who are responsible for the first meetings with parents set a pattern for future contacts. The fundamental requirement is that they should be welcoming. The reported experience of many schools is that once parents are put off for any reason it may not be easy to re-establish the links. In junior and infant schools the reception class teacher has the best opportunity for making contacts with mothers, because at this age the children are too young to go to school alone and most often it is the mother who escorts the child and may help him to change shoes and hang up his coat. There is also less likelihood that a mother with such young children will be at work.

The first step in establishing contact will be taken before the child starts at the new school.

The following extract is taken from the first pages of a leaflet sent to parents by an infant school:

This book is to help you to know and understand our school. You will find in it:
    Names of the people who work in school
    School dates and times
    What happens in school
    Why it happens and
    Your part in it.
Before school:
    As soon as you bring your child to school to put his name down, we like you to feel that you can join in with whatever is going on here. There is a lot you can do to help:

1 Talk to your child about school as a happy place – not as a frightening place.

2 Welcome us when we make a visit to your home just before your child begins school.

3 Help him to be independent of you in things like trying to dress and undress.

4 Name his things, so that, if they get lost, we can find them easily.
    (Mrs F. Robinson, Annie Osbourn School, Coventry.)

Many secondary schools also make contact before the new intake arrives. In this chapter mention has already been made of the significance of the time of transfer, and the only point to be added is that very many secondary schools produce handbooks for parents and pupils and the following headings are taken from one: (Kimberley Comprehensive School, Notts.)

Introduction, The Work of the Lower School, The Work Diary, The Work of the Main School (including the Sixth Form) General Matters: 1 Homework □ 2 School Dress □ 3 Labelling □ 4 Uniform Grants and Free School Meals □ 5 Writing to School □ 6 Telephoning the School □ 7 Basic Equipment □ 8 Reports and Interviews □ 9 The School Association.

It is perhaps useful to discuss the use of school records at some early meeting, and the information which is needed for the school to care for the child can be collected. The following sheet has been taken from a set of school records: (Annie Osbourn School).

School Record

General Information

Surname/s

Other names

Home address

Telephone number

Date of birth

Date of entry to school

Admission number

Date of leaving

Address/Telephone number in an emergency

Father ,,   ,, ,, ,, ,,

Mother ,,   ,, ,, ,, ,,

Neighbour/relative address ,, ,, ,,

Doctor's name

Doctor's telephone number

Has the child ever had anti-tetanus injection?

Father's name

Nationality (If immigrant)

Date of entry to U.K.

Mother's name

Nationality (If immigrant)

Date of entry to U.K.

Position in family
(Insert B or G for each child and ring the subject)

Position in family	1	2	3	4	5	6	7	8	9	10
Sex										

Thus far the discussion has been about attracting parental interest and Coventry LEA has demonstration classes in stores and children's pictures on the buses. Some schools, however, most often in smart suburbs, feel that there is a real need to shield the school from the excesses of parental pressure and aggressive competition. Though this may sometimes be so it might be hoped that teachers' professionalism will be a match for strident demands and the ways of working adopted by the school argued through with the parents.

There needs, too, to be a degree of realism. It is not possible nor desirable to be all things to all men and some parents may be 'turned-off' by some teachers just as some children can be, and it is only to be hoped that the good sense of the teacher will carry the relationship through. It is not suggested here that teachers should abandon their own values and standards in order to accommodate the wishes of parents.

The previous learning of the parents needs to be taken seriously. It may be difficult for parents to shake off old learning about schools and their expectations of schools, which are probably heavily coloured by their memories of their own past relationships with teachers.

Without a good pattern of contacts it is too easy for a parent's attitudes and interest to be misinterpreted. If parents never turn up at parents' evenings it is not reasonable to label them as uncooperative or unsupportive; it is very likely that there is something about the nature of the contact offered which is unattractive, and informal contacts in other settings can often reveal the extent of loving concern and support which the parent provides. The cry 'We never get the ones we want', is familiar and it may not be surprising that parents shun what may be a fairly unpleasant encounter. Though home visits might resolve many such conflicts they are extremely expensive in terms of a teacher's time and energy.

The National Survey conducted by the Project revealed the importance of the home and its neighbourhood as a setting for the early moral learning of children. The school does not begin its work in moral education with a blank sheet and the school must decide how it is going to relate to this prior values learning. One approach might be to ignore all other influences and attempt to build an entirely new pattern, but with no points of contact the learning is sterile and formal and in the long run it is mostly likely to be ignored, although children may conform to the school's procedural requirements during the school day. Far better would be an attempt to understand and acknowledge the home-provided learning, and for this to take place some real contacts must be made between the school and the home and between the school and the immediate community which it serves. This approach would make it possible for the school to build on existing patterns, to reinforce positive patterns of behaviour and to offer the opportunity for children to continue and extend their moral learning.

Contacts between home and school also make it possible for teachers to see more of the total pattern of which the child's behaviour at school is a part. Children will have learned to respond to the social requirements of their parents (see p. 9) and they will have acquired patterns for gaining attention or gaining control in the home. These techniques, the sulky mood or the winning smile, will be tried out in school. The contact will make it possible for teachers and parents to realise that they share a concern for the same child and they can exchange information.

Teacher: 'He's so quiet it's difficult to get him to say anything.'
Mother: 'He's a real chatterbox. He's never quiet for an instant; he's always up to tricks.'

Contacts can also modify a teacher's view of a child, which may be affected, and not necessarily consciously, by relatively superficial factors. The child who is clean and well spoken may be thought to be more able and contacts with the home can widen the perception of the child's interests and abilities. At the same time it may make it obvious where some less attractive characteristics are acquired. In the case of the boy who is sometimes difficult at school:

Mother: 'He's such a darling rogue, just like his father was. I can't bring myself to tell him off. I do like boys to be boyish, don't you?'

These moves towards a home–school partnership will help to provide the child with some consistency in moral education and some continuity too. It may be that the major intention in forging the link is to increase the support for academic learning which the child receives at home, and at times teachers may feel that they are providing something similar to an adult education scheme on such matters as how to encourage your child to read more or what is meant by modern maths, but in some areas of the curriculum there may be a need for rather more of a two-way exchange on, for example, the school's approach to sex education. Occasionally there are straightforward cries for help, such as 'Please tell her to do as I tell her' or 'How can I get him to go to bed on time?' All these contacts should move towards developing some mutual respect. Children can pick up the social meaning of teachers' comments and the hidden curriculum may be conveyed through unintended signals. Some remarks contain a clear criticism of home values, such as:

'You may do that at home but we're not going to allow it here.'

There are even pitfalls in the alternative form:

'I'm sure your mummy doesn't let you do that at home, so you're not going to do it here.'

Mummy may indeed tolerate such behaviour.

Teachers are reliant to quite a considerable extent on the support of the parents. When children arrive home full of the interesting things they have done at school, and then complain of being bored at home, or when they are full of what teacher has said, and teacher seems to be always right, parents can be excused for feelings of jealousy. When teacher seems to have been wrong many parents do not challenge the teacher because of a proper fear that they might be undermining the child's motivation to learn which operates at a very personal level. Where parents feel that they are being challenged for a position of influence and esteem in their children's eyes they may all too easily enter into a secret competition with the teachers which is wasteful and unnecessary and, because it falls within the teacher's realm, may encourage the child not to be concerned about his performance in academic work.

Very many schools encourage parental involvement during the school day, and a variety of approaches are successful. Some education authorities provide a parents' room which can be a base for a variety of activities; it may be a social room where parents can call in and make coffee, or they may function more like workshops, for there is always something needing to be done – for example, making up flashcards or costumes for a play – but it needs to be emphasised that the purpose is to provide the opportunity for meeting, the exchange of views and the development of a climate of trust and respect rather than to offer a source of free labour. Such involvement does not require that there should be a special room set aside and in many cases the staff room is used.

Parents may also be able to help in the classroom – listening to reading, helping with craft activities or music. Mothers may help to supervise swimming activities and to dry the little ones. Fathers may help by offering additional sports coaching. For the younger child, seeing a parent in school can be very helpful; it can aid the creation of harmony and unity in the child's world, with the significant adults in his life working together. For these arrangements to be successful, the parents need to feel welcomed in school and able to behave naturally and to acknowledge their child in a natural fashion, and perhaps to support the teachers by exercising some control over their child. The alternative artificial pretence that the child is not there could be most confusing.

Parent–teacher or school associations are extremely common and the role that they can play should not be overlooked, providing as they do the opportunity for information and discussion sessions as well as social meeting. These associations are also the most common channel for parent representation on the school's board of management.

Finally the school's links with the community and its concern for moral education may coincide if it brings into school for talks with the children key figures in the life of the community, such as policemen, local councillors or doctors.

These three aspects of the organisation of schools all have a part to play in creating a community which promotes moral learning; care for the pattern of relationships and encounters within the school; opportunities for children to endeavour to behave responsibly and show initiative; and contacts with parents and the local community to attempt to provide consistency and continuity in the child's moral development.

Reference

1. Stone, J. and Taylor, Felicity, 1975. 'Three causes in search of a campaign', *Observer*, 23 February.

6 Materials

The Project's materials approaches are *Photoplay*, *Choosing* and *Growing*.

Photoplay

The *Photoplay* Units 1 and 2 are based on the reports of almost 4,000 children about situations of personal concern. These situations focused on five main moods: happiness, unhappiness, fright, anger and uncertainty. In describing how and when they felt these different moods and how they related to others, children reported many non-verbal facets of behaviour. Different types of facial expression, body gesture and movements were reported as forms of communication and means of understanding others' personal needs. Children without this understanding or the means to perceive and express non-verbal behaviour felt isolated and socially insecure. It is clear from our work[1] and that of others[2] that in the majority of social situations the key means by which inter-personal attitudes, beliefs and feelings are communicated are non-verbal. Indeed, children learn morality from the treatment they receive and the behaviour of those close to them, rather than from discussion of what might or ought to be done.

The aim of the *Photoplay* Units is therefore to achieve the following changes in children's social ability and behaviour towards others.

1 To heighten individual's perception of other people's needs, attitudes and feelings.
2 To encourage the development of basic social skills particularly non-verbal.

3 To provide a practical base for better personal relationships.

4 To increase the individual's freedom to make moral choices by developing the capacity to suggest a variety of alternative forms of considerate action.

5 To improve interpersonal communication further by exploring the relationships between the communication styles people use and their personal means of expression through a range of creative activities.

By working with a wide range of photographs of people from different cultures, in different moods and situations, children develop their abilities to interpret and be at ease with non-verbal interpersonal communication. By the use of stories, labels and workcards, children then apply this increased sensitivity to interpreting the messages people send. They become better at understanding the needs of others and subsequently at expressing their own responses unambiguously.

By considering their own reactions children are encouraged to become more flexible in their responses to the viewpoints and actions of others. Greater choice becomes a practical possibility, through additional workcard activities, in which an increasing number of choices for considerate action are generated by the children themselves, using the photographs as a visual basis. Individuals develop better personal relationships when they are able to exercise a degree of flexibility in deciding on the most appropriate course of action.

Photoplay is divided into two Units to facilitate the implementation of its basic aims (see Fig. 4). Unit 1 consists of large photoposters that illustrate simple stories based on children's reported needs and concerns. In class work and play, children match the photoposters to individual people described in the family stories, by identifying visually and with labels what their moods, feelings and probable behaviours are. Children become more expert at differentiating between facial expression and body gestures and the personal relationships they indicate in the stories. The range of everyday family incidents used motivates children and requires them to make their own moral decisions about what to do.

Figure 4 **Photoplay Units 1 and 2**

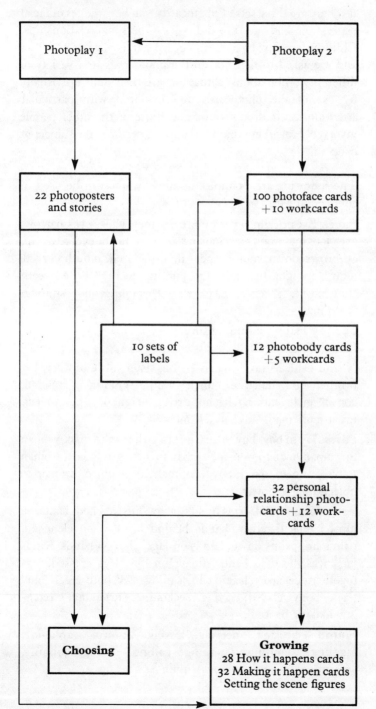

Photoplay Unit 2 reinforces and then extends interpersonal sensitivity and the related skills learnt in work with *Photoplay* 1. There are three sets of photocards, showing ranges of facial expression, body gesture and types of personal relationships. Children are involved in photocard game-playing activities and are asked to fit labels to the photocards in a variety of different combinations. Situations are then built up visually by use of the photocards and explored with particular attention to children's views and those of the other people involved. How they would feel and act becomes the subject of concern.

The following are examples of labels which can be used in connection with *Photoplay*.

Faces Eyes bright, eyes dull, eyes open wide, eyes narrow, eyes looking away, eyes looking at, eyes down, eyebrows up, eyebrows down, mouth open, mouth closed, mouth curved, mouth straight, lips tight, lips pouting, teeth clenched, teeth showing, face tense, face relaxed, smiling, not smiling, frowning.

Feeling Happy, afraid, unsure, uncertain, angry, cross, sad, thoughtful, interested, disgusted.

Name Dad, Mum, little sister, big sister, little brother, big brother, son, daughter, uncle, auntie, grandma, grandad, cousin, girlfriend, boyfriend, driver, neighbour, pet, object, toy, friend, man, lady, myself/me.

Pairs Boy to boy, boy to girl, girl to girl, man to man, woman to woman, man to woman, woman to man, girl to boy, woman to boy, woman to girl, boy to animal, girl to object, woman to object, man to object.

Body Arms folded, arms by side, arms outstretched, hands on hips, hands together, hands behind head, hand clenched, palms up, palms down, hands on face, chin on hands, hands on knees, head in hands, finger on lips, legs crossed, legs together, feet apart, leaning on, leaning back, body erect, body tense, body relaxed, waving, beckoning, shrugging, stretching, looking back.

Sound Cheering, sneering, kissing, grunting, groaning, giggling, shouting, laughing, calling, crying, sobbing, screaming, sighing, singing, whining, swearing.

Action Kicking, hitting, pushing, biting, stamping, sucking, holding, cuddling, stroking, hugging, squeezing, sitting apart, sitting on, standing on, standing close, looking at, looking away, talking to, not talking to, listening, not listening to.

Relating Aggressive, jealous, criticising, admiring, dominating, accusing, blaming, disapproving, refusing, arguing, warning, embarrassing, submitting, mocking, punishing, praising, suspicious, confusing, ignoring, loving, considering, caring, comforting, defending, agreeing, friendly, copying, forgiving, admitting, persuading, trusting, pleasing, tempting, tricking, trying, teasing, wanting, playing, telling.

Thinking I don't know. I feel a little worried. I feel fine. I'm hot and excited. I am nervous. I want to be on my own. Nobody understands me. I can't do it. I'm bored. I'm angry. I don't like it.

Saying What do you mean? I don't know what to do. Will you help me? What do you want? Should I? Who me? Do you want me? It's great. That was kind. Can I really? That's a laugh. They always do what I say. Hey listen to this. Go away. Leave me alone. I'm sorry. It didn't work. I can't do it. It's not fair. Don't touch me. I don't like you. I want to go. You wouldn't dare. You're scared. Help! Are you sure? Don't do that. Didn't you hear me? I love you. What did you say? Do as you're told. Listen to me. You're always doing that. Stop it. Come here you. Be quiet. Who do you think you are? It was you. See what I mean? I think you're nice. Thank you. Would you like to come too?

The following list indicates which mood or action the people were asked to show for the camera. The corresponding poster and the story it goes with are indicated in brackets. This is, of course, only a guide as the posters can be used with many stories.

Faces

1 Happy	9 Interested
2 Sad	10 Uncertain (Poster G, Story 2)
3 Afraid	11 Happy (Poster A, Story 1)
4 Disgusted	12 Angry (Poster C, Story 1)
5 Uncertain	13 Disgusted
6 Happy	14 Uncertain (Poster D, Story 1)
7 Angry	15 Interested
8 Afraid	16 Happy

17 Sad
18 Angry
19 Disgusted
20 Uncertain
21 Happy
22 Sad
23 Angry (Poster B, Story 1)
24 Afraid
25 Uncertain
26 Happy
27 Sad
28 Angry
29 Uncertain
30 Afraid
31 Happy
32 Sad
33 Angry
34 Afraid
35 Uncertain
36 Happy
37 Sad (Poster H, Story 2)
38 Angry (Poster I, Story 2)
39 Afraid
40 Interested
41 Happy
42 Sad
43 Angry
44 Interested
45 Uncertain (Poster F, Story 1)
46 Happy
47 Sad
48 Afraid
49 Uncertain
50 Angry (Poster N, Story 2)
51 Happy
52 Sad (Poster E, Story 1)
53 Uncertain
54 Disgusted
55 Frightened
56 Happy
57 Sad
58 Angry (Poster M, Story 2)
59 Afraid
60 Uncertain
61 Happy
62 Sad
63 Angry
64 Uncertain
65 Afraid
66 Happy
67 Sad
68 Uncertain
69 Interested

70 Angry
71 Happy
72 Sad
73 Angry
74 Afraid
75 Uncertain
76 Happy
77 Sad
78 Angry
79 Afraid
80 Disgusted
81 Happy
82 Sad
83 Angry
84 Disgusted
85 Interested
86 Happy
87 Sad
88 Uncertain
89 Angry (Poster R, Story 4)
90 Interested
91 Happy
92 Sad
93 Angry
94 Afraid
95 Disgusted
96 Happy
97 Sad
98 Angry
99 Interested
100 Uncertain

Bodies

101 Laughing
102 Very happy
103 Pacifying
104 Nervous
105 Bewildered (Poster N, Story 3)
106 Dejected
107 Welcoming
108 Uncertain (Poster U, Story 4)
109 Angry
110 Friendly parting
111 Angry (Poster T, Story 4)
112 Beckoning

Relationships

113 Agreeing (Poster M, Story 3)
114 Warning (Poster O, Story 3)
115 Wanting
116 Admiring
117 Loving (Poster L, Story 3)
118 Protecting (Poster P, Story 3)

Children are led to consider the practical outcomes of behaviour by using both workcards and the creative activities suggested. A chart suggesting how work may develop is shown on p. 126.

Both the *Photoplay* Units have been designed to facilitate flexibility in approach and application. Any one poster, photograph, story, label set or workcard can be used on its own for group or individual work, or in any combination that seems appropriate.

Photoplay is also designed to use, and be used to extend, work in *Choosing* and *Growing*. For example, a workcard or photograph can be used in combination with any of the situations in *Choosing* or *How it happens*, be illustrated by *Setting the scene* figures or be expressed through any activity in *Making it happen*. In this way work using a *Photoplay* approach can be extended almost indefinitely and materials and additional techniques developed in relation to the specific interests of teachers and children.

Choosing

The stories in the *Choosing* books are taken from those collected in the National Survey described in Chapter 9. They cover the most important themes of the children's responses.

1 Making decisions about what to do, where to play and whom to play with. ·

2 Carrying out their decisions and taking the initiative in social action and then coping with the consequences.

Figure 5 Diagram showing a suggested sequence for using the Photoplay 2 after introducing the posters and stories of Photoplay 1.

1	2	3	4	5	6	7
100 Photo-face cards showing facial expression. Portraits of one black and one white family. 20 individuals each one shown in 5 different moods.	Face labels describing aspects of facial expression. e.g. eyes bright, teeth clenched, smiling, frowning, face relaxed, lips pouting, mouth straight, eyebrows up, eyes down, eyes looking away, eyes narrow, eyes open wide.	Feeling labels. e.g. thinking, afraid, disgusted, uncertain, sad, happy, cross. Describing the particular mood of a person in the photo packs.	Name labels. e.g. mum, dad, sister, brother, uncle, auntie, cousin, neighbour.	12 Photo-body cards showing body gesture. Full length portraits of family members shown in different body stances indicating their mood and feelings.	Body labels e.g. hands behind head, arms folded, hand clenched, palms down, chin on hands, finger on lips, legs crossed, hands on hips, feet apart, body tense, waving, struggling. Describing features of an individual's body gesture.	32 Photocards of relationships. Photographs of 2 or 3 people in a particular relationship. Pets and objects included in some photographs.

8	9	10	11	12	13
Pair labels. e.g. boy to girl; man to woman; girl to boy.	Sound labels. e.g. sneering, laughing, crying, sighing, screaming, swearing. Sounds one individual is making in response to another.	Action labels. e.g. kicking, pushing, cuddling, standing close, looking at. What one individual is doing to another.	Thinking labels. e.g. 'I feel fine', 'I am nervous', 'Nobody understands me', 'I'm angry'. What an individual is thinking.	Saying labels. e.g. 'What do you mean?', 'That was kind', 'I'm sorry', 'It's not fair'. What individuals say to each other.	Relating labels. e.g. blaming, arguing, praising, caring, forgiving, aggressive, jealous, loving, trying. The types of relationship individuals have.

3 Dealing with groups effectively. Relating well with their friends and coping with their demands.

4 The treatment of animals.

5 A concern for the environment.

6 Relationships with old people.

7 The beginnings of romantic relationships with the opposite sex.

8 How to cope with new situations, when visiting other people's houses, meeting strangers and in problem situations at school.

The stories are arranged according to the age group of the children who provided them, and in which these types of situations were most common. There is no reason why children of secondary school age should not find in all the stories a reflection of their own experience to which they can respond, but obviously the last three booklets are especially suitable. In the same way junior school children would probably find the first three of most relevance. They provide an opportunity to raise many of the concerns of children in this age range, and provide the challenges in response to which social growth can take place.

The children are able, by progressing from discussion to acting, simulation and other expressive work, not only to understand better the relationships and behaviour described here, but also, because they become a part of the action, to develop a caring life-style rather than only making statements about what should be done.

By raising these issues in the classroom the pupils can explore the implications of the action from the other person's point of view. They can discover the consequences of their decisions and actions without the real-life consequences, and they can be helped to move towards a positive caring response to other people's needs, feelings and interests.

A number of activities are suggested with each of the stories. It is of course for the individual teacher to decide which activities to undertake, in what order they should be tackled and whether the work is to be done by the whole class at once or in smaller groups. However, from experience with trials of the materials, it is suggested that, when practicable, a small group is better than a whole class; that discussion should be followed by and intermixed with simulation and expressive work; and that written work should be kept to a minimum in order to encourage a lively participation on the part of all the pupils. There should be no attempt to reach a class consensus on moral judgement, as each child, if he is truly involved, will be looking at the situation from his own previous experiences and in terms of his insights gained during the work.

The stories are short, there has been no attempt to increase the complexity of the actions described by the children, and there is little characterisation. This is because the work is not intended as a series of 'comprehension' exercises. There is sufficient detail to provide an event and characters to which children can relate, and the extension is provided by the children working with the materials.

Sensitivity may be called for when handling the work based on these stories, because children may reveal much about their lives. Though the stories provide a link with real life, they also provide a context to which children's attention can return if it is felt desirable to reduce tension or embarrassment. In discussion it is desirable to encourage honest statements and a thoughtful approach, with some attention paid to the reasons for making the statements. However, the intention of this work is to affect what people do, not only what they say. Simulation can produce honest responses and provide the link to real life behaviour.

Among the intentions of these books is the hope that they will help children to realise that they can alter the pattern of events; they can take the initiative and in the course of the classroom activities gain the confidence to act. All the time attention should be drawn towards behaving with sensitivity towards others and with regard to the consequences.

It has been found that an exploration of the situation as seen from the point of view of each of the people involved is particularly helpful as children work out possible courses of action.

Possible lines of follow-up work can be found in the pack of activity cards *Making it happen*; the situation cards *How it happens* provide children with an opportunity to explore related situations; and both the *Photoplay* cards and the *Setting the scene* figures provide media through which the work can be continued.

128

Growing – resource bank

Growing is the *Startline* programme's resource bank. It is made up of three sections: *How it happens, Making it happen,* and *Setting the scene*, all of which can be used separately but which, when used together, form an integrated approach. It is possible to follow the integrated approach independently or to employ it to extend *Photoplay* or *Choosing* work. Further, teachers can use *Growing*, or its individual component parts, to work with any of the situations which the children cited during the Project's research and which have not been used in any of the programme materials but are listed in Appendix E of this book. Ultimately, as advocated in Chapter 7, we hope, not only that teachers will use a 'growing' approach with the happy, unhappy and uncertain situations they are given by the children they teach, but will also move on to evolve their own moral education techniques for use with the children's day-to-day circumstances in the context of all the school's work.

How it happens uses fifty-four children's happy, unhappy and uncertain situations which are illustrated on cards in a variety of ways likely to positively motivate different individuals to work with them and apply their 'solutions'. In most cases the cards also have a brief description of the situation printed on them. However, the impact of the illustrations is intended to involve the children and stimulate their understanding and imagination rather than a verbal description of what may be happening.

Making it happen is made up of twenty-eight double-sided cards on which are printed work suggestions. These are also designed to motivate children not only to increase their understanding of what makes people 'tick' and to decide on considerate courses of action, but also to help them become part of the action emotionally as well as rationally. The aim is for the children to use every possible expressive activity to identify with considerate courses of action and to adopt concerned behaviour so that it becomes part of their daily repertoire. Although *Making it happen* cards are intended for independent use by boys and girls, we encourage the teacher to act as an intermediary, particularly with eight and nine year olds, children with learning difficulties, or indeed on any occasion when it is deemed useful to simplify, explain, abstract or modify what is on a card.   129

Setting the scene consists of (42) cut-out figures of adults, children, animals and toys which the children are encouraged to arrange in any spatial relationship to illustrate a social encounter and 'set the scene' for further work, during the course of which the figures may be moved to show the progress of the interaction and the relationships involved.

The figures were selected during the trials as those most useful to children in their work. It is a multicultural selection, but inevitably there will be gaps as far as the requirements of particular groups of children are concerned. In almost every case these figures are not intended to be identified in a specific role, but there are obvious intentions behind the selection; the man in the dark uniform could be, amongst other possibilities, a policeman, a security guard, a bus driver or a postman, and the man in the white coat could be a science teacher, a vet, a doctor or a dentist. The expressions of the figures have been kept as neutral as possible so that there is the minimum pressure to inhibit pupils from investing them with roles and emotions.

In many cases during the trials the children have supplemented the range of figures by drawing their own by making additional props. Because the magnetic strips will work through a single sheet of paper it is possible for children to produce a background, perhaps a room in a house, a street scene or a recreation ground.

These figures can be arranged in any groupings to illustrate social encounters. They set the scene for further work during the course of which the figures may be moved to show the progress of the interaction and the relationships involved. The figures can be entirely controlled by pupils and they can give form to an abstract understanding of relationships.

These figures have been used successfully with pupils throughout the entire eight to thirteen age range. They are especially useful for work with children whose linguistic competence is limited and valuable in providing a stimulus to language development. Obviously as a basic resource they can be employed in many ways and some trial schools have even used them in number work.

The use of these figures can provide a controlled approach to improvised drama; a group of children by selecting and arranging the figures can agree on the characters involved and with the relationships expressed visually can work towards an agreed pattern of events.

Another use of these figures during trials has been for the teacher to set up a group of figures and objects and ask the pupils to provide an interpretation of what might be happening and how the situation might develop.

On some occasions children have worked with the figures on their own and the teacher has been able to use this in counselling, as the child works through a pattern of events which may have particular significance for him. Individual children have also arranged the figures to represent the patterns of relationships with which they are familiar but as yet cannot understand clearly.

Just as these figures may be particularly useful when working with eight to thirteen year old children who have difficulty with written language, so they may also be used effectively with much younger children in the context of language as well as social development.

In general it has been found that work with *Setting the scene* is most effective with relatively small groups or individual pupils.

As a basic resource, these figures can help activities throughout the moral education programme. Some of the *Making it happen* activities make specific use of them. During trials, a set of twelve trigger situations was provided which would start the work with the figures, and situations can also be taken from many parts of the programme from *Choosing*, *How it happens* and the descriptions in Appendix E of this book.

By using the figures, boys and girls are helped to work through from the simple organisation of a discussion, by way of writing and acting a play and briefed role-play, to free simulation in which they are fully involved rationally, emotionally and creatively.

Growing provides the encouragement to take a situation, work actively on it and then decide what to do next. Teachers should not be fearful of developing their own combinations and permutations, when using not only the constituent parts of *Growing* but also those parts with *Photoplay* and *Choosing*. Variety of approach is obviously highly motivating for teacher and children.

The integrated approach within *Growing* basically involves taking a situation from *How it happens*, choosing an activity to apply to it from *Making it happen* and starting work using *Setting the scene*.

Likewise *Growing* enables individuals to extend the work of *Choosing* and *Photoplay* by introducing additional situations and a greater variety of questions and ways of working.

The ultimate aim of the work is to help individuals respond with consideration and imagination to any situations in which they find themselves.

The rationale of the total *Growing* approach and ways of working should be related to what is written on learning process, creativity, school organisation, the growth model and materials and techniques in this book. The diagram on the following page may clarify what we have in mind.

Finding out

Finally, we suggest that teachers may like children to use a *finding out* approach by asking the three basic questions used in our research (see p. 163). The answers can be used as curriculum material for many classroom activities. Because the answers are drawn from the experience of the children, the maximum relevance and positive motivation are guaranteed for those children. We have found, working this way, that teachers and children learn more about each other's personal needs, interests, feelings and attitudes. The open-ended nature of the approach allows the exploration and development of materials and techniques relevant to those involved. In this way teachers and children develop independence from the Project's published materials and can use the approaches they evolve themselves. Similarly, children gain greater freedom of choice and action by developing their own materials and approaches jointly with their teachers. Our ultimate aim is to increase the autonomy of teachers and children. To do so is to put concern for moral learning into action.

Children appreciate a genuine concern with their personal needs. This appreciation is often expressed by excitement and willingness to explore new ways of working that are personally rewarding, and also by their growing ability to understand

132

Figure 6 How *Growing* relates to the total programme

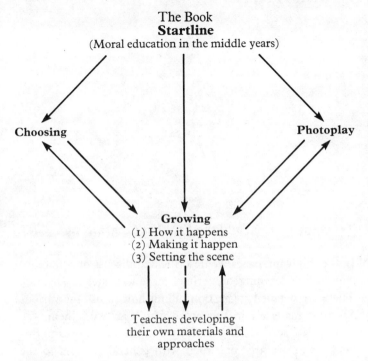

The Book
Startline
(Moral education in the middle years)

Choosing

Photoplay

Growing
(1) How it happens
(2) Making it happen
(3) Setting the scene

Teachers developing
their own materials and
approaches

and consider others. The concern is contagious.

The three questions about happy, unhappy and uncertain situations enable children to reveal the key moral learning areas of their experience. Their answers to the supplementary questions about what they did next provide them and others with direct evidence of the behaviour learning process. A special advantage of asking the questions of specific groups of children in particular areas is that the answers provide us with the information we require to make sure that moral education is as domestic, and therefore as relevant, as possible. The creative activities described in Appendices F and I may be of special use to teachers in following up a *finding out* approach.

References

1. Middleton, D., 1975. Creativity in Children's Social and Moral Learning, unpublished M.A. thesis, London University Institute Library.
2. Argyle, M., 1975 *Bodily Communication*, Methuen.

133

7 Techniques

Teaching method and the *Startline* programme

In the following pages we describe and discuss our practical approach to 'teaching' or, perhaps more accurately, 'learning'. There are detailed suggestions about how to use the various *Startline* materials in the notes which go with them, the appropriate sections of Chapter 6 and the appendices to this book. Here we are concerned with general answers to the following questions:

1 How do you use the kinds of material in this programme most effectively?

2 Why do the suggested approaches work?

3 Why do members of the team favour some methods rather than others at certain times?

4 How do I approach drama, role-play and simulation work?

5 Is there scope for introducing ways of working not mentioned in the published programme and, if so, what are the criteria which should decide us to work in a particular way?

The brief answer to the first question is that you use material most effectively when you maximise the children's positive motivation – their enthusiasm and involvement, their disposition or inclination to work or play with that material. This means that you have to guarantee relevance and personal involvement as often as possible and for as many children as possible. Professional skill in this area is the ability to do this and the key to developing professional skill is to build up and sustain two way verbal and non-verbal communication between teacher and children.

Specifically, there are a number of things which can be done to ensure the relevance of the situations portrayed in the material, all of which have the initial advantage of being those which children have told us are important to them.

a We can encourage the children to choose the material they prefer to work with. This will generally match their ability to identify, comprehend and respond.

b We can avoid ever automatically working through a list of situations in the order in which they are presented and without omitting any of them.

c The boys' and girls' confidence to be honest has to be built up gradually by making it clear to them in action that nothing they say will be used against them for punishment or ridicule. In this respect it helps to start working with the attractive events which are less emotionally fraught for the children and which allow them to work from the third person (acting for 'him' or for 'her') to the first person (being myself).

d The length of time devoted to any situation should be a function of the interest in it rather than the time the teacher, considers it is worth, or 'ought' to be spent on it. There will always be other opportunities for the message to come out!

e It is often good for positive motivation to switch from one material approach to another and then back again (for example from *Choosing* to *Photoplay* to *Choosing*) rather than using a sequential, and once-and-for-all, work technique.

f Motivation is always improved when boys and girls are encouraged, after working with *Startline* material for some time, to introduce their own significant situations. Work on what the children are currently experiencing in the home, in the street and in the school almost always increases relevance and raises interest if the topic is not too threatening and has not been 'worked to death' in some other context (staff-room communication is essential to moral education!) A material approach is always a 'starter' and the best approaches stimulate the most follow-up and development. That is how they should be judged.

When it comes to deciding which methods and techniques

are best to use with the material there are basic considerations which affect motivation.

1 The methods which motivate most are generally those which actively involve as many individuals as possible. Individual boys and girls need the opportunity to contract out (to 'coast' on occasions), especially the younger children during the afternoons, but a basic question is 'Does everyone have the opportunity to contribute?'

2 A further question concerns whether the method is active rather than passive in the sense that it requires a boy or girl to do something over and above speaking or writing.

3 The technique used should preferably be one the teacher employing it likes and is good at; though learning with the children can sometimes be motivating for teacher and child.

4 The best method at a particular time is the one which suits the mood of the child. Generally children throughout the age range we are concerned with enjoy working and playing together; but it is not always the case, and when a child has enough socialising for one day, solitary techniques have their place. This fitting-in with the mood of the child stresses the value of being able to work with groups of varying sizes, even if one teacher is responsible for a large class and can only use small groups because there is not enough room to put space between them. Mercifully, mood is contagious, especially towards the beginning and end of the day so that not everyone is calling out for different treatment all the time.

5 The methods children prefer working with are generally those which match (and encourage the growth of) their abilities, but sometimes the teacher can introduce new motivational impetus only by giving the children challenges which they are at first reluctant to accept. The art of teaching is so much a matter of introducing such challenges, making them attractive, and letting boys and girls discover their own triumphs. Bitter and critical attitudes destroy the capacities for wonder, discovery and success.

As in the case of choosing the best materials, discovering the most effective methods depends on the quality of teacher ↔ child and child ↔ teacher communication. If the 'morality of communication' discussed in Chapter 1 is a feature of school life, we need have little anxiety about relevance or motivation.

At this point it may be of value to list and very briefly comment on the principal teaching–learning techniques suggested for use with project materials.

1 *Expressive and communicational activities* which can, but do not have to be, carried out alone, including speaking; writing prose, poetry and plays; painting; modelling; making things; photography and so on. Used intelligently expressive activities can encourage greater honesty and innovatory solutions to problems. The key, as always, is motivation, and positive motivation depends on choice and variety. Clearly the writing of answers to moral problems or dilemmas for *x* minutes or hours at the same time, or times, each week is not motivating to most children.

2 *Discussion* can be involving and productive when the subject is of interest, but it is over-rated by many teachers who sometimes do not notice how few members of this age group may take part and are good at it. It can become a rather dishonest business which widens the gulf between theory and practice. Unfortunately it is often used by people who cannot think what else to do. Later in this chapter a way of enlivening discussion by translating it into simulation is described.

3 *Drama* is very popular with children, especially between the ages of eight and eleven, but somewhat less so with many teachers! Children who would be embarrassed and confused by being pitched into role-play or simulation often enjoy acting a part with a script. Boys and girls will write plays and act them, especially if there is an opportunity for performing before a live audience. (Parents are useful here but can become evasive if they receive too many invitations.) Moralising plays are popular with younger children and may temporarily widen the gap between 'how I see myself' and 'how I really am'!

4 *Role-play* in which individuals are given roles and briefed, provides a situation of maximum power for the teacher and as we know 'power corrupts, absolute power corrupts absolutely'. Typecasting is seductively attractive. The writer was only partially comforted by the head teacher who said of a small boy, 'He always seems to play little old ladies, but he is

not really like that. He has the makings of a good scrum-half.'
Nevertheless role-play based on the children's situations and
handled sensitively can greatly increase their understanding
of how the world wags. Again it is a useful step towards
simulation.

5 *Simulation.* Writing about other work techniques as useful
steps towards simulation may make it sound as if simulation
were always the ideal way of working. Certainly we believe
that simulation – meaning an unscripted and unprepared
playing out of a situation in which individuals literally 'do
their own thing' – represents an ideal approach in many cases,
because of the way in which it can be tailored to be relevant to
individual needs and to involve people totally. Later in the
chapter, when we answer the question why team members
favour certain methods at certain times and in the discussion
of drama, role-play and simulation, this argument is
developed. However, simulation is not ideal for everyone at all
times. It demands a great deal of understanding and trust
between teachers and children, and some find it difficult
to get into straight away. Being yourself can be the most
embarrassing thing ever asked of you. Nervous children may
seize up or overcompensate by being 'silly'. Most children will
test the sincerity of the teacher by overdoing the aggressive
destructive responses when first involved in simulation. They
will literally push their grannies off a bus. Many teachers are
too nervous to persist until the time, which always comes,
when the concern begins to show, though children anxious to
please may (on the other hand) be as unbelievably 'good' and
sycophantic, as when they script their own drama. In some
parts of the UK the problem is how to start simulation, in
others how to stop it. A simulation exercise conducted
anywhere reflects local anxieties and response to assumed
expectations. This aspect of simulation can be handled
constructively or destructively by teachers, as a growth point
or as the trigger for frightened repression. Perhaps the
greatest danger is that simulation may be used in the attempt
to force an invasion of privacy, to put too much pressure on
individuals, to feed 'living by proxy' or 'voyeurism' on the
part of the teacher. To work in this way, we teachers ideally
need to know ourselves and our own motivation well. There
is, however, a basic safeguard. Children working in groups

138

resist strongly the invasion of privacy, and, even if the teacher has not at first seen simulation as only a voluntary exercise, he soon will do so if he has any reception and interpretation ability. If he ignores the signs, the play (the work) simply grinds to a halt. The same applies to pathological psycho-analysing when using simulation – a continuous analytic concern with the children's motivation for behaviour rather than letting the action develop without comment and the feedback work.

6 *Real-life involvement* is the final exercise, test and 'evaluation in action' of moral education. It is both a method and an end in itself. Helping people is the best practice for helping people. The only danger is that what should always be a natural, voluntary activity can be used to exploit children with little regard for their needs. As always the capacity to receive response and interpret it is basic. Even where children are full of tender feeling and want to help, say, old people or the disabled we owe them a realistic understanding of what they are approaching and the opportunity to work initially in the less traumatic situations. Information, role-play and simulation are invaluable in deciding what to do and preparing for it.

Why do the suggested approaches work?

Approaches work when they dispose boys and girls to treat life and the whole of creation with respect for need, feeling and interest. The process by which this happens was the subject of Chapter 1. The Project's materials and techniques are designed to stimulate that process. However, in general terms learning potential is greatest at a certain level of arousal. One of the key teaching skills is to identify this level of arousal. Perhaps a conceptual graph of the type first used I believe by D. O. Hebb[1] will clarify the general position. (The writer alone is responsible for the details of this graph.)

At optimum learning potential children give a number of cues which the good teacher picks up and interprets, often subliminally. Children who are really involved pass somewhat different verbal and non-verbal messages depending on their personal characteristics and the activity they are involved in,

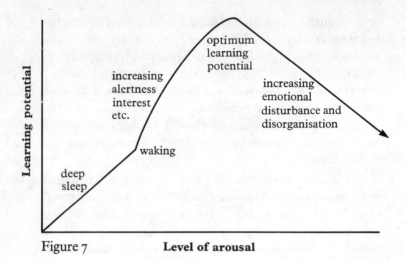

Figure 7   **Level of arousal**

but there are more or less persistent behaviour traits. When learning potential is high some of the things which happen are:

1 children are difficult to distract;
2 they give happy or at least contented cues (for example humming to themselves);
3 their direction of gaze is at the job or activity in hand;
4 their eyes are bright;
5 body inclination is forward towards whatever is happening;
6 they are generally slightly restless, vigorous and, if they are working with others, they use more gestures than usual;
7 they try to take over if someone else is involved in the action;
8 they ask for more as soon as a job or piece of play is completed;
9 involved in some activity, they draw attention to themselves, for example by saying 'look at me' or by jumping up and down;
10 their colour is usually good (for them);
11 they respond quickly to questions and suggestions.

Teachers will no doubt think of cues they believe important which are not included in this list. Indeed it is useful at least once to draw up your own list as a 'rain check'. The important thing is to be your own observer, to keep noticing and trying to interpret the cues children give as an indication of their needs and, specifically, that they are learning.

140

Too much arousal inhibits learning. Children only learn fear, anxiety and destruction in a phrenetic, hysterical atmosphere. They even tell us 'There will soon be tears!'

To those who associate learning with the style of Rodin's *Thinker*, with a quiet, reflective contemplative posture, it may be difficult to accept that the cues described above are associated with learning. But the 'thinker' is not a child of between eight and thirteen, learning largely from experiencing and responding, but an adult organising his experience and we hope making sense of it. As children grow older they need progressively more time in which to withdraw and consider, to relate events, to think laterally and to conceptualise, but the cherubic young philosopher, head in hands, is certainly not typical of the child of eight to thirteen learning morally and socially.

It is, of course, possible to train young children to behave in what looks like an adult way, to restrict them to sitting 'thinking', but if too much of each day (the signs are easy to read) is spent behaving in this way most young children learn to dislike school and the learning approaches it uses including what it calls 'thinking'. A few may flourish under such conditions. They should be catered for in any system which takes the trouble to read the signs. Most will be put off 'thinking', and those who ultimately learn to think effectively are likely to do so later outside the context of the school.

Balance is everything and the members of the project favour using different methods at different times, depending on the needs of the children, which can only be identified on the spot.

The *Startline* programme is designed to give children practice in experiencing, understanding, feeling sympathy, deciding, and speaking and acting to convey a message. All the material provides this practice directly or indirectly across the board though the emphases of, for example, *Photoplay* and *Choosing* are different, as their authors explain in the sections on specific materials in Chapter 6.

A word about 'deciding': the younger children in our age range, if they are treated with consideration, will often respond considerately without giving reasons, or even being able to give them when asked. It just is 'the way to treat people'. As children grow up, we tend to give them increasing practice in consciously working out 'good' courses of action. Provided we understand what we are doing and do it realistically, this matches and extends the child's increasing verbal capacity and ability to handle ideas and logical sequences.

However, there are a number of important points we must remember if we are to keep natural style and argument in balance.

1 Our prime interest is in behaviour, not verbal formulae.

2 We can accept (1) and still encourage and help individuals to develop and articulate personal choice.

3 We should avoid the 'rational-status-of-man' anxiety which prefers a good verbal offering to a good deed.

4 If we suggest to children that life is a continuous series of conscious decisions about interpersonal behaviour we exaggerate the decision-taking function. Furthermore to encourage a preoccupation with making decisions by denigrating tender feeling, sensitivity and spontaneous action can lead to a neurotic and self-destructive concern for 'why?', the terminal stage of which is paralysis in the face of a call for action.

5 We must not assume that goodness correlates positively with intelligence.

6 We should distinguish conceptually, and in practice when we can, between the reasons given for action and reasons for action, because understanding and honesty are central to moral growth.

7 In general, decision-taking process is best reserved for situations in which there is a real problem about what to do and to which the child's natural style does not offer a solution.

8 Even where a theoretical decision about what to do is worked out the details of how to proceed always have to come from an empirical investigation – a study of the real-life situation itself.

9 Growing children increasingly ask 'why?' in their struggle to become independent of outside authority. Tedious as this sometimes is for parents we always owe them answers except when immediate unquestioning action is needed to save or

protect life – that is, if we want them to become adults independent as adults should be.

10 Finally, when we ask children 'Why did you do that?' or 'Why do you intend to do that?' we should monitor what we are attempting so as to discourage the search for spurious reasons.

We have discussed in general why members of the team favour using certain methods at certain times and special attention has been given to expressive activity and decision-taking. What we propose to do now is to look at a group of techniques – drama, role-play and simulation – already introduced on p. 137, and to suggest why and when they are important, how to use them and what the significant differences are between them.

Basically the techniques are valuable because they are active rather than passive. They call for commitment to do something. If we refer back to the arousal-learning potential graph on p. 140, it is obvious that motivation increases when you are doing something that you want to do and that the only technique which is likely to produce sleep is being talked at. These techniques cater for the attraction to children of finding out about themselves, finding out about how others see them and discovering what their relations with others are, and may be. According to Eric Erikson, the children are helped to develop 'ego-identity'. Because much pre-adolescent and adolescent moral learning is by trial and error, i.e. by play and social experiment, these techniques provide a low-risk context for natural learning process. Mistakes can be made without serious casualties, or irreversible steps being taken. They provide a microcosm of life without much of the anxiety. The natural tendency to risk-taking can be handled in the work and put in proportion. Another advantage of these techniques is that when using them children get immediate feedback and learn directly the attractions of the personal success which follows making appropriate moves. For many children these techniques have the attraction of novelty or being used relatively infrequently, and provide a motivating change from normal school work. It is possible for these ways of working, when used with contemporary situations, to provide a first-rate context for essential education for change. In the play–work children learn not only to cope and to adjust, but also to create, to evolve and try out innovation, to become the companions and controllers of their environment. Finally, the work helps children to put themselves in others' shoes – an essential basis for moral behaviour.

The decision of when to use these techniques should depend on the teachers' recognition of the children's need for a certain level of involvement, to be part of a bridge-building exercise between theory and real-life experience. The points about gauging the motivation and the motivational opportunity have already been made. Although we are discussing when to use drama, role-play and simulation, it is important to remember that the ladder of involvement ascends from acting in a play to 'doing your own thing', and the technique which it is most effective to use depends on the child's level of confidence, which the teacher and children can only identify there and then. We are only able to discuss the three techniques together on the assumption that drama here refers to children writing and acting their own plays.

If the sessions can be sound-taped or, better still, video-taped, a dimension will be added to the work. The details of how to organise the work will depend on whether drama, role-play or simulation is used. The general moves in each case are as follows:

1 The class is divided up into groups, ideally not larger than ten or smaller than four.

2 The situations to be used are selected by the groups for their interest and relevance.

3 The detailed information (if any) required by the participants is provided by the teacher, or the boys and girls are told where they can find it. [Slow-learning children generally require more background detail whether because of poor imagination, weak memory or the inability to relate situations to their own experience.]

4. In phase one of this work, the key question is 'As x in this situation what do you do?' In phase two the question is 'As x in this situation what would you do?'

5 If drama is to be used, the children base their script-writing on their answers to the first or second questions in 4 and their answers to further questions about what y, z, etc. (the

other characters in the situation) would do in this situation. If the intention is to use role-play, instead of a script being prepared general briefs are drawn up for the principal characters giving the attitudes of these characters and the sorts of things they are likely to say, but not the actual words they are to use. In the case of simulation those to take part are merely told to be prepared to do what they do, or would do, in the situation.

6 Anyone not immediately taking part is told to be prepared to take part or to comment on what is going on.

7 The participants act, role-play or simulate the situation

8 As long as the boys and girls are interested they can take each other's parts, respond to the script in their own way, react to the briefing or simply do what they do or would do in the situation.

9 The final stage is for the teacher to be available to discuss with the children what happened and their ideas about why it happened. This work can lead into all sorts of creative endeavours especially if a sound or video-tape is available. A word of warning, however, the teacher's enthusiasm can exceed that of the children and spin out the session in a demotivating and unproductive way.

A variation on this standard procedure is with one-to-one (dyadic) situations to put the emphasis on getting into the other person's shoes by using role-reversal. The moves are:

1 Choose a situation which involves two characters who have different points of view.

2 Support the situation with a cartoon, straight drawing or photograph which you show to those about to take part.

3 The two participants play out what they would do, having taken the point of view to which they are naturally inclined.

4 The other members of the group watch and decide how they would react 'in' both parts.

5 The participants reverse roles and play the situation out again from the other's point of view.

6 Those taking part revert to their original roles and play out the situation again.

Generally the final simulation shows more consideration

for the other's needs, feelings and interests from both the participants. There is some experimental evidence that this consideration is, at least to some extent, subsequently shown in real-life. Those who watch the exercise can themselves participate in further sessions. For this reason it is useful to have even numbers in the groups. A critical follow-up discussion may be included if it seems likely to be useful.

Whereas discussion can be valuable, simulation in particular is more effective in a number of ways. In particular:

1 It frequently involves those who for various reasons do not take part in discussion;

2 Those who simulate become personally involved and more part of the situation than those who discuss it, the result being that there is greater honesty about what would happen and so a more realistic basis for behaviour change;

3 The preparation for real life is intimate and direct, based as it is on interaction which has really taken place and is of importance to those taking part.

Figure 8   **Simulation moves from**

1 Discussion

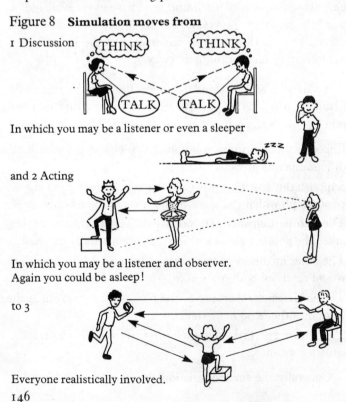

In which you may be a listener or even a sleeper

and 2 Acting

In which you may be a listener and observer.
Again you could be asleep!

to 3

Everyone realistically involved.

146

Some teachers, and to a lesser extent some children, are convinced that simulation is not their 'thing' and they may be right, but more often it is simply that no-one has helped them into what is for them a novel, mysterious and somewhat intimate activity.

One easy way of moving directly from discussion to simulation, even with a whole class, goes like this: when a boy or girl is describing what he or she would do in a given situation, the teacher interrupts with 'Imagine you are x and say it or do it' or even more simply 'Say it or do it.' The move is from reported speech from the 'As I said in Blackpool' of the politician to direct speech and action towards someone. The next step is for the teacher to withdraw as a point of reference, to sit down or to move away, perhaps into a corner, and when addressed to say something such as 'Don't tell me, tell him; he's y' (the magistrate or whoever it may be). By continuing to use this technique the teacher unobtrusively 'casts' the simulation, perhaps sometimes by asking for volunteers, and encourages the members of the class or group to speak and react directly to each other. It is surprising how many children, even from a class of over thirty pupils, can be involved in this way when the room may be too crowded to allow them to move from their desks. You can always tell when the technique is working because more and more children look away from the teacher. Instead, they look at the active participants and get into the action. If there is a bell they may even not hear it.

In answer to our last question there is always scope for introducing ways of working not mentioned in the published programme, and the criterion for introducing them is an affirmative answer to the question 'Do they help children behave with concern?' The criteria for using specific types of approach have already been discussed in this chapter and Chapter 6. Indeed, as is spelt out in Chapter 8 of this book on a 'growth model' it is the purpose of our stimulus approach to encourage this and as far as possible ultimately to make people independent of the programme. Teachers will have their own ideas about how to make the best use of any special advantages which they, the children, the class situation or the school may have. Different kinds of equipment make different kinds of work possible. In particular strategies for work in the

147

community, the final stage in moral education, can only be realistically worked out in the context of a particular school.

It is not extravagant to claim that, when a school actively develops the dimension of education which concerns us in this book, it becomes progressively less necessary specifically to timetable the work.

Expressive arts

Throughout our approach to working with children we have continually stressed the importance of creative activities as a means of expressing personal moral interests, concerns and solutions. This chapter discusses the relative merits of some forms of expressive activity, and extensive suggestions for creative activities in the classroom are outlined in Appendices F, G, H and I and in the *Making it Happen* section of *Growing*.

Involvement in making things and expressive artistic activity is fundamental to our moral education approach. Children are motivated to respond by using various forms of creative expression because these involve them in enjoyable and practical activity. Theoretical concern is supplanted by creative practice. Morality becomes active.

Through expressive artistic work, honesty and directness of personal communication are encouraged. Children, by creating different versions of themselves and their relationships with others, can externalise their emotions and reactions. They can review their efforts to create and to understand themselves and their reactions better. We maintain this is especially so in group work in drama and simulation, when the children's own ideas about, and other possibilities for, behaviour are modified in the light of others' reactions. In this play or work the group creates a continuing joint morality that is relevant to the individuals involved in its processes.

We have not suggested in our programme that the whole gamut of the expressive arts is equally appropriate to moral education, though some may believe that is the case. Certainly, any form of artistic expression which enables children to make an active statement can increase their practical concern.

148

Dramatic activities described and discussed earlier in this chapter involve children in reading the messages others send and in sending clear, unambivalent responses – undersubscribed moral skills.

Other forms of visual communication are encouraged throughout our programme. Cartooning, drawing and painting are advocated as they also increase visual communication understanding. They provide a vehicle and a focus for non-verbal elements of communiciation so fundamental in establishing personal relationships. Chapter 4 on children's drawings illustrates the value of this approach to moral education. Both improved visual perception and the mastery of body language can be combined with aural and verbal communication work.

Taking the trouble to look, listen and respond is considerate behaviour – morality in action.

Using the forms of the expressive arts supports the growth of personal creativity, encourages imagination and variety of response. We have suggested in Chapter 3 that the growth of creative ability provides the means for considerate behaviour. By applying creative ability to the expressive arts we support the growth of moral autonomy. If, for example, we heighten interpersonal perception and sensitivity to others' behaviour by picture appreciation or drawing, we can then develop open-ended activities that allow the expression of a number of alternative strategies for action rather than just one. We are enabled to encourage the generation of a number of ideas in the search for the best solution, rather than recognising and adopting only one course of action. Imagination is basic to being able to identify with others and show concern for them. Flexibility in thought and action are nurtured by expressive artistic activity, and this flexibility enables children to modify and adapt their behaviour in the face of change. Both society and education are changing so rapidly that teaching flexibility as an example for problem solving and imaginative person-centred action has never been more of a priority. It is upon the quality of personal relationships that the success of society and education depends. Treating others honestly and considerately is the basis of morality and a better society.

Our programme, through its materials and techniques, provides many opportunities for developing children's creative abilities. Most children's creativity is restricted by educational processes which do not allow individual exploration and invention to emerge in normal school activity. By the use of situational material in our programme, children are encouraged to identify needs and meet them. By generating other possible choices for action they are testing the social and moral parameters of the situation. By using their imagination, curiosity, invention in social experimentation, children increase their creative abilities and develop a flexible, adaptive and yet committed personal style. The amount of creative growth is dependent on the degree of freedom allowed in expressing and exploring, linked to the degree of sensitivity the individual possesses to what is seen, heard, touched and experienced generally.

The child of creativity is appropriate action. We have suggested many ways in which this action can be expressed but whether it will be expressed is dependent on teachers' attitudes and behaviour. We can increase creativity if we give children a sure, predictable and loving base while encouraging them to learn on their own, or in their groups, through social interaction, without their feeling dominated or consistently monitored. They need to try out moral behaviour, to fail, to succeed, to evolve and develop their own attitudes, beliefs and behaviour. When adults do not govern their every action, they can avoid the misconception that adults are all-knowing. They will discover and act in the knowledge that adults have needs and feelings; for example, that teachers are entitled to consideration too.

The part adults play is crucial. Children need our security, support and encouragement to independence in order to grow creatively. In talking, discussing, painting, or drama, we can open up new possibilities, encourage different endings, and ideas of what may be appropriate. We can, through the expressive arts supply emotional satisfaction to children. We can value children's own contributions as worthwhile. By supplying a flexible structure in the programmes, both teachers and children can plan their own activities, generate their own situations and solutions and use material in any combination they choose. Other ways of ordering time and activity are always possible. Class organisation and activity can be decided by personal needs rather than by administrative and school organisation. The need for the individual to be operative and instrumental in any situation is fundamental to moral education, whether that individual be pupil or teacher. Work in the expressive arts ensures that the teacher is relieved of the anxiety of wondering how to introduce or timetable 'moral education'. Everything which needs to be done can be done in the course of the school's normal activities.

Reference

1. Hebb, D. O., 1955. 'Drives and the conceptional nervous system', *Psychological Review*, 62, 243–54.

8 Learning research, materials and techniques – a growth model

Figure 9 on p. 157 shows the project's approach to moral learning research, curriculum research and development. Although, like all diagrams, an oversimplification in some respects, it represents accurately the way in which the project has worked and would like to see work develop.

The diagram also illustrates in general terms how the Schools Council Adolescent Moral Education Project worked in the University of Oxford between 1967 and 1972. There are, however, the following differences:

1 The Oxford Project evolved its whole way of working. The Cambridge University work followed a specific proposal to the Schools Council which was modified in practice.

2 In the case of the adolescent work the learning research was well advanced before the Project was established. The 8–13 Project has carried out its learning research during the life of the Project.

3 The 8–13 'significant-situation' moral learning research technique was a development of the 'critical-incident' technique evolved and used for the first time in moral learning research in the University of Oxford between 1964 and 1969.

4 Teachers were directly involved in collecting the 8–13 survey data.

5 Members of the Cambridge Project team have worked directly with teachers *in their schools* to develop materials and techniques.

6 During the life of the present project we have become increasingly convinced of the central status of continuous

support for children, teachers and parents, if worthwhile behaviour change is to be effected.

7 We are now sure that a reform of teacher education is urgently required if the education system is to contribute effectively to a better quality of life in this country. This reform should ensure that teacher education institutions continuously use an inductive approach which asks questions to discover the wants, expectations and aspirations of children, teachers and parents; analyses the answers to identify their needs, learning process, and motivation; and applies the findings to teacher education. Without such an effort we shall never establish sufficient relevance in the curriculum. A narrow understanding by some of what education is about has helped politicians to rationalise the reduction of expenditure on education by putting the basic emphasis on literacy, numeracy and specific skills when socially and *economically* the national priority is the generation of enthusiasm and commitment.

We have mentioned these evolutionary changes in some detail because they illustrate in practice, and we hope graphically, what is meant by 'growth'. It is the limitation of so much learning research, curriculum research and development work that its short-term, *ad hoc*, nature means that any insights which are gained are abandoned, if we are lucky to be rediscovered at a later date. The present system for funding and administering work is wasteful and frustrating. Present committees and working parties, supposed to be democratically appointed, are frequently composed of representatives of influential bodies who use meetings to state established positions and refight old battles.

The key points about the approach illustrated in the diagram are:

1 That a project or unit to be of maximum use must have a way of working which actively encourages response, feedback, at every stage.

2 The whole cycle in its school application depends at every point on teacher education and in-service support, particularly the emotional support made essential by innovation which initially poses a threat as well as the possibility of better things.

3   The ultimate aim is to de-professionalise the handling of the
    learning process so that each individual enjoys, and becomes
    responsible for, his own learning. The teacher, the researcher
    and the curriculum-developer are facilitators. They are
    needed and should be available to help others meet their
    needs. At the same time they share the responsibility of
    making individuals as independent as possible.

    There are a number of things which the diagram cannot
make explicit. The first concerns the origin of the work, based
as it is on learning research in the field. It is sometimes argued,
falsely in our opinion, that the basis of inductive work
must always be unstated rational–logical assumptions. Logic
does ascribe priority to finding out how children learn their
moral behaviour and what the motivation is for different kinds
of behaviour. However, the conviction that learning research
is basic comes from practical experience as schoolchild,
teacher or parent, and our response to it. We experience, we
feel, we decide and in this case logical priority confirms the
decision.

    There would be no money and therefore no learning
research and curriculum research and development sequence,
if some individual or body did not support the conviction that
work was needed in the area proposed. This is where the
Schools Council has made a unique contribution since the
mid-sixties. It has made possible work of the first importance
which for commercial or political reasons would not otherwise
have been done. Other countries, borrowing and developing
as they do ideas which have come from council projects, are
often frankly envious. A particularly valuable feature of
council support has been that so far, whatever the reasons for
council backing and whatever council committees' ideas
about the form which work should take, projects have
generally been left to develop and modify from experience the
approach originally suggested by their directors and approved
in committee. Such tolerance and flexibility are essential if
work is to be relevant and have integrity.

    The second feature of the work which cannot be adequately
expressed on the diagram concerns sequence. The 'stages' of
the work are numbered on the diagram from I 'Learning
research in the field' back to I again through, finally, VIII

'Use of the programme as a research tool'. This correctly gives the impression of the general order in which jobs were tackled and are projected, and of continuing process rather than a once and for all linear programme. However, the two-dimensional temporal sequence is an over-simplification. The order of events is not necessarily as represented. Sometimes in practice different activities go on at the same time or a backtracking or repetition phase is included for some specific purpose. People join in at different points and for different reasons. They may not see or understand the whole process. They may, at any point, move off to abandon the work, or into a curriculum research and development sequence of their own. Communication is multi-directional and not simply from A to B to C.

The third point which the diagram leaves to be clarified is the scope of the second 'stage', 'identification of the needs, motivation and learning process of those involved in the learning situation'. The team has done a great deal to identify the needs, motivation and learning of children and teachers and the work is described in this book. What has disappointed us has been the difficulty of involving parents, not because of parents' unwillingness but more because of political anxieties and the view that our brief did not extend to parents (or for that matter to teacher education). The effective general involvement of parents is essential to the future extension of this work. Our experience when we have involved parents suggests that the effort will be very much worthwhile and the approach problem free, if it is handled with sensitivity. Political and professional anxieties limit research far more than is generally realised, even when all proposed involvement is voluntary and rigorously protected by guarantees of anonymity and the possibility of withdrawal at any time.

The fourth point which the diagram does not make clear is that all the work from VI 'Publication' onwards is a projection, the expression of hope. We hope it will happen that way and we are sure that it should happen that way. We cannot say that it will happen.

The fifth comment concerns 'Evaluation'. It is our conviction that by far the most informative and valuable form of evaluation is evaluation of the programme in use. Our experience of this in the 8–13 work and in the development of

155

Lifeline is extensive and most encouraging. On the diagram completed 'evaluation in use' is represented by stages IV and V. Unfortunately publication in this country has tended to be once and for all and even though the programme we are offering may finally be extensively used in half a dozen, or more, countries, including the vast market of the United States, no provision has been made for evaluation, revision, development and extension in use. What could be an exciting and valuable beginning might be an end in itself, apart, of course, from the further work we hope it stimulates elsewhere.

The sixth point is that VIII 'Use of the programme as a research tool, producing data for further research and development, teachers' curriculum research and development sequences and learning insights, may, without active support and encouragement, remain an idea.

Seventh is that the same very much applies to the aims of continuing support and dissemination by the Project members. The time of one Project member is guaranteed until August 1978 but the extent to which anyone will be available after that time is uncertain.

There are those who believe that a model of the kind we have introduced is too project-centred. It does describe the work and hopes of a project but, as we have already stressed, we are acutely aware of our responsibility to make teachers and children independent of us. Indeed, we want to de-professionalise learning whenever possible and the teachers' curriculum research and development sequences which are shown as a 'Spin off' from stages VII and VIII on the diagram not only could occur at any stage of the diagram sequence but are themselves intermediate stages on the way to independent and interdependent creative living which does not require such strategies. However, a realistic look at the present situation in schools suggests that teachers' capacity to be self-evaluating and self-servicing is, largely through no fault of their own, strictly limited. The poor links with parents in most schools illustrate the problem. (But there are dramatic exceptions.) Until there is an honest national recognition of need priorities in education, including the best use of schools, better treatment for teachers (especially the enthusiastic young who have often been trained, only to be unemployed later), higher staffing ratios, more time, recognition and

156

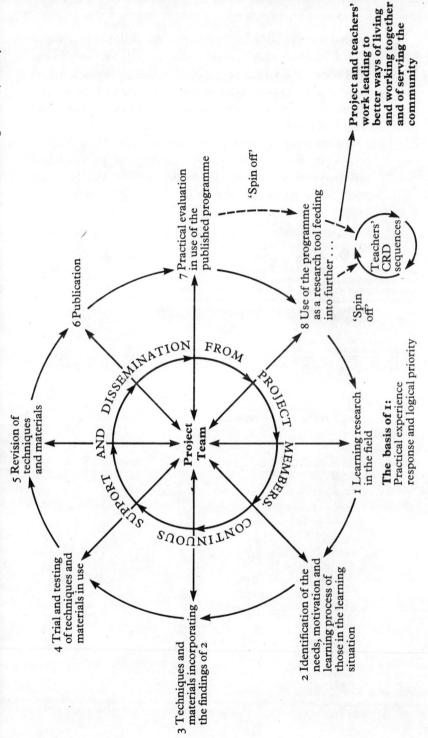

Project and teachers' work leading to better ways of living and working together and of serving the community

'Spin off'

7 Practical evaluation in use of the published programme

6 Publication

Teachers' CRD sequences

8 Use of the programme as a research tool feeding into further . . . .

'Spin off'

DISSEMINATION FROM

Project Team

PROJECT MEMBERS'

SUPPORT AND

CONTINUOUS

5 Revision of techniques and materials

1 Learning research in the field

The basis of 1:
Practical experience response and logical priority

4 Trial and testing of techniques and materials in use

3 Techniques and materials incorporating the findings of 2

2 Identification of the needs, motivation and learning process of those in the learning situation

know-how, available teachers are going to need every bit of outside support they can get. Such an improvement in the education service, in spite of its cost, makes economic sense. It could transform our society by generating the enthusiasm and commitment we so urgently need. The return on investment would be unrivalled.

Ultimately the value of all this work is to be judged practically in terms of a better quality of personal and interpersonal life and service to the community. The final phase in moral education is doing things with and for other people.

9 The research approach

The Schools Council Moral Education 8–13 Project was established to continue the work of the 11–17 Moral Education Project. The latter project is sometimes described as covering the thirteen to sixteen year age range, when in fact the research work surveyed the eleven to seventeen age group in order to be able to make projections for both the thirteen and sixteen year olds.

The earlier work was based in the Department of Educational Studies of the University of Oxford. The move to the Cambridge University Department of Education as a base for the 8–13 work provided an impetus to establish a fresh pattern of working relationships with schools. The new team extended the goodwill which the previous project had secured under the same director.

The work of the 11–17 Project is widely known through the *Lifeline* programme, published in 1972, and the 8–13 Project continued with the same basic emphasis on understanding and practice. We set out to examine and describe the moral climate in which children of this age range learn their behaviour and to identify the process by which that behaviour is learned. By asking children to describe situations in which they were treated with or without consideration, it became possible to understand the depth and perspective of their moral environment.

Each child was also asked to describe a situation in which he or she was not sure what to do. The answers to this question brought out the extent of the children's understanding of others' behaviour and of their own capacity for action.

Finally, the children were asked what they did, if anything, in response to the situations they described. The answers to these questions are packed with vital information. For instance, you can discover from them the circumstances in which consideration is, or is not, shown to others. You can identify the people who show, or fail to show, consideration so that it becomes clear which situations pose behaviour problems for children, how these situations were initiated and what happened. When we analysed the children's responses we not only understood better how they felt in different social contexts but also the effects of considerate and inconsiderate treatment on their behaviour.

Children adjust to circumstances and learn to create new states of affairs. Our central concern relevant to action is the nature of the learning and how it takes place. We include at this point a diagram of the whole survey and research procedure used to enable us to understand this learning and to apply the understanding to the development of learning materials and techniques.

The members of the Project team tried in practice and finalised the form of the questions to be put to the children. The general, relatively open-ended, inductive approach and type of question had been established prior to the initial submission to the Schools Council by Peter McPhail in 1971. At that time it had been decided to use a 'significant situation' technique similar to, and developed from, that previously used in the adolescent study.

There was much preliminary discussion with teachers about research and its relevance to meeting children's needs and the work greatly benefited from their support and constructive criticism. There were two basic considerations: the questions should be simple, yet specific; at the same time any change in a question should be directed towards increasing the child's involvement and, with it, the 'depth' of the response. The medium of the child's response was indicated in the instruction, for example: 'Write about . . . and draw . . .'. As a result of this work with teachers and the evaluation of trial questions with children in school the form and content of the National Survey questions were finalised. Using writing and drawing rather than interview, except in the cases of some children who it was considered might have

The survey and analytic procedure

1971–72
The development of questions and possible procedures

1973
Discussions with teachers and others
First trial of questions with children
Analysis of results; discussion and modification of procedures and questions
Discussions with teachers and others
Detailed plans for administration of questions
Formation of sample
Second trial of questions with children
Analysis discussion and modification, as appropriate
Separate administration of questions by each of the four team members
Analysis, leading to the final version of the questions and of the administration procedures

Oct.–Dec. 1973
Use of the questions in the National Survey: 3,475 children and control groups

---

1974–76

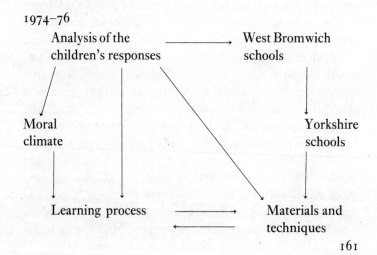

Analysis of the children's responses ⟶ West Bromwich schools

Moral climate

Yorkshire schools

Learning process ⟶ Materials and techniques

difficulties in expressing themselves in these ways, not only made it much easier to standardise conditions for the many individuals asking the questions but also to interpret the children's responses.

We had thought it best that class teachers should ask the questions of their pupils in the chosen schools, and preliminary discussions with teachers confirmed this viewpoint. Teachers are likely to know their children and can encourage their cooperation. Furthermore the group is an efficient context in which to collect the large amount of data needed in a survey of this kind.

In order to try to discover whether the teacher had an effect on the nature of the situations reported by the children, the questions were given to a number of control classes by members of the project team. These control classes were established in large schools by obtaining two matched classes of pupils in the same year. One of each pair of classes had the questions given to it by the class teacher, the other by a team member. This comparison suggested that it made little difference who put the questions.

Although the data were collected from the whole class, individual pupil anonymity was preserved to ensure that the children felt free to report whatever they chose. Every child was given paper and an envelope. After responding to both parts of the three questions each child was asked to put his response into the envelope and, after his third answer, to seal it. Names were not written on either the paper or the envelope, although the latter contained the pupil's reference number to make it possible for us to assign the child's age, sex and other personal details to the response. Teachers were asked not to alter the layout of desks or tables in the classroom, so that the likelihood of children feeling that they were in a test situation was minimised. Other details of the approach to children similarly played down the notion of a test. The situations quoted by children in their answers were to be drawn from personal experience. The children were asked not to talk to others about what they were going to write and draw. Teachers, when giving supplementary information, were asked not to give the class illustrative examples of possible answers. Help with spelling or understanding the questions was, however, to be available on request. No time limit, for answering any or all of the following questions was set by the Project:

1 Write and draw about a time when somebody made you feel pleased or happy.
Describe what you did as a result.

2 Write and draw about a time when somebody made you feel frightened, angry or unhappy.
Describe what you did as a result.

3 Write and draw about a time when you were with somebody else (or other people) and you were not sure what to do.
What did you do?

As well as the questions being on display, they were read to the children by the teacher.

It may surprise some people that the Project chose to ask children questions about happiness and uncertainty. There was a number of reasons for doing this.

First, we found questions about 'good' and 'bad' experiences were difficult for children in the age range to handle.

Secondly, responses to questions about good and bad treatment often resulted in eight to thirteen year olds attempting to reflect adult ideas about 'goodness' and 'badness'.

Thirdly, questions about happiness, unhappiness and uncertainty gave us an excellent start motivationally. They made the children keen to pass on the whole range of their experience and reactions to it.

Fourthly, our preliminary evidence suggested that children from eight to thirteen might build up their understanding of what is good and bad from their personal feelings about the various kinds of treatment they receive. The growth, logically and psychologically, is from the 'smile and frown' 'yea and nay' conditioning of the young child through personal experience to an understanding of others' needs from an understanding of self. This understanding of self and others can then be analysed and understood in conceptual terms, though to behave morally always involves observation and the recognition of the influence our actions have on others, as well as ideas about right and wrong.

In brief, to base work in moral learning process on the

happiness, unhappiness and uncertainty of children is not to sell out to a crude utilitarianism. A satisfied pig can still be compared morally with a dissatisfied Socrates if there is any purpose to be served in doing so. All we do assume is that man is born with the potential for considerateness; that people need people; and that morality is the servant of man as well as his adopted master and can be a means to his great well being. It is imperfect moral systems, the product of the limited perspectives of their time, which restrict, cause suffering and destroy.

We decided to build on our network of contacts with Local Education Authorities all over the country, with whom the project had worked between 1967 and 1972. These authorities were invited to say whether they would like to participate in the National Survey. They were asked if they could nominate groups of schools which would be likely to cooperate with the survey, were close enough geographically for the teachers to meet together with one of the Project team, and whose work could be coordinated by some representative of the Authority, who was usually either a member of the advisory staff, or the leader of a teachers' centre. In deciding which Authorities and schools to include in the sample, middle schools were given precedence where they were being established. For this reason the sample was not fully representative of the national status quo as the number of pupils in middle schools in our sample was greater than it would otherwise have been. We took trouble to include examples of all types of non-selective school, in terms of both organisation and size. We also included a group of small rural schools, which have an important though often neglected place in our national education system. The groups of schools were located throughout the country, with as wide a range of settings and catchment areas as possible. The list in Appendix C shows the distribution of the forty-three schools which took part in the main survey and the locations of the schools used in the preliminary work.

The priorities we adopted in establishing our sample meant that, although it was not statistically ideal, it gave us groups of schools with which individual team members would establish highly effective partnerships.

Each teacher who was to take part in the survey met the

164

team member working in that region of the country. Discussions took place to clarify the aims of the survey and procedural details. Teachers' reports at follow-up meetings indicated that the arrangements for data gathering worked satisfactorily.

It is worth reiterating that the data was to be used in three distinct ways:

1 as a description of the children's moral situation;
2 as a way of collecting evidence about how children learn their behaviour;
3 as a means of identifying the nature of the children's moral concerns and of incorporating these concerns with the learning understanding in the development of teaching materials and techniques.

The children's response to each of the three questions were read and categorised, re-read and re-categorised according to different criteria. In order to cope adequately with the large number of personal variables for each child, as well as with the salient features of the children's responses, it was decided to code as many of these variables as possible for computer analysis. Although the flavour and quality of a verbal response is lost in such coding, the computer analysis should be seen as being complementary to the reading, and more qualitative categorisation, of the children's writing and drawing using topic sheets. The computer supplied the quantitative description while the topic sheets recorded any unusual vivid characterisation by the child. Other items recorded on the sheet included creative response, and drawings of special interest, especially where relationships were depicted or described.

Earlier reading of the children's responses made possible the construction of coded-response categories. A list of fifty-two 'theme categories' was derived which represented the major concerns of the children. Eight categories of 'significant other' mentioned in the child's responses as the key characters in situations were listed. These ranged from human beings and animals to spirits and other fictitious figures. The eight broad categories were subdivided into twenty-eight distinct codes. Other coding dimensions included the kind of reaction described by the child; the context in which the situation occurred, the time and place as well as the degree of involvement; the nature of the response, whether constructive, destructive, active or passive; and the number of responses to the situation reported by each child. The classification of responses adopted was a shortened version of that developed by Peter McPhail as a result of his 11–17 'significant situation' work between 1964 and 1967. More details of the procedures of the survey can be found in the research report[1].

As shown on the simplified diagram, two aspects of the work were carried out in West Bromwich and Yorkshire schools only.

The West Bromwich study involved two schools. It was concerned with questions such as: 'What are the principal moral concerns of those children who have learning and communication difficulties?' and 'How can they be helped to express their concerns?' The answer to the first question was that the principle concerns of these children did not differ significantly from those identified from the National Survey except that they reported a high incidence of personal injury. The answer to the second was that the children expressed their concerns most effectively by expressive artistic activity, especially by 'acting out' their situations and using cartoon strips.

In addition to the use of painting, drawing, written responses and the tape-recording of conversations, new procedures, such as drawing a cartoon strip were evolved. This approach of giving the children a sequence of five labelled but otherwise blank boxes in which to draw their response was productive and popular.

The use of other means of responding, developed in West Bromwich, was followed up as part of the Yorkshire schools survey[2], but here the aims were somewhat different. A small scale reliability study was carried out by re-questioning, after a delay of some nine months, the same children in three Yorkshire schools who had previously taken part in the national survey. After the re-questioning, the children were given a choice of using painting, drawing or the cartoon strip as alternative methods of representing their responses to the questions. In addition, children from two other schools which had not previously been involved in the survey were asked to respond to the questions using the same chosen means of expression.

We were interested to find out if the children who were re-questioned reported similar significant situations after the time lapse. They did. We also wanted to know if a wider means of response helped children to add to what they had already expressed in writing and drawing. The answer in this case was a definite yes. Finally, was it the case in all five schools that the public nature of the response was affected by the use of these different means of expression? It was in that what the children had written was expanded by drawing, while a discussion of the drawings with the artist even further expanded his statement.

A central theme of all the Yorkshire schools work was to establish the degree of 'creativity-innovation' children reported using in their thinking and behaviour. During the sound-taped interview, children were asked a number of questions about their reported situations, based on general abilities and traits of creativity. All the responses were then analysed and the creative social interaction model in Chapter 3 was developed from the results. Variety of perceptual comprehension was the key to the degree of sensitivity shown by the children.

The richness of the children's responses gathered in the National Survey and through continued contact with children in schools over subsequent years had led to the understanding of how they learn their behaviour, described and discussed in Chapters 1, 2 and 3. This understanding is the foundation of our work in developing curriculum materials and approaches and, coupled with our close working partnership with teachers, has made it possible for us to progress towards meeting the expressed needs of children in the ways discussed in this book.

References

1. Ungoed-Thomas, J. R., 1978. *The Moral Situation of Children*, Schools Council.
2. Middleton, D., 1975. Creativity in Children's Social and Moral Learning, unpublished M.A. thesis, London University Institute Library.

Postscript –
The challenge of change

The children, parents and teachers generally make us optimistic about the future. We just cannot believe that, whatever the economic constraints, the progress made towards relating education in this country to the needs of these groups will be lost. However, we would be less than honest if we did not conclude with a mention of the current trends which we passionately believe should be resisted.

First, there is a marked tendency to rationalise the results of economic restriction and to move towards a backwoods education. Literacy, numeracy and other basic skills are important but there is no reason why they should be sacrificed or why excellence in basic skills should constitute a threat to greater relevance in the education of our children. The key problem facing the country at present is a lack of motivation and commitment which can only be remedied by greater concern for need and an educational system which is better at meeting need. The school must be a listening post for society, not simply an institution devoted to turning out whatever persons are in short supply in order to meet short-term economic pressures.

We may have seriously to discuss the preconceptions of the economic model for society. Standard of life, and assumptions about the need for ever increasing purchasing power conflict with the quality-of-life ambitions of many children to whom time is in shorter supply than money. Materialism is producing the jealous society obsessed with economic comparison and a God-given structure of pay differentials which can never be agreed. Vandalism, dishonesty, aggression, sneering and 'knocking' other people are the by-products of such a society.

Children need love and security which cannot spring from these origins. Without them we shall not have the health and happiness which are still man's principle aims. They come from a sense of purpose and commitment to a cause. We hope our work can make some contribution to such purpose and commitment.

Appendix A

**Schools Council Moral Education Project 8–13
in the University of Cambridge, 1972–76**

Staff

Director
Peter McPhail, M.A.
(1972–76)

Deputy Director
(September 1972–April 1975)
Jasper Ungoed-Thomas, M.A., D.Phil.
(May 1975–August 1976)
David Ingram, M.A.

Research Officers
David Ingram, M.A., 1973–75
David Middleton, M.A., 1973–76
Caroline Rennie, B.A., 1973–75

Information Officer
Charlotte Bird, M.A.

Secretary
Sarah Williams, B.A.

Consultant (computing and statistics)
John Sutcliffe, M.A., M.Sc.

Visitor 1975–76
Peter Hudson, B.A. of Ontario, Canada.
Jo Pelly (Assistant in research) 1976

Appendix B

Schools Council Moral Education Project 8–13

Members of Consultative Committee

Professor P. H. Hirst (Chairman)
Mr T. I. Ambrose, H.M.I.
Miss P. M. Bell
Mr G. W. Cooksey
Mr C. R. Jacobs
Sir Desmond Lee
Mr J. Malone
Mr A. I. L. Morgan
Alderman C. J. Peers
Mr A. Razzell
Miss A. Richards
Mr M. Rogers
Mr G. W. Scotney
Mr I. Sutherland
Mr J. R. G. Tomlinson
Mr J. R. Ungoed-Thomas, H.M.I.
Mr C. Wigglesworth
Miss M. Wileman

Appendix C

Those who have helped us

We are grateful for the support of the Directors of Education of the Authorities in which we have worked.

Overmead County Primary School, Oxford.
John Fisher Roman Catholic Primary School, Oxford.
Bishop Kirk Junior School, Oxford.
Blackbird Leys Junior School, Oxford.
Greenmere Junior School, Didcot, Berkshire.
North Hinksey Church of England Junior School, Oxford.
Preswood Junior School, Great Missenden, Bucks.
St Mary and St John Junior School, Oxford.
Wolvercote Primary School, Oxford.
Carterton Comprehensive School, Oxon.
Headington County Secondary School, Oxford.
Milham Ford Secondary School, Oxford.
Westley Middle School, Bury St Edmunds, Suffolk.
Caldecote Junior School, Abingdon, Berks.
The Alec Hunter High School, Braintree, Essex.
Newbiggin Hall Cheviot County First School, Newcastle upon Tyne.
Throckley Vallum County First School, Newcastle upon Tyne.
West Denton County First School, Newcastle upon Tyne.
Newbiggin Hall Cheviot County Middle School, Newcastle upon Tyne.
Throckley County Middle School, Newcastle upon Tyne.
West Denton County Middle School, Newcastle upon Tyne.
Grove Street School, Norton, Yorks.
Langton School, Malton, Yorks.

Settrington School, Malton, Yorks.
Westow School, Yorks.
Northside Junior School, Workington, Cumbria.
Victoria Junior School, Workington, Cumbria.
Moorclose Boys' Secondary School, Workington, Cumbria.
Newlands Girls' School, Workington, Cumbria.
Bishops Middle School, Blacon, Cheshire.
Cherry Grove Middle School, Chester.
Newton Middle School, Chester.
St Thomas of Canterbury Middle School, Chester
Charnwood Junior School, Lichfield, Staffs.
Chase Terrace Junior School, Lichfield, Staffs.
Chase Terrace Comprehensive School, Lichfield, Staffs.
Carlton Gedling Stanhope Junior School, Nottingham.
Kimberley Comprehensive School, Nottingham.
West Bridgford Comprehensive School, Nottingham.
Yew Tree Junior School, Walsall, Staffs.
Sawston Village College, Cambridge.
Barkway School, Royston, Herts.
Icknield Walk Junior Modern School, Royston, Herts.
Bridgwater School, Berkhamsted, Herts.
The Greenway School, Royston, Herts.
The Thomas Bourne Middle School, Berkhamsted, Herts.
Furness Junior Modern School, London NW10.
Salisbury Junior Modern School, London NW6.
Bessemer Grange Junior School, London SE5.
Langdon School, London, E6.
Llanedeyrn Primary School, Cardiff.
Marlborough Junior School, Cardiff.
Roath Park Junior School, Cardiff.
Llanedeyrn High School, Cardiff.
Cranborne County Middle School, Wimborne, Dorset.
Ferndown County Middle School, Wimborne, Dorset.
St Michael's C. of E. Middle School, Wimborne, Dorset.
Bow Primary School, Crediton, Devon.
The Queen Elizabeth Comprehensive School, Crediton, Devon.
Hayward County Primary School, Crediton, Devon.
Eldene Junior School, Swindon, Wilts.
Walcot Junior High School, Swindon, Wilts.
Roger de Clare First School, Puckeridge, Herts.

Bective Middle School, Northampton.
Boothville Middle School, Northampton.
Angley School, Cranbrook, Kent.
Grantchester Primary School, Cambridge.
Thriplow County Primary School, Royston, Herts.
Houghton County Primary School, Huntingdon.
Studlands Rise First School, Royston, Herts.
Bottisham County Primary School, Cambridge.
Oulton Broad Middle School, Lowestoft, Suffolk.
The Harris Middle School, Lowestoft, Suffolk.
Ryburn School, Sowerby Bridge, Nr. Halifax, Yorks.
Rillington School, Malton, Yorks.
Overleigh Middle School, Chester.
George Salter High School, West Bromwich, Staffs.
Wood Green Junior School, Wednesbury, Staffs.
Annie Osbourn Infants School, Coventry.
Blackwood Middle School, Streetley.
Clothier St Primary School, Willenhall.
Alice Stevens ESN School, Coventry.
Corley Residential School, Coventry.
Deedmore ESN School, Coventry.
The Meadows Residential School, Coventry.
Three Spires ESN School, Coventry.
Town Thorns ESN School, Easenhall.
Wainbody Wood Maladjusted School, Coventry.
St Margaret's ESN School, Bedworth, Staffs.
John Mason High School, Abingdon, Berks.
Shepherds Hill Middle School, Blackbird Leys, Oxford.
St Joseph's School, Hertford.
The Augustus Smith School, Berkhamsted, Herts.
Chantry Secondary School, Ipswich, Suffolk.
Fulbourn Junior School, Cambridge.
Birchwood Middle School, Lincoln.
Monks Abbey Middle School, Lincoln.
St Faith's Middle School, Lincoln.
Gainsborough North County Primary School, Gains-
    borough.
Upper School, Northlands, Basildon.
Arthur Bugler County Primary School, Stanford-le-Hope.
Harlesden Junior Middle Infants School, London NW10.
The Church of England Middle School, Newport, I.O.W.

University of Durham Institute of Education.
College of St Hilda & St Bede, Durham.
Curriculum Development Centre, Madeley College of Education.
C. F. Mott College of Higher Education, Prescot.
Homerton College, Cambridge.
Moray House College of Education, Edinburgh.

Mr G. Miller, R.E. Adviser, Newcastle upon Tyne.
Mrs D. Edwards, Newcastle upon Tyne.
Mr S. Londesborough, Scarborough.
Mr R. Leach, Tenbury Wells, Worcs.
Mr M. Stevens, R.E. Adviser, Leicester.
Mr I. Wragg, R.E. Adviser, Derby.
Mr P. East, Special Education Adviser, Coventry.
Miss P. Firkins, R.E. Adviser, Welwyn Garden City, Herts.
Mr G. Oliver, R.E. Adviser, Redbridge, London.
Mr J. Kettle, Adviser for Compensatory Education, Brent, London.
Mr P. King, R.E. Adviser, Exeter.
Mr D. Treharne, R.E. Adviser, Cardiff.
Mr J. W. Brimer, R.E. Adviser, Newcastle upon Tyne.
Miss P. Bell, Newcastle upon Tyne.
Mr P. Gartside, Warden, The Teachers' Centre, Workington.
Mr K. McWilliams, Senior Organiser for R.E., Chester.
Mr G. Hughes, County Adviser, Stafford.
Mr D. E. Bennett, General Adviser, Nottingham.
Dr T. Jones, Cardiff.
Mr R. Cocks, R.E. Adviser, Dorset.
Mr B. Oastler, Warden, Wimborne Teachers' Centre.
Mr J. Dumpleton, Warden Crediton & Tiverton Teachers Centre.
Mr T. Phillips, Curriculum Study & Development Centre, Swindon.
Mr A. Greenwood, Gorse Hill Teachers' Centre, Swindon.
Mr J. Bailey, R.E. Adviser, Lincoln.
Mr D. Burch, R.E. Adviser, West Glamorgan.
Mr J. Boylan, Drama Adviser, Huntingdon.
Mrs J. Pelly, Assistant in Research (Moral Education Project).

Appendix D

Relevant papers and publications

McPhail, P., 1974. 'The Schools Council moral education projects', *Ideas* (University of London, Goldsmith's College), No. 28, June.

McPhail, P., 1974. 'Lifeline and moral education', *Special Education: Forward Trends*, March.

McPhail, P., 1975. 'Adult-adolescent relations and moral education in school', *Education News* (Australia), Summer.

McPhail, P., 1975. 'To role play or do your thing?', *The History and Social Science Teacher* (Canada), 11 (1), Fall.

McPhail, P., 1975. 'Moral education', *New Ways*, Fall, Charles F. Kettering Foundation, Ohio, USA.

Ungoed-Thomas, J. R., 1974. 'Process, dissemination and training', *Cambridge Journal of Education*, June.

Ungoed-Thomas, J. R., 1975. 'Conditions for dialogue in moral education between teachers and educational philosophers', in *Progress and Problems in Moral Education*, ed. Taylor, M., 9th edn, NFER.

Ingram, D., 1974. 'International understanding – a social learning model', *London Educational Review*, June.

Ingram, D., 1974. 'Between people, between peoples', *New Era*, October.

Ingram, D., 1975. 'Building bridges between people: the work of the Schools Council Moral Education Project', in *Education for Peace* – Reflection and Action, ed. Haavelsrud, M., IPC Press.

Ingram, D., 1976. 'Children are people too', *Education 3–13*, 4 (1), April.

Ingram, D., 1976. 'Moral education today', *De Moralist*, 100th edn, Belgian Humanist League.

176

Appendix E

How it happens (List I)
(Some happy situations)

8–9 Boys

1 I went to a school fair – there was a model railway and the man let me drive it.
2 I liked going to the swimming baths when there were only a few people there.
3 When a concrete slab fell on my leg on a building site my cousin got a workman to help me.
4 My brother saved me in the pool when I was learning to swim.
5 Gran gave me a game that I'd wanted for a long time as a Christmas present.
6 A new boy came to school when I didn't have a friend, and we became friends.
7 We went on holiday to an hotel with 2 pools and a car park.
8 Getting a bicycle *before* my birthday as all my friends already had one made me very happy.
9 Mum gave me 10p and said 'Good boy' after I'd tidied the garden.
10 I was pleased when my sisters let me play their records and cassettes.
11 A friend of mine came and 'sorted out' a fight I was in.
12 Mum let me wash my hair by myself.

8–9 Girls

13 I won a competition and everyone clapped.
14 I made friends at my new school.
15 When I found my tortoise!

16 My sister found my rubber dolphin when I didn't think I'd see it again.

17 I was given a budgie.

18 I did some shopping for someone and she gave me 20p.

19 I'd saved up and bought Mum and Dad a present and they were very pleased.

20 My friend let me ride her bike which was new.

21 When I got my spelling badge I was very happy.

22 When Mum and Dad kiss me.

23 When we go on holiday.

24 Going with Dad to order my bike for Christmas was great.

25 We went to buy me a new coat.

26 When I was a bridesmaid I felt good.

27 My brother came to help me when two boys were teasing me.

9–10 Boys

28 One day our friend took us for a ride in his Rolls-Royce.

29 When Dad took me to a football match.

30 If our school football team wins I'm happy

31 When I get presents I really want.

32 I was in the park with my girl friend.

33 Going on a surprise holiday. That was not knowing about it until we were just off.

34 When I went to where Dad works and saw all the men working.

35 We got a new car.

36 I played football and scored a goal.

37 Going to the beach and finding it empty.

9–10 Girls

38 I was on holiday in Spain and the hotel made me a birthday cake.

39 I went to a Christmas party at Dad's works and I sat next to a boy who said he liked me.

40 A friend cut her knee on some glass. I helped her and went to see her in hospital and she was glad to see me.

41 I stayed with my pen friend for the night.

42 I was staying with my uncle in London. He said 'Let's go to Brighton' and we did.

43 We got a new dog. I picked him up and he licked me.

44 Mum asked if I'd like to start ballet and bought me some ballet kit and I liked it very much.

45 I went to the seaside for the first time in my life and saw rock being made.

46 When we got a new house, it had a stable and Dad bought me a pony.

47 My Dad had made me an Easter bonnet and I won the Easter bonnet competition.

48 When I saw Dad for the first time in 6 years I was so excited I couldn't sleep that night.

49 My sister took me skating and I got some boots after 6 weeks.

50 I always enjoy it when we have Drama at school.

10–11 Boys

51 When I was playing bouncing on my bed, my neck hurt and I had an X-ray. I had a displaced bone and had to be away from school.

52 I had help from friends to make a large bonfire for Guy Fawkes.

53 At Judo Class the big boys kept jeering at me, until I made friends with the biggest one of them all.

54 I found £5 and took it to the Police Station. It was an old lady's pension and she was very grateful.

55 My father plays with me and it keeps us fit.

56 I wanted to go to the fair and Dad said no, so I cut the grass and he gave me a £1 and took me on nearly everything.

57 I got into the highest group of spelling tests and passed 'everything'.

58 When I went to stay with my aunt, Mum gave me 50p and Dad gave me £1.

59 The teacher said that I could go on a school trip.

60 I caught more fish than my brother.

61 Dad took me on a walk and we called at the 'Travellers' Rest'. I had a shandy.

62 I was happy when my eczema went away and everyone seemed to like me.

63 I went to a car rally with a school master.

64 The NZ rugby team was coming to play but it was a school day, and then our school master said we could go and see it.

65 When I beat the steel worker's Chess Champion.

66 My greyhound broke the track record.

10–11 Girls

67 I went to a dancing competition and won a bronze medal.

68 The teacher told me my work was good and he put it on the wall. I am no longer ashamed of my work.

69 I sat next to a girl I didn't like and my work was bad. I got tummy pains and was sick – I plucked up courage and asked to be moved. Teacher said 'no'. Other girls asked for me and he said yes – I was so happy.

70 I asked if I could go riding. Mum said 'some day' and then fixed up a lesson for me two weeks later.

71 Getting into the netball team was ace.

72 When my sister told me jokes and made me laugh.

73 I went to the shore with the class and our student teacher during school.

74 My father won a goldfish for me at the fair.

11–12 Boys

75 My uncle brought me an elephant's tusk from India.

76 My pocket caught fire from a firework and Uncle Joe took it out – I laughed my head off.

77 Mum and Dad bought me a new stereo and it didn't work. Dad mended it.

78 I was picked for the football team.

79 When mummy told me my real Daddy was coming to see me (I am a Fostered boy).

80 We stayed at a big hotel.

81 Mum said she'd buy me a new bike if I stopped sucking my finger and biting my nails.

82 Going to a 'Reproduction' lesson, drawing and learning all about 'it'.

83 When I learnt to read, because I was very slow – Dad had been very encouraging.

180

11–12 Girls

84 My Aunt and Uncle were made Mayor and Mayoress of Richmond and they asked me to present them flowers.

85 My favourite teacher asked me to look after the class for a few minutes.

86 When Dad and Mum took us to Blackpool for a holiday – it was very good as Dad was out of work and he and Mum 'went without' to save up.

87 Dad left home, but after a month came back and we were happy.

88 I went deaf and Doctor took a dolls shoe from my nose. I was better.

89 My cousin is a great artist and when I showed him my drawing he said I would be good.

90 When my mother and father got married.

91 When I worked in Grandma's shop.

92 Mum had my baby sister.

93 The Headmistress asked me to play the Angel Gabriel. On the night all the parents looked at me as I had Big Silver Wings.

94 When my brother came back from 5 months in hospital (burns).

95 I danced with my aunts and drank beer.

12–13 Boys

96 Listening to good music makes me happy.

97 Being on my own is good.

98 When my guinea pig gave birth.

99 I won 2 scout awards.

100 My father cooked a lovely meal.

101 When my mother re-married a man we all love.

102 My friend lent me 10p to get into the Youth Club.

103 When my father left the R.A.F. and we stopped travelling round and my asthma got better.

104 Sitting on the Captain's table at sea on my birthday.

105 Not being able to go to church.

12–13 Girls

106 When a boy taught me how to climb a tree.

107 Mum told me she was going to have a baby.

108 A boy I liked asked me to go to a disco with him.

109 When my friend let me ride her pony.

110 I was moody and lost a friend – but I spent 2 months being patient and interesting and 'won her back'.

111 When I went back to Africa. I hadn't seen my parents for $1\frac{1}{2}$ years.

112 I was nervous about swimming and the Headmaster made a special effort to help me.

113 Being given a real sewing machine.

114 When Gran paid for me to go to Spain with the school trip.

115 Moving house to one next door to my best friend.

116 6 friends and I did a concert in aid of Blind Babies and got £5 and were asked to do it again to O.A.Ps.

117 I made some buns and my mum's friend asked what shop Mum bought them from as they were *so* good.

118 I watched a mother sheep give birth.

How it happens (List I)

(Some unhappy, frightened and angry situations)

8–9 Boys

119 A dog jumped out at me.

120 Dad switched off the lights at Halloween.

121 When Dad took me up in an aeroplane.

122 The time my friend fell off a swing.

123 When we broke down.

124 Once a boy threw a stone at me.

125 A girl wouldn't play 'tig' so I squeezed her arm and she cried.

126 I tripped and hit Gran in the tummy and she cried.

127 When I ripped my trousers.

128 One day I was told I couldn't play football as it was too cold.

129 Sometimes I'm called 'four eyes' as I wear specs, and no-one plays with me.

8–9 Girls

130 If my brother throws my dolls about.

131 When I'm 'smacked special'.
132 Teacher said I was no good at playing the recorder.
133 I was in bed and a ball came in through the window, break-
   ing it.
134 My sister told me we had a ghost and I was frightened in bed.
135 If boys frighten me with fireworks.
136 When my Dad goes off on a trip and won't be back for a while.
137 Mum blamed me for something I didn't do.
138 Ann keeps jumping out at me.
139 I felt frightened feeding the elephants.
140 Once Daddy got stopped for going too fast.
141 I got my sums wrong and I had to do a lot extra.

9–10 Boys

142 I fell in a hole and hurt my arm when I was playing with
   friends.
143 My pigeon couldn't fly. My brother fixed its wing but when I
   came back from school my mum had given it away.
144 I wanted to go to a film with a friend but mum made me go
   and buy school uniform.
145 I was in my canoe when I got 'knocked into' and went into a
   barrier.
146 When I was in a little boat and the sea started to get very
   rough.
147 One day I was knocked down by a car.
148 When I got a fish hook in my lip.
149 Walking to my friend's in the dark. I saw a figure and a bright
   light. I ran and the figure chased me. I shone my torch and
   saw it was my friend.
150 I lost a ball down a deep hole and my friend went after it and
   fell in. We had to get a rope to get him out.
151 The time our old cat died and we buried her.
152 A big boy called me names and took my sweets.
153 When I got lost in an orchard.
154 Last year I nearly fell out of the flat window in Bahrain.
155 My bike was stolen from outside a shop while I was in buying
   a ball.

9–10 *Girls*

156 Our car broke down on the way to see my sister in Birmingham.

157 When my brother torments me. He reads or sings aloud when I'm trying to get to sleep.

158 The doctor found out that my brother had a hole in his heart.

159 I had to go to hospital and my mummy wasn't with me.

160 The other day my brother ate the ice-cream that had been saved for me.

161 The mortgage rates were too high and we couldn't buy a new house.

162 My friend, who was staying with me, messed up my bed after I'd just made it and I got told off.

163 Dad put a luminous green 'monster' (free with my comic) on my window, and when I woke in the night it was shining and I was frightened.

164 I cut my leg and I had to have stitches in. Dad said 'wait' till you have them taken out and you'll see how it hurts'.

165 When I've been away and get 'left behind' in maths.

10–11 *Boys*

166 When I had an accident because two of us were on a 'chopper'.

167 I won my swimming badge and it took a very long time before the badges came.

168 I was playing on a building site. The night watchman set his dog on me and it bit my leg.

169 I had the cane for throwing stones.

170 I lent my ball to a friend and he burst it.

171 When my dog broke his leg.

172 The caretaker picks on me and when I lost my plimsoles he never said he'd got them until my mum had bought me some more.

173 When my mum and dad go out drinking and I'm alone.

174 One day I was in the wood when the gamekeeper told me to get my dog away and fired his gun. My dog was so frightened she was sick.

175 Once a 'banger' went off in my anorak hood.

176 My eczema came back and the boys said 'Happy Eczemas'.

184

177 When I nearly fell overboard on the way to Australia, my father made me 'stay in' for the rest of the week.

178 My big sister locked my friend and me in a shed at 12 (noon) and didn't come back until 3 p.m.

10–11 Girls

179 The boys fooled about with fireworks near me.

180 My friend told me she didn't like me any more.

181 I was walking home in the dark and a man followed me.

182 My boy friend didn't turn up every night for a week.

183 I wanted to sit next to my friend but another girl wouldn't move.

184 I wouldn't clean my father's shoes as he was nagging me. He forbade me to go to gym club, piano lessons, dancing and film club.

185 When we were on the shore the tide came in very fast and I thought we were trapped.

186 My dog chased the neighbour's cat and the neighbour hit my dog with a broomstick.

187 When my sister and her two children moved house away from us.

188 At a new school I was told off for touching apparatus.

189 Going round the Chamber of Horrors on my own was terrifying.

190 If I have to cross a wide main road I'm very frightened.

11–12 Boys

191 I had an argument with my father one day and I punched him and kicked and then ran out of the house and had to sneak back through the window.

192 My friend and I were exploring the attic of an old house and we were caught by a man who was cross and sent us home.

193 My brother wanted to put his bed and chair in my room and my father encouraged him. I ran up, put my bed in the middle of the room and tore off the wallpaper as I was so mad.

194 Some of my friends asked me to put money in the kitty towards fireworks which I did. Then they said I couldn't go to the bonfire.

195 When we were playing round a building site we got stuck in a

store room and had to climb out through a hole in the roof.

196 My brother threw my golliwog into the lavatory after I had just had a pee.

197 One day I looked at a present bought for my brother. My mum hit me and sent me to bed.

198 Some big boys fought me. They put me on a hedge and took my bus money.

199 I couldn't understand why our dog had to be put down. He was such a good dog.

200 A lady gave us a cocker spaniel and then asked for it back a few days later.

11–12 Girls

201 I couldn't believe it when my mum and dad told me they were going to separate.

202 One day when we came home we found that the house had been burgled.

203 There is a girl I know who always boasts about her car and her holiday.

204 Grandma lives in a big house and she asked me to fetch something in the dark and I didn't know where the switches were and I don't like the dark.

205 I was leading a horse with a young child on its back and she was thrown. When I got back to the stables I was asked to leave.

206 I was on a boat going to Sweden and I couldn't get the door unlocked and so I had to wait for a long time for help.

207 My puppy ran out on to a busy road and I couldn't get to him because of the traffic.

208 I rang my friend and she said she couldn't come out. Then later I saw her with another girl.

209 Our headmaster saw me kissing a boy and he told mum. Dad walloped me.

210 The day I heard that I had failed my 11 + I was very sad.

211 I had jaundice at Easter time. I had to go on a diet which meant no chocolate eggs.

12–13 Boys

212 I hate to be called by my nickname.

213 I was walking along and a car just missed hitting me.

214 My father was building us a new house and we lived temporarily in a caravan. I was called a gypsy.

215 I worry when a teacher has a quiet voice and I can't hear what he says. He gets into a temper if I keep asking him to speak up.

12–13 Girls

216 I hate it in netball matches when the ref. is biased.

217 All the class took my friends side in a personal argument and I loathed going to school for ages after that.

218 My mum started bringing her 'love' home. His visits became more and more frequent. I can't love mum any more.

219 I was upset going to a new school as I miss my best friend so much.

220 We were stacking straw bales on a friends farm and were going to sunbathe after. My spoilt cousin just lay in the sun while we were working and when we finished she said we had to go home, so no sunbathing.

221 A boy wanted to go out with my friend Susan. She said she wanted to be with me. The boy said he'd throw me in the river if she didn't go with him and he did it. I had to swim with my shoes on. Susan only thinks of herself.

222 My dad's greyhound kept running off the track and dad said he had to be put down. I said please not to do that but dad took no notice.

223 I nearly drowned in the pool trying to be clever. The pool attendant jumped in to save me and then the teacher hit me.

224 We moved house to where none of my friends were and where Grandma was not coming.

How it happens (List II)
(Some happy situations)

9+–12+ Boys and girls

225 I passed my proficiency test on my bicycle.

226 I got a hamster for my birthday and it didn't bite.

227 I was asked to read something in assembly and I was very nervous but I did it and everyone said it was very good.

228 Dad taught me to surf and bought me a board when we were in Cornwall.

229 When it was icy and we could slide on the puddles.

230 Dad made me a super bird table.

231 When my family are happy and I'm doing my favourite things like playing music and dancing I feel a different person.

232 Our school started a 'Tuesday Club' with all kinds of activities and dancing and a 'pup and crisp' shop. I look forward to it all week and work much better now.

233 I like building a den and being able to keep it.

234 My parents let me have the wheels off an old pram to build a go-kart.

235 My Mum takes an interest in my hobbies.

236 I saved up a lot of money by doing jobs to go on a school trip. I was £10 short but Dad lent it to me until I could pay it back.

237 I won a gold fish at the fair.

238 I was chosen for a basketball team to go to the Crystal Palace.

239 My friends and I had great fun making a tree house.

240 I had had bad eyes since measles (9 years ago). Then I had an operation and after that the Doctor said 'no more glasses'.

241 I was given a patch of garden of my own.

242 I was fishing and fell asleep. When I woke there was a 10 lb fish on my line.

243 I won a bronze medal for swimming.

244 My friend and I went for a walk in a wood and it got dusk thought I was lost but unknown to me my friend had been unrolling a ball of wool to mark our way and we were OK.

245 I gave Mum a box of chocs for her birthday. She knew that I liked them and shared them with me.

246 I got an autograph of a famous pop star when I saw him in a shop.

247 My uncle gave me 50p to help me buy Christmas presents.

248 When I plucked up courage to dive in the pool I was very happy.

249 My parents started talking to each other after a row lasting a week.

250 We moved to a new house and it was very near my best friend.

How it happens (List II)

(Some unhappy, frightened and angry situations)

9+–12+ Boys and girls

251 I took my dog for a walk and another dog kept following me.

252 I couldn't do my sums and the teacher made me cry. My friends laughed at me.

253 I bought a chocolate flake with my last money and dropped it in a dirty puddle.

254 My cousin pulled me under the water when I was learning to swim.

255 The school bus had to go up a very steep hill (in Persia) and the driver drove very fast. There was a sheer drop on the side I was on.

256 Some friends and I made a camp and some boys came and barricaded us in and said they would set fire to it. We got out.

257 A boy pushed me into the canal and ran away.

258 My friend and I were walking down a country road and a car backed out of a drive right at us. He was going very slowly so we didn't get very hurt.

259 My sister was run over by a car. She had to have her spleen removed and her leg was broken and is now 2" shorter. She can't play with us now.

260 My friend and I collect soldiers and paint them. We kept them all at his house and he has lost half of my soldiers and all my paints.

261 My sister told Mummy that I had hit her which was a lie, but Mummy believed her.

262 I did a very good drawing of a flower and the teacher took it for an exhibition. I wanted it back but she said I couldn't have it as it was for the school collection.

263 Dad frightened me when he came into the room with one of my Mum's wigs on and lipstick on his cheeks.

264 We were climbing up a mountain and I stepped on a rock which got dislodged and hit my sister on the head and knocked her into the stream. Dad got her out and she had to go to hospital.

265 I'm scared of things not being done in the 'right way' in case someone says it is all hopeless.

266 When my sister makes a noise on purpose when I'm watching TV.

267 I was in hospital and wanted Mummy. The horrible nurses told me to stop and not be silly.

268 My dog chased a rat and I ran after him. The rat jumped up and bit me.

269 When my parents separated.

270 Having a den knocked down or messed about upsets me.

271 We ran out of petrol 30 miles from home in the dark.

272 When my best friend and I 'broke friends'.

273 I lost my rod and spinner in the stream.

274 I was in the library and when I came out I found my tyres had been let down. I had no pump and I had to walk home pushing my bike.

275 I had injections at school.

276 Dad was going to let me drive the car up the lane but my brother took the car out.

277 I was followed home by a man and when I ran so did he.

278 I enjoy playing the clarinet and art and singing and the boys laugh at me and call me names.

279 I was left alone with my brother and the gas fire was on. We got hot but we didn't know how to turn it off.

280 I found some matches in a field and lit one. The grass caught alight and I couldn't put it out. My friends father came along just in time.

281 My best friend went missing one night and the next day we heard she had been murdered.

282 Some friends and I were playing noisily on some ice puddles near some flats. An old man came down and started choking my friend. She got away.

283 A friend and I made a bridge over a river on to an island and found a tramp was living there.

284 There was a sale on at a shop and I got knocked over by the crowds rushing in.

285 My friend tipped me out of a dingy and I got my clothes all wet and cold.

286 I was promised a rabbit for Christmas and I got a football instead. I cried.

287 I was not allowed to sit next to my best friend at school.

288 When a girl cut my new cardigan.

289 Having to wear a dress that I hate at a party.

290 On my uncle's farm I drove his tractor without his permission. The throttle stuck and we skidded in a field and ran into a hedge.

291 Dad collapsed at work and had to go into hospital for an emergency operation for a brain tumour.

292 We were not allowed to practice a dance routine for a school 'club night' at school, or use the school record player.

How it happens (List II)

(Some uncertain situations)

9+–12+ Boys and girls

293 I went to a museum and 'the man' asked me a question. I couldn't answer it.

294 My Dad left me standing on the pavement while he went up the hill to park the car.

295 My friend cut his head and I helped him home, but his Mum and Dad weren't there.

296 My friend dropped his guinea pig by accident. It lay very still and we didn't know if it was alive.

297 My friend and I were coming home from school and we saw a man with no clothes on.

298 When I haven't been listening in class.

299 I was at my friends house for tea I didn't know what time to go home. Mum hadn't said and I didn't know how to ask my friend's parents.

300 When I have a present I never know how to say 'thank you' nicely, though I'm very grateful inside.

301 I forgot my lines in a school play.

302 My pony ran away with me on his back.

303 We Brownies went to a competition but didn't know where to go or what to do. In the end somebody said to a grown up, 'will you look after us?'

(Some unhappy situations)

304 I was very unhappy when Auntie died and I cried when

Grandma talked about it.

305 I was thinking about my homework because I could not do it. At school exams teacher kept me in. I was whacked by teacher.

306 Running home from school a bully stopped me and made me smoke a cigarette. He said he would burn my hair if I didn't.

307 I was frightened when I saw a monster on TV. As a result I hid behind the chair.

308 When I went to babysit for my aunt I was very frightened.

309 My mummy makes me unhappy when she says I can't help her in the kitchen because I will get in her way.

310 I was very unhappy when my dad's dad died. Everybody in the house was crying except my dog, hamster and my budgie.

(A happy situation)

311 Helen gave me an invitation to a party on Saturday and mummy said I could go.

Appendix F

Making it happen

1 Find a photoface from *Photoplay* and decide how you think the person is feeling. Try and draw the things in the face that give you clues about how they feel. For instance, if you think it is the eyes, draw what it is about them. Are they bigger or smaller when the person is feeling happy or frightened?

   Find more photofaces showing different feelings. See if you can draw more faces showing the same feelings. You could do several drawings of different moods.

   Can you think of something which happened to go with the faces you've drawn?

2 Find a situation in *Choosing* or *How it happens* in which members of a family are doing something together. Paint your own family doing something like it. Put yourself in the picture to show what's happening, and what you did. What could you have done to change the situation? Paint the ending you like best.

3 Find a *relating* label from the *Photoplay* pack which tells you how people feel about each other. The people may feel nasty towards or interested in each other. Can you think of a situation which goes with the label you have chosen? Move some of the *Setting the scene* figures around to show how they are getting on with each other. When you have done this, move them around again and try to fit them into another situation.

4 Find some *Photoplay* photocards or *Setting the scene* figures of people who you think are in the same mood. Put them into groups. They may be frightened, uncertain, angry, happy or sad.

   Find a situation to fit one group. Move the people about to

show how they would be feeling, and where they would be. Act out a play of why they are feeling like that and what they do.

See how many different ways of changing the situation you can work out by moving the people. Who changes what happens?

5 Look through the *Setting the scene* figures or *Photoplay* photographs and find someone like you. Pick out more figures or photos and show a situation/story you remember in which you were happy. Draw a cartoon story to show what happened. Then fit *Photoplay* labels to each drawing to show what's happening. How many different labels can you use?

6 Find a *Choosing* or *How it happens* situation where someone is unhappy. Choose *Setting the scene* figures plus photocards to fit the situation. Lay them out in front of you. What would you do to make the person happy? Try adding more photos and figures to help make this a happy situation. Make a picture to show the ending that you like best.

7 Find a situation card and fit *Setting the scene* or *Photoplay* figures to it. Work out what would happen in the end. Try and act this out.

When you have done this once change two of the figures around so that Mum now takes Dad's place or the brother takes the part of his sister. Now act out how this will change what happens. Have you really got another story? In which of the two stories are the characters thinking about each other most?

8 From *Photoplay* find three or four *name* labels. From *Setting the scene* and *Photoplay* find people to fit the jobs, for example if you can find a teacher, doctor or a policeman put the labels next to them.

Can you think of situations in which these people might work together? Do you know of a short story in which they might take part? You can find a situation card to help you if you want to. Put down who else might be involved. Say why they feel and act as they do.

9 Think of an animal you know or find a situation with a pet in it. How do the animal and the people feel? Do they treat each other well? Draw several pictures to show people and animals together. Draw each one to show how the animal and the

194

person are feeling. How many can you draw? Can you mime the story of your best picture?

10 Find *Photoplay* photocards or figures from *Setting the scene* like some people you know well to fit a *Choosing* or *How it happens* situation. They can be in your family. Think of several times when you were all unhappy, or angry with each other or other people. Move the figures and photos to try to make this better. Can people be unkind or pleasant? Can people change? Make a picture of a pleasant ending for everyone.

11 Look for a *Choosing* or a *How it happens* situation which describes something which has happened to you. Choose any activity card or photograph or figures to help you work out what you would do. How would you make the situation better?

12 Can you remember a time when you were very happy? Draw your face in a happy mood. Try to add colour to help show what the mood is. You and your friends can cut out your faces when you have finished and stick them together on one sheet of paper for the wall. While you are working on your face think about other happenings that make you happy. Write a few words to describe your drawings.

13 Divide your paper into squares or oblongs. Try to draw a comic strip or cartoon story about yourself showing anger towards other people. Remember to draw how you look and act when you are angry. Can other people tell from your comic strip what the story is? How many different endings can you draw? Show how you could alter the story. Can you show how other people in your cartoon feel? For example, you could give them word or thought bubbles to show how they are feeling and thinking.

14 Think of a situation in which someone is feeling sad. Draw the person's face and body to show how sad he or she feels. Draw the other people in the story to show their feelings too. Then make a picture of what might happen in the end. Put in all the people and other things that are important. Give your drawing a title and see how many more endings you can draw.

15 Describe a situation that led to someone's property being smashed. Describe how our surroundings can be spoilt by people smoking inside a building, eating while walking along the road or having a picnic by the side of the road. Paint or

make a poster to show what happens and the people who are affected.

16 Take a situation from *Choosing* or *How it happens*. Paint or draw what you think would happen next. Show clearly anyone who is thinking about others. See how many different endings you can draw.

17 Make an imaginary frightening creature from odds and ends. Describe a situation from your own experience in which the thing you have made could play a part. Make and tape-record the noises in your situation.

18 Use some thin card to cut out a mask for an animal or person. Paint a different expression on each side. You can use this cut-out to act stories on the following themes: hunting, dancing, playing and dying. Afterwards make a 'mobile' by hanging them where they can turn round in the wind. You could stick them in groups on the wall.

19 Collect pictures from magazines and newspapers. You can use them for one or more of the following activities:
    a Creating a creature half-human, half-animal
    b Making groups of pets
    c Illustrating a situation card

20 Use chalk, biro, charcoal or pencil to draw a picture of one of these:
a A place I know well
b My favourite place
c Where I go sometimes
Add some colour if you want to. Put yourself in the picture to show what you are doing and how you feel. Describe what happens next.

21 Paint how you feel inside after thinking about any situation you choose.

22 How does your family act when they go out in the car? Draw what goes on inside your family's car and write about what is happening. Who else may get involved as well as your family?

23 Draw or paint your favourite room with you in it. Tape-record what you do there. Can others guess which room it is or whose it is? If so, how do they guess?

24 Make a picture to show how people are feeling when
a in the doctor's waiting room

b at the fair
c in church
d at the dentist
e at a disco
f in the headteacher's room
   Write under your picture how different people feel and why.
   What can happen to make things better?

25 Draw a comic strip or cartoon to show some of the things that
   can happen in your street, home or neighbourhood. You could
   use speech or think-bubbles to help you. What sort of things
   can you do? What happens in the end? What else could have
   happened? What could be altered to make things better?

26 Invent and draw a special vehicle to help people in some way,
   perhaps old, young or handicapped people. Imagine how it
   could change someone's life. How would they feel at first?
   Would their feelings change? How can other people help?

27 Think about the places that we travel through, like stations,
   airports, docks, towns and villages. How do you think the
   people there feel? Why do they feel as they do? Are some
   happy and others unhappy? Why is this so? Draw some
   changes in these places which would make people feel better.

28 Make a mask for yourself showing one mood. Try and
   emphasize the mood by making parts of the mask very large.
   You can make your mask from a paper carrier bag, cereal
   packets, a box or from papier mâché on a wire frame. Can you
   use your mask in a play?

29 Try and make an identikit for faces. See if you can make an
   angry, happy, unhappy and frightened mouth. Cut them out
   and colour them. Now make eyes, nose, eyebrows, mous-
   taches and even beards and hair. Cut out face shapes and stick
   the parts on them. Does the whole shape of the face change for
   different moods? Are sad faces longer and thinner than happy
   faces? See how many different sorts of faces you can make.
   Can your friends guess the mood?

30 Make a card figure with separate arms, legs, head and body.
   Use a paper fastener for the joints. Try to move the body parts
   to show different moods. Make faces to fit the different body
   moods. If you want to, you could make background scenes for
   your figures. These could be kitchen, bedroom, classroom,
   playground, street or seaside or any you can think of. You can

then act out events and situations by moving the arms and legs of your figures. How many situations can you think of? Are people kind to each other? What else can people do? How do different people feel in the story at different times? Do they change their moods?

31 You could make a puppet from a paper bag, old glove or sock. Stick on or paint the face and clothes. Can you make several puppets and act out a play around a family story? Some puppet heads can be made from plasticine, clay or papier mâché.

32 Try and make a TV set or stage or puppet theatre from an old cardboard box. Use it to play with any of the figures you have made. Try these as story titles, 'When we're frightened', 'What happens when we want to play', 'People we meet'.

33 Try making the following in clay or plasticine. 'Mother and child', 'Father and son'. Try to show how they are feeling towards each other. Now try a group of people all doing one thing. Perhaps playing or working together.

34 Make a shape or shapes to show a mood. Try fright or sadness to start with, then make up others of your own. When do you feel like your shape? What makes you feel like that?

35 Here are two things to make:
1 Draw a pin figure or animal on one of the outside corners of a notebook. Make each drawing slightly different from the one you drew on the page before. Flip the pages and watch how moods change. You could make one for faces too!
2 Fill a small cardboard box with objects that feel different, e.g. soft wool, crinkly paper, hard nuts and bolts. Make a hole in the top big enough for a hand. Can your friends describe what's in the box? Can they say how it feels? Can they draw what they feel inside without looking? Does it make a difference when you cannot see what you feel?

36 You can make creatures in many different ways. Choose one way to start with. They can be wild, zoo creatures or even pets and farm animals. For example, model from clay. Think about the way the animal is standing, the gestures it is making and its attitude. What do these things tell you about how it feels? Add a texture or markings for its coat or skin.

37 Try with your friends to make a frieze for the wall. You can paint the background first then stick on cut-out people and

animals. Some can be made from small boxes and junk. Here are some ideas. Can you think of more of your own?

a Our town, our street or where we live – paper or card buildings.

b Zoo, circus, safari park – material scraps – small box cages.

c Markets, fairs and carnivals – drawn and painted paper cut-outs, materials and objects stuck on.

When you have finished, imagine what the people and animals would be doing. Use some of the *How it happens* cards to help you. Write stories about the places and the people. Did people enjoy themselves? What did and didn't they like about the place? Write about the time you were in a similar place.

38 If you want to act out a situation you can make some simple scenery:

a Stick boxes of different sizes onto a flat background or room divider and paint them to show furniture, cupboards and drawers.

b Make things to stand up, use big boxes or things that hang down. Use paper torn or shredded into strips, nets, wire and string.

39 Be a famous person – someone we all know, a TV star or a comic character. Can your friends guess who you are? How did they do it? What was it about you that told them? Can you suggest better ways of showing who you are? Try being other people.

40 Lead your friend on a short journey over and under things. They must trust you and have their eyes closed. When you stop, can they guess where they've been? Now do it again with your friend's eyes open. Take turns.

41 Feel your partner's face with your eyes closed. Describe what you feel. Form a small circle, one of you in the middle with eyes closed. Someone leads you round to feel a face. Guess who it is. How do you know? Try it again but ask this person to change mood. You can also identify people with your eyes shut from the sounds they make.

42 In pairs, take the parts of doctor and patient, nurse and wounded person, policeman and young person, teacher and pupil, judge and criminal and others you can think of. Act out a story with one of you in charge. Do you treat each other well? When you have finished one story, be someone else, and

act it again. Does this make you feel and act differently? Why is this?

43 Make as many gestures as you can with your body. Start with head-shaking, waving, fist-shaking and hand-shaking. What do they mean to other people? Make up stories using them, but don't use words. Can others guess what is meant, what is happening, what will happen in the end?

44 Tape-record an interview with someone in authority about changing something. It can be about houses, travelling, club or school rules. You and your friend take turns. Can you say what happens next? Who is better or worse off because of the changes? Why are they? Show how you would feel if it were you!

45 By acting, can you make other people change their minds or their moods? Start by making your group laugh. Think of situations in which this might happen.

46 Mime some ways that people and animals communicate with others. Try rubbing, patting, scratching to start with. Your friend can guess what the messages are. How many messages can you send? Noises can help you.

47 Form a group. Join together to make an animal. See if your animal is friendly, angry, frightening, sad or uncertain. Make a story round your animal and act it out.

48 Do you know any songs, records or poems about birds, animals or fish? You can make up some of your own. Make movements to fit the words or music. Try to think of as many ways as you can of changing the ending. Can you write your own song about a creature which does not know what to do?

49 Dramatize, in any way you wish, some situations in which animals and people are: angry, wanting something, not liking each other or loving and being pleasant. Can you act out some more?

50 Act out one of the following: arriving at school, at a new house, at hospital, at camp, at a holiday home. Try and show what you would see, how you would feel and what you would do there on the first day. Then try to show how you would behave on your last day there. Would your actions be very different on the two different days?

51 Act being in a frightening place. How can you show fear? Does the person you are with help you or not?

do you find out about your friend, the place and yourself?

52 Act out how a family can start out happy and excited but end up unhappy. Show how this can happen. Act the situation out again with different endings. What could be done to make everyone happy again?

53 Write about yourself saying what you look like, what your personality is like and the sorts of things you do when you are with the other people. Draw yourself doing something you enjoy.

54 Talk and write a poem about what other people do that makes you happy or angry or frightened. Why is this? What sort of things can you do about it? How could other people help?

55 Write two different stories about the same people. In one story people care about others. In the other story they do not care. Talk about the two stories with someone else. Which story do you both like best? Why is this?

56 Try a tape-recorded interview with:
 a someone who is doing what he or she likes
 b a friend who is telling you how other people see you
 c two friends finding out why they are friends.
 Also ask someone to describe his or her best friend. Can other people guess who it is afterwards?

57 Do our clothes show something about us? Which things make you feel good? What do our clothes tell other people about you? Draw and write about your rings, clothes, belts, hats, scarves, haircuts, shoes, and ties. Show what they mean to you and then to someone else who sees you wearing them.

58 Think of as many phrases or sayings as you can which you use and that tell other people something about you. They can be commands, requests, answers to questions about how you feel. Try tape-recording some. Change how you say certain things. For example, how many different ways can you say 'come here'? Try it slowly, fast, soft and loud. Can you say when and where they might be used? Do animals use sounds in the same way? Can a lion roar in different ways? If it can, why?

59 Write a poem about a lonely or solitary place. Do you need to get away from people sometimes? If so, why is this?

60 Find illustrations and photographs of places in the news or well-known places. They could be beauty spots, historic

201

buildings, seaside or towns. What do you like/dislike about them? Think of open spaces, new things to do, tourists, crowds, litter, pollution and traffic. How do they affect people in these places. Write a short play showing different points of view about these places. You could perhaps use a policeman and a driver or hitch-hiker and a local councillor. Do people care enough about others? Can you tape-record your play?

61 Write a poem about secret places, tree houses, dens, shelters and rubbish dumps. Make a picture to show what you like best about your secret place. Do we all need to be secret sometimes?

62 Act out moods without speaking or changing expression using only hand gestures.

The seven symbols in the *Making it happen* cards are used to indicate the following activities:

1 Writing poems and prose
2 Drawing, cartooning
3 Painting and adding colour
4 Talking, labelling, discussing
5 Cutting, making things, modelling, gluing
6 Recording tapes and listening
7 Acting, miming, moving

This list is an indication of the activities which are recommended first, however any of the seven activity areas can be used with each card for follow-up work. For example, children and teachers will obviously want to talk (symbol 4) about all the cards.

The use of symbols on the cards serves as a guide to the teacher on lesson preparation. For example, some cards call for paint, paper or drama space so the symbols will draw the teacher's attention to the facilities needed.

Appendix G

Photoplay Units 1 and 2

Classroom techniques

Unit 1 – The stories and posters

Each suggestion can be treated as a separate lesson or as a stimulus to further work with *Photoplay* 1 and 2 or as a lead into follow-up work with other *Startline* material.

1 Teacher reminds class of the stories and photoposters that fit them. Each photoposter shows someone in a family, some from different cultures, in different moods. Children match labels describing the mood to one photoposter and give alternatives. Discuss how they recognise the mood. Children now match *face* labels describing facial expression. Class draws the face and writes matching labels. Can repeat with another photoposter.

2 Any photoposter. Class discusses, mimes and matches, *face* and *feeling* labels. Introduction of *name* labels to build up idea of personality, e.g. auntie/neighbour who may be shop assistant (Poster K). Children add details of age, sex, race and job and whatever else class discussion reveals as appropriate. Add why the person feels as they do. What's just happened? What might happen? Can repeat using any other single photoposter.

3 Teacher and class select any two photoposters. Discuss, make and match labels. Introduce *pair* labels to suggest who is interacting with whom, e.g. girl to boy. Children put people into a situation of interaction and imagine the result. Write about, draw and discuss which actions are the most considerate. Can repeat using more photoposters to increase complexity of situations and decision-making.

203

4 Teacher and class select several photoposters of different people all in the same mood or in similar relationships. Can children guess what the relationship is and the visual similarities and differences in the photoposters? Introduce *sound* labels, e.g. sighing and grunting, to match photoposters. Work focuses on where the people in the photoposters are, what's happening and what the children would do. Use *Making it happen* cards to facilitate this work.

5 Select several photoposters with one odd one out, e.g. poster A is happy but posters H and E are sad. Can children spot the odd one out and say how they recognise it? Class imagines, illustrates or acts out what has put these people, who are in the same set, in different moods. How do their moods and reactions affect others in the situation? Are people generally being considerate?

6 Starting with any number of photoposters, give and make labels. Put them into a situation and see if changing their roles changes their viewpoints and behaviour. Try role play and role reversal in pairs. Can the children think of more situations, perhaps from the stories or their own past life experience? Labels naming relationships can be made and matched to more photoposters if required.

7a Class discussion centred on any photoposter about family size and make-up. Describe and draw an ideal family and discuss the problems of small and large families. Do children know someone from a family of a different culture? Does it matter if a dad or a mum, brother or sister are from a different culture?

b Write and draw about the children's role in their family. Are they like any of the posters? Which jobs do they do? Are some jobs for boys or girls only? Who do they get on well with? Are family roles changing? Does Dad help with the housework and Mum go out to work? Any *Making it happen* cards can provide the vehicle for creative expression here.

8a Find two or three photoface posters to make up a family. Using *name* labels can children identify who is who? It can include aunties, uncles, pets, grandparents and close friends. Children can draw and write about the sort of people the photoposters show and how they know. Introduce *thinking* and *saying* labels and imagine a family situation. Then record or dramatize what happens.

204

b Class draws their own family doing something together or helping someone else. How well do people get on with each other? How can they make things better?

9 By looking at the photobody posters can children compile case studies of each person? They can use labels to describe their appearance, build up mood and personality and specify the nature of their interaction with others.

10 Find two or three photoposters showing the same people. Make and match *relating* labels for them and discuss how and when people change how they feel. Discuss how people's changing mood and relationships change situations they are in. Think of situations where this has happened. Use *How it happens* and *Making it happen* for creative arts follow-up.

Unit 2 – The photocards

Photoface cards

1 Teacher explains the photoface pack structure i.e. each photocard shows the face of someone from a large family. Each person is shown in five moods. They are happy, unhappy, angry, frightened and unsure. *Name, feeling* and *face* labels describing aspects of facial expression can be matched to the photoface cards and posters.

2 Teacher writes list of moods on board and children match them to photoposters held or pinned on board. Children build up own list.

3 Teacher writes list of roles on board and children relate particular photofaces to particular roles. Children extend list.

4 Teacher writes verbal description of facial expression on board, children relate them to particular photofaces. Children extend list.

5 Teacher can pin up several photofaces, children 'spot' odd one out, discuss how they know. Class discuss or illustrates what has happened to a particular person to put them in that mood. Can evolve own situations around particular photo-faces. How do their actions and reactions in situations affect others? Are people in the situation being considerate to others' needs, feelings and interests?

6 Teacher selects several photofaces, from different individuals, all in the same mood. Can children guess what the mood is?

Can they use the descriptive labels to help them to do this? Can they spot the visual similarities between the photofaces? Teacher writes a few facial expression descriptions on board, children draw the faces. Then children choose labels from the list on board and describe the appropriate face.

7 Teacher asks children if changing roles can change how a person feels in a situation. Can they think of examples? If necessary, teacher can refer them to instances in the stories already used.

8 Discussion on family size and make-up. Their ideal family. Difficulties of small and large families. Class family graph. Are they part of a multi-cultural family? Do they know anyone who is? Does it/should it make any difference if Mum or Dad, brother or sisters are from different cultures? Why does it? Which role do they play in their family? Which jobs do they do or help with? Do they think it helps others in the family? Who do they get on best with? Do they think girls should do certain particular jobs and boys others. Are family roles changing? Does Dad help with the housework? Does Mum earn some money as well?

9 Teacher pins up two or three photofaces and make up a family from them. Can children identify who is who? The family can include grandparents, aunties, uncles and friends. Children discuss what they think family members are like from their photofaces.

10 Children draw their own family doing something together or in a situation of helping. Discussion precedes drawing.

11 Children can mime family situations and produce alternative endings.

Starting from class lesson, children can work as individuals or in small groups using the photoface workcards.

Photobody cards
The photobody pack can be introduced after the work with the facial expressions to extend children's understanding of the part body gesture plays in inter-personal communication. Work with the photobody cards may follow the general outline of that described below for use with photofaces.

Relationship cards

Once children have worked with both facial expression and body gesture photocards they are ready to consider the relationships individuals will experience. The relationship photocards show people, animals and objects in different relationships.

12 Teacher explains the structure of the relationships pack i.e. a series of photographs showing the range of people, animals, and objects in different relationships to each other. Children have to spot the nature of the relationship, using the *relating* labels. To help them do this, other labels are used. These include: *pair* labels, that is labelling who is doing what to whom; *sound* labels describing non-verbal sounds that people in the photographs may be making; *action* labels, describing what they are actually doing to the others; *thinking* and *saying* labels to indicate what people in the photographs may be thinking to themselves or actually saying to each other.

13 Teacher pins up one relationship photoposter. Children discuss the individuals, animals or objects shown, identify their moods, using *feeling* labels to start with.

14 Teacher introduces idea of *pair* labels, perhaps written on board. Children state who is reacting to whom in photograph. Choose appropriate label or extend list on the board.

15 Teacher can then show several relationship photoposters and children discuss similarities and contrasts in the relationships shown. This would include detailed descriptions of the individuals, animals and objects in the situation.

Teacher introduces labels of non-verbal sounds. Children attempt to relate them to individuals in the posters. Children generate their own labels and add to list. How important are non-verbal sounds as a means of communication to humans, animals and birds? Can children tape some of their own sounds? Do they know a baby under nineteen months whose communications are mostly non-verbal? How is it done? What other gestures are important?

Teacher introduces the labels describing actions. Children can relate them to photographs. Are they adequate? Can more be added? Do these labels help find out the type of relationship that exists?

16 Children can write or make a cartoon drawing showing

relationships between individuals, animals or objects emphasising their roles, sounds and actions.

What is the result of such relationships?

17 *Thinking* labels can be related to the photographs in any of the packs, as can the *sound* labels. Children can discuss what they think people may be thinking and sounds they may be making. The class can draw a cartoon story illustrating this. An interesting area for class discussion arises from people in relationships who are thinking one thing, but doing another. Children can be encouraged to spot where they think this is happening in the photographs. Interesting combinations of thought and action can arise in this way.

18 Teacher may feel that introducing variations and flexibility in label use is valid at this point. The class can discuss roles and how they may affect what is thought and what is done in a particular relationship situation. How does role reversal change the nature of the interaction?

19 The *saying* labels are included as pointers in certain directions and cannot possibly cover everything that people may say to each other in interactional situations. Teachers may like to link *saying* labels to one individual in the photograph, with class cooperation. Children can then write the replies of the others in the situation. Dual dialogues between individuals in photographs which can lead to script writing or taping conversation can be built up in this way.

20 Teacher may write a phrase list on board and children match them to *thinking* labels using particular photographs as reference. Class discussion as to why what people think may be different from what they say and then do. Introduction of *role* labels at this stage can often change phrases, thought and action.

21 The *relating* labels will lead to the consideration of a number of facets of communication that are represented by the other labels. In the process of choosing *relating* labels children will have to consider in some detail not only the individual's facial expression and body gestures, but also the roles they may have in the situation, what they are thinking and saying as well as what they are doing. If children are introduced to each label area gradually they will gain a better understanding of the complexity of personal interaction and become practised in its use.

208

22 Lists of one, two or three label categories can be considered to find the common elements for particular moods. For example a *pair* label 'girl to animal' may relate to sound 'sighing'. This in turn may relate to the action 'cuddling' and thinking 'nobody understands me'. Children in this way are encouraged to build up patterns of meaning in communication. Individual work is encouraged in the workcards which ask children to relate labels from all categories to one relationship photograph.

23 Further work can encourage children to generate their own label categories and extend those already provided to suit other photographs from the press or magazines that may be available. In addition, children may like to take a series of their own photographs or even slides to build up a class or school *Photoplay* pack.

24 The importance of the *Photoplay* work is the application of the interpersonal knowledge children gain. Mime and dramatic work as well as simulations, based on real life situations, help this happen. Those with video equipment are exceptionally lucky as this enables children to see instant playback of themselves interacting with others, and making moral and social decisions.

Appendix H

Photoplay **workcards**

Photoface workcards

1a Look through the *Photoplay* face cards numbered 1–100 and find someone looking happy. Try numbers 1, 6 and 11 to start with and then find more like them.

  b Make a pile of all the happy faces you can find. Write down their numbers. Now find the *faces* labels and fit some to the faces. Is it only the mouth or eyes that make happy faces look happy or is it other things as well? Make up some of your own labels to fit happy faces.

  c Draw a happy face and then make your own face change from happy to sad. Can your friend guess how you feel?

  d Write down the things that make you feel happy and draw yourself in a happy situation.

2a Sort out the *Photoplay* faces into happy, sad and angry piles. Numbers 16, 17 and 18 can start you off. Now find *feeling* labels for them. Can you make up more labels to fit the faces? Write them down.

  b From the *faces* labels find some to fit the happy, sad and angry faces. Now make your own labels. Write down what makes the faces different from each other. Do the mouth and eyes change? If so, write and draw what you notice.

  c With a friend, show each other your own faces when happy, sad and angry. Can you guess which face is which? Tell each other how you can tell.

  d Write and draw about yourself when you were angry or sad. Use some *faces* and *feeling* labels to help you.

3a Find *Photoplay* face numbers 3, 4, 5 and 9. Each face shows a different mood. Can you find and make *feeling* labels for each one? Now sort out any other *Photoplay* faces like these and put them in piles.

b From the *faces* labels find one for each photocard you have in front of you. Make up more if you need them. Now write and draw about the differences you see between the faces in different moods.

c Change your own face from being afraid to disgusted and then from uncertain to interested. Can your friend guess how you feel each time?

d Can you remember a time when you felt afraid, disgusted, uncertain or interested? Draw a strip cartoon of yourself to show what happened.

4a Find a friend to work with. Deal out ten *Photoplay* face cards each, face down. Now turn over the top card and ask your friend what mood it shows. When they have guessed they turn their top card over for you to say what mood it shows. Take it in turns until you have turned over all the cards.

b Shuffle the pack and play again. This time fit *face* and *feeling* labels to the cards when you turn them over.

c Put the cards in 'feeling' sets such as happy, sad and choose a different feeling each. You could choose happy, your friend sad. Now make up a story with a happy and sad person in it. Draw a cartoon strip to show what happens and write with each picture what people are thinking and saying. Do the people in your story care what happens to each other?

5a Find *Photoplay* face numbers 23, 30, 36, 44, 50, 52 and 84 and lay them in front of you. Make up more *face* and *feeling* labels to fit them. Write and draw the differences you notice most of all between them. Think of their age, sex and race, as well as their differences in face moods. Which one looks most like you?

b Give each person a name that fits them and say if they are a sister, brother, mum or dad or whatever. Make some more *name* labels to help you do this. Now put them all in a story that describes who they are, what they look like and how they acted.

c Paint or draw a picture of one moment in your story where

someone was being kind to someone else. Show in detail how they looked.

6a Find five *Photoplay* faces of the same person. Try 21 to 25 or 36 to 40. Lay them out in front of you and find the *sound* labels to fit them. You can make up some of your own. Write down each card number and say how you can tell which of these labels fit it – *sound, face, feeling*.

b Now find another five *Photoplay* faces of someone else. Lay them out underneath the first five and fit labels to them as well. Now give each person a name. If they were talking to each other write down what they would think and say. This would make a script that you could tape-record with a friend if you each took a part. Think of these situations for your story – admiring, blaming, punishing, caring or teasing.

c When you have recorded it, try acting it out. How many changes can you make to what happens? Try taking each other's parts without using the script.

7 Photosnap
This is a game of Snap for two people to play. Halve the *Photoplay* face card pack and hold them face down. Now turn one card over from each pack at the same time. When two photofaces show the same person, shout 'snap'. The first person to shout takes the other player's cards which have been turned over. Now play again after shuffling the pack. You can also snap moods. When two photofaces show the same mood shout 'snap' and pick up the other person's cards. This is harder as it is more difficult to see moods so quickly. You will get better at it, the more you play. Can you think of the things to 'snap'? Think about age, sex, name and race to start you off. Can you invent games like it with the *Photoplay* body cards?

8 Photoset
a This is a game like Happy Families for two, three or four of you to play. Each player has to collect *Photoplay* faces of one person in five different moods. Put the pack face down on the table. Each player takes five cards from the top without showing them to anyone. To start, the first player takes the top card to see if it's the person he wants. If it is he keeps it and throws down one by putting it face up next to the pack. If it is

not the person he wants he can throw it down. You can choose to either pick up a card from the pack or from the pile next to the pack. The first person to collect the five photoface moods of one person wins the game.

b Another way to play is to collect five *Photoplay* faces of the same mood. So you could collect five sad people, for example.

c When you have finished the games lay out your five *Photoplay* faces in front of you and draw or write a story about them. Use *Making it happen* cards and *How it happens* cards to help you.

d Can you play other games with these photocards? Try a game of Dominoes, matching moods, Whist or Beat Your Neighbour. Try to invent similar games with the *Photoplay* body cards.

9 Storychance

This is a card game for two or more people. Find three *Photoplay* faces of the same person each and hold them in your hand. Start by laying a photoface and saying who it is and what mood they are in. For example, you could choose Mum and say she is feeling angry. You must say what made Mum angry. The next player lays a card and chooses a mood because Mum is angry. For example, the brother is looking sad because Mum is angry with him. Play all the cards in turn until the game is over. Then talk about the story you have made and say whether people were pleasant and cared about each other or not. You can use a *Making it happen* and *How it happens* card to help you write, draw, paint or act the story. Anyone can challenge a mood put down if it doesn't fit the story. All of you can talk and vote on it. If you are voted wrong, you pick up your card and try again. You can play *Storychance* another way by taking any three *Photoplay* faces but not choosing which people they show. Play just like before. Find other ways of playing *Storychance* with more cards and more players. Try using the *Photoplay* body cards also.

10 Cheating

a Five or six of you can play this game. Deal out all the photocards face down. Each player picks his cards up and sorts them into moods but does not let anyone see them. One person starts by laying, face down, any number of cards. If the cards are not in the same mood the player pretends they are. The player says what the mood is. The cards laid could be four happy or three sad faces. If another player disagrees and thinks they are not all in the same mood, that player says 'cheat'. Everyone then looks at the cards and decides if they are in the same mood. If they are not the same, the player has cheated. He or she must then pick up all the pack. If they are the same and the player has not cheated then the person who called 'cheat' has to pick up all the cards instead. See who is first to get rid of all their cards.

b Another way to play *Cheating* is to lay down cards all of the same person and say who it is. If they are not the same then that player has cheated and has to pick up all the cards, just like before.

Relationships workcards

1a Find the *Photoplay* relationship cards which are numbered from 113 to 144. Choose one and fit a *relating* label to it to show how people feel about each other. For example, the *relating* label for card 117 is 'loving', as one girl loves the other. Find a card and label of your own.

b Now find or make a *pair* label. This shows who is doing what. For example, the *pair* label for card 117 is 'girl to girl', as one girl is hugging the other. Now choose a card and label of your own and write them down.

c Write down who the people are in your card, where they are and what is happening. You can use *name* labels to help. Draw a cartoon story to show what happens next. Could people be nicer to each other in your story? If so, how?

2a Choose any *Photoplay* relationship card and find labels to show how each person is feeling. One could be certain, the other angry. If one is certain and one angry, what is the relationship between them? Find a label to fit the relationship.

b People in different moods make different sounds. Make and find *sound* labels for the people in your relationship card. Write them down and say what is happening. Fit *name* labels too.

c Change some of the labels. Does this change who they are,

214

how they are feeling towards each other and what could happen next? Make up some stories to show how things could change.

d Use *Making it happen* or *How it happens* cards to show your story where people are kindest to each other.

3a Look very closely at people's faces in one relationship card. Can you see then draw how they feel? Are they, for example, looking at each other or not? Use and make *face* labels to help you.

b Find *body* labels, *relating* and *action* labels to show what people are doing and how they are relating. Think of a time when you were in a situation like this and use *Making it happen* and *How it happens* cards to help you tell what happened. Were people considerate to you?

4a Find a relationship card showing several children together. Write down who they are, what they are doing and where they are. Use the *action*, *relating* and *name* labels to help you.

b If you were one of the children what would you do next? How would the other children react? Write a short script to show what is said.

c Use *Making it happen* and *How it happens* cards to show different stories from the one relationship card you choose. Which is the story that shows the most consideration for other people?

5a Find a happy relationship card and fit as many different labels to it as you can. Make more of your own.

b Fit your card into a cartoon story showing a loving relationship. Use the *thinking* and *saying* labels to write underneath what is happening. The relationship card could start or finish your cartoon story.

c Use *Making it happen* and *How it happens* cards to show your story in other ways. Can you think up other endings also?

6a Choose two or three *saying* labels and find *Photoplay* relationship cards to fit them. Make some more *thinking* and *saying* labels of your own and put them down in a script to show what people say to each other. Does anyone change their mind? Are some people unkind or unfair? When is this?

b What else could these people say or do to change the situation or the ending? How many endings could you have? Can you tape-record the ending that pleases most people? Use any labels to help you.

c When you have finished the tape-recording use *Making it happen* and *How it happens* cards to help you paint or draw pictures to show different parts of the story. Pin your pictures up, in order, on the wall, then show them to other people and play the tape. Ask other people what they would think and do in the story.

7a Take several *Photoplay* relationship cards and lay them out in front of you to make a short story. Use *thinking, saying* and *relating* labels for each photograph. Write the story and draw what happens next.

b Write about a situation you have been in like your story and write about what you did. Say what happened next.

c How can you alter what happens in the story by changing the photographs around? Write down how the situation changes. Put down how different people react and who it is who thinks of other people most. Now use your story with any *Making it happen* or *How it happens* cards.

8a Find a *Photoplay* face card, body card and relationship card of the same person. Lay them out in front of you and decide how the person is feeling in each photo. Write and draw a story that shows this person changing their feelings. Say who affects them and why they change moods.

b Keeping the same cards, describe what kind of person they show. Are they generally angry or bad tempered or kind and loving? How does this person affect other people? What does the relationship card show you about them?

c Use the relationship card with *Making it happen* and *How it happens* in any way you wish.

9a Take a *Photoplay* relationship card with an animal or object in it. Write down what is happening and where they are. Name the people, animals and objects and say who they belong to. Draw and then write what is going to happen next.

b Now try and imagine other endings and see how many you can draw. Choose the one you like best and say why you like it.

c Look at the relationship card and change things round. This should change what happens. Use *Making it happen* and *How it happens* cards to show what these changes are.

10a Lay the *sound* labels in front of you. Put them in sets or groups of similar sounds and then write more labels of your own.

b Match relationship cards to your *sound* set. Write down in a script what the people are thinking and saying.

c Use the script as a story and describe actions and relationships. Say what you would do in a situation like this. Who else could be affected by what you did?

d Use *Making it happen* and *How it happens* cards to help you.

11a Take a *Photoplay* relationship card and say what sort of relationship it shows. Find and make as many labels as you can for one of the people shown. Now do it for the others and draw people like them. Write underneath about these people and their relationships with each other.

b Take a situation card from *How it happens* that fits a relationship photocard. Using *Making it happen* cards see how many answers you can find to the situation. Start by looking at it from different people's points of view. How would you feel? How would you change your feelings and actions?

12a Take any *Photoplay* relationship card and imagine yourself as one of the people. Ask friends to be the other people in the situation. Find out how people in the photographs relate to each other by using the *relating* labels or by making your own.

b Now mime (without speaking) what happens next. Show how people are feeling by using faces and bodies clearly. Look at the *face*, *body* and *action* labels to help you.

c Now try again but this time have names and talk. Use both the *name*, *thinking* and *saying* labels to help. Work out the most pleasant way to act towards others by being kind and caring.

d Use more *How it happens* with *Making it happen* cards for more stories and things to do.

Photobody workcards

1a Lay out the twelve *Photoplay* body cards in front of you, numbers 101 to 112. Some of them are from the posters. Can you spot which ones they are? Write down the numbers and how people are feeling.

b Find *feeling* labels to fit the photobody cards. You will have to make up more labels of your own. For example, photobody 103 shows quietening. Write down the card numbers and how the people on the cards are feeling.

c Some of the same people in the photofaces are in these photobody cards. For example photofaces 1 to 5 show the same girl as in photobody 101. How many more can you find that match? Write their numbers down.

d Give *name* labels to those that fit together. Write and draw about how they feel and what they are doing. Can you use *Making it happen* and *How it happens* cards to act out what happens?

2a Put the twelve *Photoplay* body cards in front of you. Now find the photoface that shows the same mood as the body. For example, photobody 107 shows Mum happy and matches photoface 41. How many more can you match? Write down their numbers.

b Use the *body* labels to see why people look different in some moods. Is it how they stand or what they do with their arms only? Fit *body* labels to the photobody cards.

c Find *feeling*, *name* and *sound* labels for each card. Put the people into a story by writing what they say and think. Draw a cartoon strip of your story.

d Draw yourself when you looked and felt like one of these photobody cards. Also write what happened.

3a Match a happy Photoplay body card to a happy *Photoplay* face card. Choose *face* and *body* labels for them and draw the person.

b Now match a sad photobody to a sad photoface. Find *face*

218

and *body* labels and make up more of your own. Now draw this person.

c Put your happy and sad person into a situation and draw and write what happened. You can use *feeling, name* and *relating* labels to help you. Start with a comforting or caring situation.

d Now use *Making it happen* and *How it happens* cards to show yourself in a situation like that.

4a Find a friend to work with and shuffle the *Photoplay* body cards. Deal out six cards each face down. Start by laying a card face up and asking your friend which mood it shows. Take it in turn with all the cards. You can play more games asking about age, sex, race, character and other things about a person.

b Shuffle the pack and play again. This time fit as many labels as as you can to each card. Try to use *feeling, name, body, face* and *sound* to start with. Write down the numbers and the labels that fit together.

c Choose one photobody card each and change your own body to show that mood. Can your friend guess what it is? Take it in turns showing the mood your cards show. Talk about the differences you find in each position and ways of showing the mood better. Can you mime two people who change their moods because of each other? You can use sounds but not words.

5a Find a *Photoplay* body card that shows the same person as a *Photoplay* face card, for example, photobody 103 and photofaces 21 to 25. Now instead of matching the same moods try doing the opposite. That is, where the face is in one mood but the body shows another! For example, photobody 109 shows Dad's angry body but photoface 51 shows Dad's happy face. Put the two cards together for a mis-match. How many more can you find? Write down each body card number and the photoface number it mis-matches.

Appendix I

'Finding out': Practical creative activities for the classroom

1 Making pictures.
2 Making things.
3 Talking and writing.
4 Drama.

It is intended that this appendix be used as a support and reference for teachers wishing to develop their own range of moral education activities in the classroom. These suggestions can be used to extend *Photoplay*, *Choosing*, *Growing* or *Finding Out* work whenever or however it may be seen as useful.

For specific examples of creative activities outlined in the published materials, see the *Making it happen* cards which form part of the *Growing* material.

Making pictures

Children enjoy making *portraits*, facial or full length, which can be cut out and stuck together as a class gallery or crowd. When children have painted themselves in a mood or series of moods, of their own choice, they can use the paintings in mood guessing games with others. Some may like to make the limbs and heads articulate using pins, to reinforce ideas about the body gestures related to different moods and feelings. Alternatively, the portraits can be grouped according to mood and stuck together. Children can then try to recognise each other in the groups and describe any similarities or contrasts they perceive between people in the same mood, or between people in different moods.

220

We have found that *variation in the thickness of paint* emphasises a mood with texture and movement. Van Gogh's portraits are useful as a starter here to show how thick paint strokes can produce bold emotional statements, particularly when using unnatural mixtures of colours. Paul Klee's many dreamy paintings illustrate the effects of thinned colour on the mood represented.

Children often enjoy emphasising mood by the emotional *use of colour*, e.g. red for anger, white for fear. Colour use can be extended to include unnatural face colouring. This changes the feeling the face projects and emphasises the importance of using the appropriate colours to make elements look 'right' or 'fit', depending on the overall aim of the picture. Unnatural colour can help children over any racial problems that arise, especially if they represent themselves in a variety of different colours or hues.

Children often involve themselves in *discussion* on how faces change to show different moods. Verbal description of what actually happens visually to eyes, mouths and noses helps children to paint the differences they perceive in faces during mood changes. Painting and drawing self-portraits are revealing experiences for children and offer an idea of how individual children see themselves. This work can be closely related to *Photoplay*, which shows varieties of facial expression and body gesture on photocards.

Younger children like to do bright *wax crayon drawings*, washing them over with a darker contrasting paint colour to produce very effective serpents or dragons. They tend to 'emerge' from the paint during the process. Children working in a group may like to produce a long frieze of one animal or people that they all dislike or are frightened of. Serpents, dragons and huge worms are ideal as they can be curled and bent into interesting shapes and also be highly decorated. What is it about the animal they dislike?

There is obviously a wealth of visual material to be produced around farms and zoos – from individual animal paintings to families and herds. Laid out painted farms, zoos, safari parks or plans of a local nature reserve can provide backgrounds for children's wax crayon drawings, once they have been cut out. It is important that children's work is always within the context of animals living and reacting to each other. Similarities and contrasts between animal and human interaction can be explored this way. Is there a herd leader? How does he or she become herd leader? Do we choose our leaders in the same ways?

From their case studies and observations children can see if animals communicate with each other entirely through the way they look and what they do. Does noise or sound help them? Do some animals have highly developed senses, if so, how do they help them find out about others? Perhaps children could draw a hawk's eye view of their neighbourhood or keep a visual record of how animals, birds, fish, reptiles, etc., use their senses. The texture of animal coats can be expressed effectively with different materials representing the characteristic feel of different creatures.

If the imaginative *use* of both *colour and texture* is encouraged, then children can represent different animal patterns and shades, e.g. some drain-cover rubbings make excellent giraffe skin and brick rubbings bear's fur. A group of cat-lovers can prepare one large cat using various pieces of tissue and torn papers.

Ranges of warm and cold colours too may be built up on various textures and used with discretion in indicating animals that are warm and content, or cold and frightened. Children's experiments with unnatural colouring to indicate animals' feelings can develop this work.

Children who make up case studies accompanied by visual work enjoy preparing them about particular pets or animals available to the school. Children can note visually how an animal changes its shape and body position with mood. The different kinds of sound it makes for different reasons can be represented in abstract patterns or in cartoon form with sound bubbles. The importance of regular attention in terms of feeding, cleaning and sleeping can be represented by pie charts, graphs, and more cartoon work showing a day's activities. Pictographs and histograms can be used to record the animal's happy or sad moods, the times at which it sleeps and so on. A child is then able to compare the animal's behaviour patterns with his own. After some time, a class chart of, say, dog or cat body attitudes related to mood can be built up and similarities and contrasts with humans be drawn. Phrases, such as 'he's like a dog with two tails' or 'stealthy as a cat' or 'slow as a snail' may provide starters for individual picture-making in this area. Can the children generate their own phrases?

Illustrations collected from various cultures are worth scrutinising to see which type children find most pleasing and why. Studies of school buildings, both interiors and exteriors, can be made from direct observation. Children can state which features of certain buildings they like and dislike, and perhaps the aesthetic as well as the practical and social reasons for their opinions. Considering the colour ranges they find conducive to particular moods can lead to a discussion of the emotional effects of different colour areas. Should the library, for example, be blue and the gymnasium red? Does it matter? Would stripes or strongly contrasting colours be appropriate in a rest or sick room or a private study area? Should the colour suit the social activity that takes place in the room? What effects do particular interiors have on us, for example the head teacher's study, a cinema, the dentist's or doctor's waiting room, a disco, taxi, top of the bus, train, etc. What is it about such interiors that make people feel the way they do? Is it just colour, the furniture or the expectations they come to them with? How considered are their expectations of places? Can they illustrate a time when they were wrong about how an interior felt – perhaps in a strange place or an unusual building. A lot of visual work can stem from considering buildings and places and aspects of them. Would children like to re-design a school or home colour scheme to suit how they felt in certain areas? Would it also affect others in similar ways?

Through work centred on buildings and places, children realise that the private and public expectation of behaviour governs what is permitted. Do they know if people talk loudly in churches or whisper in discos? What is expected to happen in the haunted house at the fair? Can they illustrate visually their expectations, and then illustrate what actually happened, using thought bubbles? An ideal home design, complete with colours, can bring home to children the restrictions placed on social activities by particular places.

As a further activity to emphasise how places affect behaviour and individual's treatment of one another, children *working on scenes and scenery* provide different environmental

223

contexts for dramatizing situations. Large friezes, using collage, or wax and wash techniques to accompany drawing in pencil or biro can feature 'our town', 'the seaside' and backgrounds to particular personal situations experienced by class members. Places familiar to children evoke a lot of interesting and detailed work. Suggestions for a focus include the neighbourhood, our street, where my parents work, school, where we like to play, individual and secret places for hiding themselves or objects of importance. Do we need a secure place for ourselves, a family house or classroom? Could the secure place be inside us? Can children imagine places from the point of view of different creatures? Do they feel dominant or dominated by the situation? Can they paint people and animals overawed by buildings and places? How long did it take them to get to know their school buildings? Who helped them? What suggestions have they to make it easier for others? Can they put these ideas into practice? (This may well be a chance to develop simple plan-drawing and map-making.) Signposts, notices and lettering of various sorts may well emerge here if time and facilities allow. Could the children provide a school map with coloured areas to show where particular incidents or situations have taken place or are likely to occur? Health, fire and accidents are often interesting starters.

Children can take their own photographs and collect others to emphasise the differences in the areas surrounding the school, from factory to field, clean to dirty, pleasant to unpleasant, etc. Places that facilitate social activities can be illustrated and discussed. Who goes where? Do they enjoy and participate in the local social life? What improvements could they suggest? Are their parents involved in the same social life or do they have one of their own? Can they describe and illustrate different forms of social life from different viewpoints? A community portfolio relating to school can be produced in which social activities and problems can be illustrated and described. Obviously, the fortunate minority with video can consider making a community tape to be exchanged with other outside communities, nationally or internationally. Sections of the portfolio could be about the very young, the aged, local wild life and flowers, housing, work, social problems and benefits, demolition and development and so on. Tape/slide sequences or film-making for small groups focusing on a particular aspect of the portfolio, or on the whole community, can be explored if time, money and equipment permit.

Many children find *photo montage and collage* a fascinating and often humourous method for portraying others as they see them. Even public figures, politicians and stars of various sorts, can be easily adapted to take on different roles or different bodies or be put in different situations.

A variety of materials can be used by children in expressing their faces and bodies visually. Variety enables individual children to find the appropriate means of expression, so that developing ideas about themselves and other people can be explored. Using different working methods allows flexibility in the manner in which people are portrayed and develops abilities in a variety of materials. Older children very often prefer drawing with pencil and biro and adding colour later.

With children, we have often used material scraps for clothes, string and wool for hair, and buttons stuck on as themselves to accentuate a portrayed personality. After all, what is worn and how it is worn indicates a great deal about the wearer. This is often an intriguing insight for children who then want to work on stereotypes or forms of stereotype-breaking in dress and behaviour. Further relationships may be illustrated between where it happened and the behaviour displayed.

Drawings, cut-outs, photographs, illustrations and children's own paintings can be effectively used to stimulate other groups or classes to work in related areas. An interesting activity is to take two pictures and cut them into two separate series of strips, of about the same width. The first strip from one pile is stuck next to the first strip of the second pile, to form a 'tent' on a flat background. Then the rest of the strips are stuck down alternately to form the rest of the concertina. The final result if viewed from one side will present a complete picture, and if viewed from the other side, another picture. When placed in a corridor, children passing watch the picture change. Obviously, 'before' and 'after' photographs or visuals are of interest here, as they present the processes of change in a simple visual and immediate form.

Often children will draw a complete cartoon to illustrate a

225

whole story, the sequences of the interaction, and the end result. If the work stimulates the children enough, a moral education comic may emerge, full of cartoons produced in this way. Variation can be obtained by leaving end frames of the cartoons blank with the words 'what would you do?' underneath, so that children can discuss their own endings and the implications, and then draw them in.

Making things

To many people *masks* appear obviously attractive and easy to make, but children find them exasperating if the end product does not look like them or whoever else was intended. Masks representing moods or feelings avoid this difficulty as they are not expected to be representative of individuals. If children choose a mood for their masks, they are in a position to choose which features to concentrate on and emphasise. Huge grinning mouths, round red cheeks, jolly eyes and 'happy' exaggerated features are all well-known to children from TV, Disneyland and local carnival and fairground art. The masks can require the very minimum in material if made from paper bags, carrier bags, cardboard boxes or cereal packets. Papier mâché on wire frames is technically more difficult and can take a long time to complete. However, these are to be preferred if children are going to use them for mime and drama work, as obviously they are more substantial. Complete body masks can be made from larger cardboard boxes or paper sacks but they tend to restrict movement and hide some body gestures.

The social uses to which children put their masks are all-important, if the making of them is not to be an isolated and unrelated exercise. Much mime work where masks can be used based on different moods is discussed on p. 232.

Using masks of animals and birds often enables children to exaggerate their impressions of animals' facial expressions. Lions with enormous teeth and donkeys with huge ears not to mention cats with huge glowing eyes, are familiar to children. It is how these masks are used that gives them their importance. Work could begin with discussion on *Aesop's Fables*, or stories of animals and birds from other societies or primitive cultures, which can be dramatized. Again, comparisons can be made between different cultural attitudes to animals, those that are sacred in a given society and those considered to be possessed with evil spirits or magical properties. It is no bad thing if children are encouraged to be understandingly critical of the role given to animals in various cultures or fairy stories.

Making *puppets* is popular with many children. They are easily made with a small paper bag or sock with painted or stuck-on felt features. Simple cardboard box theatres of 'TV screens' can be made, and simple situations played out. If short 'mood mimes' are presented, the characters' moods can be identified and advanced ideas about individuals' roles in the situations formulated. Puppets can be given features to identify children's roles, for example pupil, dancer, musician, sportsman, bridesmaid and responsible 'adult'. They can then be used to present a dramatic sequence in ways discussed earlier in this appendix.

We have found that *modelling and carving* is both demanding of teacher time and expertise. However, they can provide children with rewarding ways of working, especially when depicting themselves. Clay, dough and plasticine are all ideal for modelling. Full-length figures can be placed in a particular social context with other figures produced in class. Movement and body gesture must be clearly modelled if the work is to be successful, and perhaps the figures grouped to show happy and/or action groups. Modelling work on family members can be extended to involve aunts, uncles, cousins, grandparents and close friends. Large cardboard boxes can be assembled to produce life-size figures, which will involve children in problems of proportion, space, size, texture and physical relationships.

Most children prefer modelling animals, together with their human counterparts, in clay. It is a malleable medium that enables fairly accurate presentation of attitude and gesture. Flat, clay slab creatures can also be produced with incised or pinched up decoration or texture. All animals, whether two- or three-dimensional can be used by children in playing out stories and situations. Perhaps several desks pushed together can form a base and different children be different animals. Humans may be involved also, so that quite

227

complex interactional situations can arise. Children can build up their own situations using a card from *How it happens*, or a story from *Choosing*, as a starter. When the lesson is finished, space permitting, the characters can be left on display at one stage of the interaction, so that other children are than asked to guess what is happening and to think out suitable endings and other courses of action.

Some groups of children may choose to model one animal, each child producing it in a different mood position. These look effective when coloured and cut out of thin card. If joints are kept mobile with a paper fastener, an animal can be moved into different positions. Children may like to supply a series of backgrounds onto which the animal can be pinned in set positions. Human figures can also be cut out and included, as children enjoy being asked to guess, talk and write about how the animal feels and why it feels that way. They can then put this animal into a total situation involving people as well as pets. This area of work is limited only by the materials available to children and the maintenance of their interest.

Many children we have worked with are concerned about aspects of the good and bad treatment of animals. Cages, aviaries, nests, dens, natural and unnatural habitats for a range of creatures may be made with some accompanying study on the treatment of animals and the forms of animal communication, together with their social habits. Do creatures have similar social needs and patterns to our own? How are they similar or different? Do they 'think' about others?

Clay and plasticine are ideal media for developing work on the idea of groups meeting, playing, etc., where figures can be moulded in conjunction with each other. The members of a thinking group can literally put their 'heads together' to provide a focus for the group composition. A frightened group, on the other hand, can fan out in panic. If each child completes a figure in an agreed mood the figures can then be grouped in a secondary stage of development. This could bring out questions of touching, feeling and grasping between group members and how these are dictated by how the group feels. Modifications may be required in the body gestures of some figures so that they will 'fit' into the group better, in terms both of attitude and feelings and of group composition.

228

Children are often keen to make *portrait heads* by modelling or carving, but if it is done in clay, an elementary knowledge of pottery techniques and use of modelling tools (old lollipop sticks?) is a great advantage. Carved heads are more difficult as any material mistakenly carved away is difficult, if not impossible, to replace or stick back on. Suitable materials that can be cut away easily to reveal form are polystyrene blocks or lumps of balsa, soft woods, plaster and sometimes blocks of salt and soap if they are available. Some soft local sandstone blocks or breeze blocks of various types can be tackled with success by older children, especially if the work is carried out in an 'art' area of the school where advice, guidance and tools may be available.

If children are encouraged to think of themselves as living, moving sculpture, perhaps through mime, they often see and feel the necessity for giving as much attention to back and side views, as to the front. When this understanding is related to how the whole body is used in movements to express feeling, three-dimensional work takes on new meaning and importance. Activities, such as guessing how people feel other than by looking at their faces, help to establish the importance of using the whole body in expression. Use of touching and feeling is important in body communication and in learning to understand how to make things. Some further work on mood communication by passing tactile messages to each other with eyes closed is useful. Also feeling others' faces blindfolded can accentuate the importance of knowledge through touch. Discussion on different textures to be used in the objects children make, together with actual touching experiences and identifying ranges of different surfaces, emphasises the importance of textural possibilities in their work. Considering how they tend to stroke surfaces and animals when they are angry or sad, and whether they grip objects and people more firmly when in particular moods, will enable children to understand how their touch varies depending on their feelings.

Herds, flocks and shoals of creatures familiar to children can be made in clay, papier mâché or junk material, to fit in a habitat which has also been created. Fish mobiles made from thin card, tissue paper, milk tops and transparent toffee papers are very effective if hung by cotton or fishing line closely together near the source of a draught. They can also be used as a background for dramatic work of various sorts or for a study of natural movements in space. Do fish really flap like this? If not, what would happen if they did? Do fish communicate with each other by different movements of head, fins, tail, mouth or body? Can the children find examples?

A two-dimensional frieze can be organised on the basis of 'our street' or a 'busy town'. It can be made by sticking small boxes of various sizes and shapes onto a flat background. The reverse side of a roll of wallpaper would do if the sky and ground is painted on first. Doors, windows and shutters can be cut out to swing open, or be made from other materials and stuck on. Roofs of various sizes and shapes, including half-domes and different pitches, can be made from corrugated scrap card or even cellophane and stuck on, together with dormer-windows, porches, arches, window sills and flower boxes, to add interest and realism. The choice of place will depend on the children's own experiences and knowledge and can be supported by a drawing trip to the local scene, perhaps with cameras. When the buildings are nearing completion, discussion on the sorts of people and activities that go on there could centre around children's own experiences in similar places. Class groups can each produce an interactional situation, perhaps someone caught stealing, or helping a shopkeeper or stall holder, these then being stuck onto the background. Much creative work could then follow about possible solutions to the situation portrayed or different courses of action for particular individuals to take. To consider how concerned these responses are in terms of others' points of view, needs and feelings is fundamental to this work.

More places, rather than buildings, often emerge from children's experiences of incidents on motorways, in woods, by rivers, in streams or at the seaside. These may be produced as two-dimensional structures that can be pinned to the wall. The class can be divided into small groups, each one producing a different place. At the end of the session, the groups could exchange different 'made' environments to continue work with animal and people cut-outs. Having moved their people and animal models, further exchanges of environment can take place and groups then repeat the process.

Drama

These notes supplement the section on drama, role-play and simulation in Chapter 6.

In all drama activities with children we have found it useful to begin with a warm-up session. This can concentrate on different body areas related to surfaces or aspects of places. The children are asked, for example to run up the railway steps, point to the roof, bounce or run along the platform, cross the station foyer, dash for the train very fast or run carrying a heavy case.

Children can try miming a place for others to identify – stretching to show the ceiling height, feeling different walls and their surfaces with hands and bodies, stepping across the floor to show its length and width, and eventually miming activities or incidents that may take place there.

Role-taking is especially enjoyed by children when it involves well-known personalities, friends and TV or comic-strip figures. Working in groups children understand themselves a little better by monitoring and understanding the group's reactions to them. Opportunity should be provided to try out 'new' roles in the safety of this situation. We have discussed the value of using *role-reversal* with children's own situations in Chapter 6.

Role-reversal is also popular when it involves a person in authority and a 'client', e.g. parent and child or magistrate and offender. This gives children further insight into how different people see the same situation. To play the magistrate or boss in a particular situation emphasises certain aspects of the player's personality, which often differ from those aspects portrayed as an offender or employee. How children 'change' to fit a role, and the different points of view about the situation that emerge from role-reversal are good starters for work with children on personal interaction.

When children try to convey personal information to one another in different ways, different facets of communication are emphasised. For example, when they try to communicate

231

with a deaf or blind person: can they take the role of such a person? and how do they convey that they understand what's being communicated? Guessing games based on partner work can extend this into a consideration of aids available to deaf and blind people and situations in which they work well or become defeated. How does it feel to see or hear other people again after being isolated, blind or deaf?

Facial mime provides a stimulating way of introducing work to children. The class can mime facially different moods, led by the teacher or a pupil. Facial expressions may be mimed, with the body hidden behind a screen to emphasise aspects of facial change. The members of the class then guess what those miming represent in terms of mood, role and feelings. An interesting partner activity is for children to build up their own repertoire of different facial expressions, then to ask others to recognise the differences of expression and mood and say in which order they came. Further work or play situations develop if children are then encouraged to say what could have occurred to make them change to the moods expressed.

Through this work children begin to realise also that body gesture is as important as facial expression in communicating needs and feelings. They can be encouraged to show a variety of moods by standing angrily or moving indecisively, etc. An emphasis on the different ways in which a particular mood may be expressed through a combination of face and body gestures can enliven posture and expression. If partners work together, they can suggest and criticise particular movements and thus help each other improve their communication. All work in this area should help children not only to express themselves a little better visually and kinetically, but to lead them to an understanding of what others are communicating through heightening perception and interpretation abilities.

Working with a group can emphasise aspects of contagious behaviour. One child can try to influence the rest of the group to think like him, change attitude or adopt the same mood. There is a place here for the 'laughing-policeman syndrome'. Alternatively, groups can show combined 'happy' or 'unhappy' movements, angry crowds, excited spectators, etc. Non-verbal sounds that accompany such moods could also be expressed. Perhaps a sound orchestra can compose a mood story non-verbally with a central figure bringing in, and fading out, groups where appropriate. We have found references to natural phenomena useful as starters, especially where they involve body movement and sound in sympathy with a mood: for example, tranquil ponds that become rippled, storms at sea, winds in the forest and the life cycles of plants and animals.

Most children love *speech, mime and dance* dramas about living creatures. These can originate from listening to stories of folk myths, perhaps on record, or even on TV programmes. How different tribes or societies treat different animals and birds can be used as the basis for improvised work. Situations around the hunting of birds of paradise, the shooting of elephants for ivory or even catching animals for vivisection can be generated from such areas of interest.

Children are often keenly interested in preventing kinds of animal ill-treatment and are able to recall instances known personally to them. After discussion on the feelings of those involved and possible alternative courses of action, a series of short simulations or five-minute plays can develop. The daily papers are often useful in supplying emotional write-ups in this area. In addition, animal ill-treatment is often seen in Tom and Jerry, Donald Duck, Mickey Mouse and various other cartoons. How far do children take these seriously? Can they remember one in detail and explore the social and moral aspects of animal and human behaviour? Would animals really survive the cartoon treatment they get?

Further work around ghostly animals or birds and other creatures that they dislike highlights children's stereotyped ideas of rats, owls and bats for example. They can act out what these animals or creatures seem like initially, then contrast this with what they actually find out about their particular habits. Could they dramatise a situation in which they make friends with a ghostly creature they thought was ferocious? The *Wizard of Oz* with its sensitive lion may be a good introduction here. Why do they dislike some creatures? Do they know how to handle them?

Children are often intrigued by small places like cupboards, holes, caves, boxes, vehicles and coffins. Miming different aspects of body movement in crouching, kneeling, squeezing, sliding, or a gradual unwinding of the body can enable exploration of intermediate spaces and places, particularly corridors, small rooms, the inside of vans, sheds and barns. Some groups can add sound effects, but not words initially, to give another dimension to their work.

Topics suggested by children can be explored to develop aspects of social awareness, e.g. 'places we didn't like at first, but want to go to again now', etc. How far does the place determine their attitudes or what happened? How much did the people involved change the situation? Situations can be played out several times and the age, moods and sex roles of individuals changed. This gives children a realistic idea of how others see the situation and how sex roles may change what is permitted or not done.

Places, too, can vary from natural and rural to artificial and residential to include pot-holes, woods, hillsides, city streets, traffic congestion and so on, and these linked to children's topics.

Dialogue situations, especially those involving places which become increasingly well known to children as they grow older, make good material, from places like child clinics and school to outside social agencies, joining the local youth club, or arguments with shop managers or even the police. If children can be encouraged to take both role of interviewer and interviewee they can experience the same situation from different people's points of view.

Talking and writing

We have encouraged a *class discussion* to arise once any sort of work is completed. How are children going to use their work, is it to be displayed or is it to form part of a joint book or topic? What does their particular work represent? Why is it different from that of others? Does it represent the most appropriate form of expression for the idea? What sorts of work situation annoy them? Which ways of working make them happy? and so on.

Alternatively *discussion* using animal sounds as a basis, can alert children to different types of animal communication and how they relate to similar types of human communication. Can they observe animal young and human babies and

234

articulate their understandings of their cries, movements and various behaviours? They can observe and listen to how feelings are shown and what the parents do in response. A short list of situations can be compiled in which the baby was frightened, content, intrigued, unhappy, etc. What are their own experiences of baby involvement?

Script writing too can be greatly enjoyed by children, especially if animals are involved. It demands that sounds the animal makes are given meaning. The addition of cartoon illustration often maintains interest and expands the value of the work.

Much written work may be organised around animals that are hunted by man or other animals, and discussion around such episodes leads to an examination of man's hunting tendency. Are blood sports fair? Why do children catch butterflies, caterpillars and fish? What is so attractive about bird nesting? How do the creatures involved feel? Can they tell us how they feel?

Children can be motivated by *creative writing* – i.e. being able to write freely what they wish to write. Such writing arises most naturally from their own personal experiences and those with pets or other animals they have encountered. Can they remember rescuing a creature or saving an animal's life? How did they find the animal and what did they do? In contrast, have they ever been surprised or helped by an animal? Do they talk to their animal and bird 'friends'? What sorts of replies do they get? How do they interpret them? Can they communicate with each other in a 'made-up' language, perhaps similar to an animal language they know?

A wealth of material exists in folk songs recorded about animal behaviour and in which creatures are often given human qualities. How far children identify with these songs is of interest and their interest can promote them to write their own blank verse, poems or folk songs. In addition, some may relate the folk song to their own personal experiences or dreams of mystical creatures.

Word lists related to particular situations can help to make children more aware of what is going on. These lists can include both what is seen, smelled, felt and heard as well as technical or specialist words appropriate to particular situations. In this way the atmosphere and feel of situations is

235

built up. In addition to collections of words, sound pictures written or made on tape by children may encourage them to write blank verse or poetry.

Types of sounds which give particular kinds of information are an interesting focus, e.g. human cries or the ringing of alarm bells, the ticking and chiming of clocks, the sounding of fog and car horns. The children may like to complete sound pictures of airports, docks, fairs and festivals, and discuss whether the sound information is accurate and easy to interpret.

Using sound *tape-recording* can be a natural follow-on to discussion and written work if the equipment is available. A class using many voices together can produce frightening or happy sounds. Small groups or individuals can describe themselves in detail and the class guess who is doing the describing or who is being described.

Interviews may be set up by children for themselves. This can be done almost anywhere in the school where quietness is assured. Children can also interview their teacher, and vice versa, to help them to understand each other's different perspectives on the same situation e.g. 'You remember when Tom was late for school, how did you feel?'

Listening to narrative extracts, including radio and TV. programmes, about how individuals see and feel themselves to be, or about times of fear or happiness, can stimulate discussion and further work using any medium. If the emphasis is on whether children would feel and act similarly in the same situations, then children are encouraged to project their own feelings into the situations and so get to know themselves and cope with themselves better.

Appendix J

Special Problems?

Early in 1975 the Coventry Education Authority held a meeting for teachers, to consider the implications of Gulliford's report 'Teaching materials for disadvantaged children', *Schools Council Curriculum Bulletin* No. 5. At that meeting all the materials recommended in the report were on display and where possible each project was represented by a team member or a local teacher who had been closely involved.

At that time the Moral Education Project was well advanced in its work with children aged eight to thirteen and discussion was inevitably extended to the possible relevance of this new work to the needs of special schools. As a direct consequence of this meeting, of the willingness of the Project to become involved in this investigation and the initiative of the Authority's staff, a working group of heads and assistants was established, drawn from seven schools, day and residential, for educationally sub-normal (moderate), maladjusted or delicate pupils. This group met regularly during 1975 and 1976, and discussed their work with the Project's materials and approaches; in addition a member of the Project team visited many of the schools to observe and participate in the work which was taking place.

This short section is an attempt to summarise the conclusions of this group. Some initial opinions changed, others did not and this report attempts to reflect these changes.

One initial concern of some teachers, reflects, in part, the balance, which has to be struck in all work with disturbed pupils, between raising and dealing with the fundamental social causes of their disturbance and concentrating on providing a new social confidence based on developing new relationships and on achievement in conventional school activities. The concern was that materials and techniques which bring to the surface the social experiences of children may be a cause of increased disturbance and may be 'dynamite' in the hands of inexperienced teachers.

As the work progressed it became clear that the Project's 'package' enabled two-way learning to take place. One teacher of maladjusted boys who were 'deemed to exhibit unacceptable standards of social and moral behaviour, though on the whole their behaviour was acceptable for their own communities', reported that this work allowed him to understand more clearly the values that the children had come to accept as normal, and at the same time children could explore their own reactions to the situations which were presented and explored without the usual consequences of real-life action.

The working group agreed that the best hopes of changing attitudes and behaviour lay in relating to a child's needs and that the quality of relationships between teachers and pupils was most important. Chapter 3 has shown how some adults can be significant in pupils' lives and that these are the ones who are most influential. Fundamentally, the child needs to care about the adult and the adult needs to be seen as caring about the child. In special schools, the staff:pupil ratio is more favourable than in normal schools, so the opportunities for close contact and the development of caring relationships are improved, though this must be set against the disturbed nature of many of the children and the learning difficulties which they experience.

One problem which was raised at an early point was that far too many of the pupils whose behaviour is undesirable have been brought up as members of 'delinquent families'. This brings two difficulties: first, if the school emphasises too strongly a clear disapproval of patterns of behaviour learned at home, behaviour tied in with loving relationships and a basic security, then the school's social patterns may be rejected and with them much else that the school has to offer; secondly if this danger of alienation is avoided and if the child identifies closely with the school and its values system, he may become

238

increasingly isolated from the family structure and the support it can offer, while the school can offer no alternative. A situation which is particularly distressing when sixteen year olds leave the security of residential schools and no strong framework of support can be provided for them.

One tension which was frequently expressed is that between the reality of the world and the protection of the school. For many pupils social reality was distressing and, though teachers generally seemed to agree that the security and caring provided in school, as in good homes, would provide a self-confidence which would help the child to cope, they could not be entirely confident that their pupils were adequately prepared. When the jobs many of the pupils might take up were considered, based on past experience, the desperate joke was made that entirely different training should be provided so that the children could be winners in the society they were going to enter.

The teachers reported that many of their children had no sense of fair play, that they were extremely selfish and that one fundamental task in their schools was to provide a firm structure where certain expectations were made clear. Most schools found that their pupils enjoyed the structure which was provided and were obedient and generally happy when the teacher made all the decisions and were at least slightly hesitant about suggestions that children might become more responsible for themselves; in much of their work the teacher needed to draw out conclusions for them and to control their learning. In terms of learning from the context of the community which is discussed in Chapter 5, residential schools have one major advantage, it is possible to create a consistent caring community. Consistent in agreed intentions at least, and involving the child care staff as well as the teachers. They did feel nevertheless that they had one problem relating to this work. Most social difficulties occurred at weekends and during holidays and the school could not respond immediately to the situation, there was not a fresh tide of outside experience such as would be found in a day school. The materials produced by the Project provided, through stories, trigger situations and photographs, the opportunity to raise issues which had lost their immediacy and this was welcomed by the school. This point of view seemed to reflect a strong optimism, not shared by all the group, about the daily life of the school as a community, and teachers from another residential school went on to discuss the forms of punishment and rewards which they used. They felt hesitant about imposing very strict rules, for many of their pupils had not encountered consistent rules and the idea of 'ought' before, and for the most part used a system of withdrawal of privilege, within a rich atmosphere full of 'carrots'. Two major points emerged, that the punishment had to be within a relationship and the child should always know why; it should always be, 'I don't like what you did' not 'I don't like you.' Even so there was still some unease about depriving a deprived child, and most agreed that a positive system of rewards and encouragement was much preferred.

When it came to working with the materials this same issue of teacher dominance came out again and it seemed to be a common experience of the group that it took several months before children and teachers became used to new ways of working, during which time the structure of control needed to be maintained. With many educationally sub-normal pupils the pattern of telling continued but it was found that if sufficient time was taken children would come out with their own ideas, even though it took a great deal of prompting from the teacher. It was clear to the group that it was important to understand as far as possible the pupils' patterns of thinking and also their social experience when carrying out this work. One teacher reported that the work made very clear the gap between his middle-class morality and that of the children, and he came to the conclusion that 'as a teacher I should not impose my values unquestioningly upon the child'. The word unquestioningly is central here, for in so much of the work, especially with the younger ones or those who are developing slowly, the teacher has to make choices and provide a framework, as shown in Chapter 1. It was not always easy to be so understanding: one case was cited where the child might appear at first sight, to the teacher, to have an unsympathetic home background, particularly as this was the view of the child who felt rejected, but the father was trying valiantly to cope, mum had disappeared after a period of almost constant rowing, there was often no-one in charge at home and dad was working so hard that he was frequently too worn out to listen.

If the social situations raised by working with the Project's materials are home-based the teachers had to tread very carefully for if they seemed to be making moral judgements about the family then the children would react by being angry or disturbed.

Often the difficulty did not lie in getting the children to talk about their social experiences, but to differentiate between fantasy and reality, and how to cope with the difference. Most agreed that the situation needed careful handling as the fantasy was important to the child as a defence. Discussion could become intensely personal and then the Project's materials became a safety valve, providing a relief route through a third-person situation. It was important too to be sympathetic, as already mentioned, to the domestic circumstances, and support the child and the family. A teacher from a residential school cited the situation of a child who proclaims, 'My Dad always writes to me', when he does not, and the careful support required rather than the intrusion of a harsh truth.

Pupils labelled maladjusted were not necessarily lacking in intellectual ability and had flashes of insight. These bright children could notice very quickly if it seemed that they were being 'got at' and the Project's non-manipulative approach was particularly valued. Again the third-person context of the material was helpful as a structure, because one way of approach through other children's problems was possible, even if the insights and experiences which make a discussion or simulation possible are personal.

In working with the Project's pupil materials one of the first concerns was accessibility and this focused on the written language. Fortunately a large part of the programme is visual rather than verbal, particularly *Photoplay* and *Setting the scene*. In the other Units the language has been deliberately kept as simple as possible; although some criticism was made of the wording of some of the suggested activities and stories in the earliest version of *Choosing*, it seemed to be within the comprehension of the majority of the children. Furthermore one of the major benefits would seem to have been within the area of language development as well as the ability to appreciate other people's problems and points of view, and to respond to these more considerately. Many of the children in

241

these schools were not able to handle abstract thought and their teachers reported that relationships were immediate and not subject to reflection and interpretation. Another important intellectual process which seemed to be developing only slowly was consequential thinking – the ability to think in terms of cause and effect. This group generally agreed that, in terms of freedom of choice and the organisation of their own courses of action, for many educationally sub-normal pupils this would not take place to any significant extent during their period at school, though the process would continue after the age of sixteen though it was one of the goals towards which they were working with all their pupils. This would not prevent the formation of loving relationships and caring behaviour; children could take direct pleasure in their friendships and even the most linguistically retarded, who would find it very difficult to explain and discuss their behaviour, would comfort a friend in trouble, for example would help to pick up a friend who had fallen over. Much learning will take place directly by modelling, imitation and social diffusion. What seems to be important is the need to support and reward such behaviour even though it might lead to inconvenience, as in the case of lost property. One child had found some money, a £1 note; the teacher praised the child, who became a focus for attention for his honesty, the class was told how the money was handed in at the police station, and the point seemed to have been well made. The children seemed to be handing in stray coins almost continuously for days afterwards, and all of them expected the same degree of attention.

One point which was much appreciated was that much of the material is a resource which can be used in a variety of ways and is not obviously age related. It does not seem to be infantile, as, because of their reading difficulties, much of what they can read is not in line with their social interests and experiences. As the programme is open-ended it was possible to feed in situations which are relevant to the pupils and in a residential school this included situations derived from within the school. The directness of approach of the written materials, and their having been derived from children, greatly increased the motivation of the pupils, providing the hook of experience which is vital to gain the children's interest, the correspondence with their own experience. Some teachers felt that the language used in early versions of *Choosing*, particularly in the suggested activities, was rather too subtle, but these parts were rewritten with this criticism in mind.

Throughout the whole of this work two issues were returned to again and again: one was the importance of the professional skills, the personality and the ability to form relationships; the second was the problem of honesty about behaviour in the classroom activities because without an honest starting point, progress will be formalised and hypothetical. Groups of pupils often revealed that they knew what the 'correct' or 'desired' responses were and they found it difficult to forget the teacher's presence as an authority figure. As an example, one group was working from the starting point, 'John was playing with my car and broke it', they acted a play showing considerable understanding and forgiveness, hoping that the teacher would be impressed, and it took quite a long time before one boy ventured to say that really he would 'kick his teeth in' and then the whole group joined in vigorously to discuss this reaction.

Those teachers who had begun the work in the belief that moral education would proceed by drawing out generalised moral conclusions, or principles, found that it was not very successful. This was largely because that type of reasoning was beyond the intellectual and linguistic capabilities of their pupils and the discussion was teacher dominated, and also because they came to realise that considerate behaviour was not necessarily produced through reasoning.

Most of the teachers felt that even though their classes were not large, groups of more than ten made progress very difficult as the children competed for attention. If the class was broken down into smaller groups it required very careful regulation and preferably some assistance though some teachers found that occasionally pupils could function quite well as group leaders, though in discussion activities a teacher was usually required, to be able to draw out comments, respond to pupil contributions and redirect attention. One of the original trial materials included slides, and it was reported that in the slightly darkened room that these required, some children felt bolder and were more prepared to contribute.

Most activities based on this material lasted successfully for between thirty and forty-five minutes, though slightly longer when drama was involved.

Before looking in more detail at work using specific parts of the programme and specific techniques, it might be worth summarising the benefits reported by this working group.

1 The development of greater insight into their own and other people's social needs.

2 A growing awareness of 'structure' in society and some of the reasons for it.

3 The development of the skills and abilities required to participate in a wider social life, especially language skills and the interpretation of non-verbal ones.

4 A growing self-confidence and improved self-image based on knowledge of how to deal with social demands and cope with new situations.

Photoplay

This unit proved to be very useful. It generated a great deal of discussion and producing an alternative system of labels provided a lot of activity. As a measure of the vitality of discussion and developing insight one teacher reported that his class provided twenty different interpretations of one of the relationships posters. There was always a lot of discussion over mood interpretation: in one case half the class decided that the person was happy and half that he was angry. This was not seen as a disadvantage and the children's interpretation ability definitely improved. One issue it raised was the role of the teacher as a transmission agent; one teacher reported, 'I did find it difficult to convince them that I didn't know the right answers all the time.'

Many pupils found that work with the 'body' pictures was the most difficult as they needed to develop a vocabulary to cope with what they wanted to say and this was in itself beneficial.

In one school it was decided to extend the work with the *Photoplay* Unit by taking pictures of the children in class in various moods. This worked well but the teacher reported that, 'At first I thought that this would be more useful than pictures of strangers but in fact I used both quite successfully and I have continued to use the *Photoplay* pictures because of the range provided.'

Setting the scene

This approach was particularly welcomed where children had severe communication difficulties for it provided a manipulative activity where social relationships and events could be handled in concrete form. It provided a focus for talk.

It could be used to raise and handle any issues of current importance to the class, and in one school it was used to explore the next day's major event, BCG injections. The situation was set up on the board and children talked through a series of reactions using the small figures as a safe context for something about which they were rather apprehensive.

Many of the children in these schools found it difficult to understand the web of their relationships, and one teacher developed an approach in which children were invited to set up a family and include themselves and then to add the other people who were important to them. All the time the children talked spontaneously about these people and their view of the world came through clearly. This teacher concluded, 'I was extremely impressed with the results and would recommend this use to anyone who has counselling situations with children.' In one case it showed that, since his parents had parted, a very disturbed boy was having difficulty in coping with two homes; what was revealed was the child's version, not mum's or the social workers. This information could then be fed into the record cards.

Choosing

In most cases the stories were read to the children rather than being given out. The greatest response came when the stories were closest to actual experience. The range of the stories has been increased since the earliest trials with this group but one teacher made the point that these children are usually emotionally and culturally deprived and the pattern of this material provides opportunities for developing and exploring a wide range of social interactions.

As a general comment the children seemed to find this work exciting and interesting. This was thought to be in part because it related to their own lives and experiences and it is as well to bear in mind one of the conclusions of the group that if the work were to be confined to the content of the materials provided then the work would lose much of its appeal and its usefulness, it would become mechanical and formal, no more than a series of intellectual puzzles. Two of the techniques used to follow the pattern of the children's interests were discussion and drama.

There was general agreement that discussion approaches needed to be built up over quite a long period of time, so that class became used to this way of working. Usually the work proceeded best when the group size was not more than ten. It took a long time to develop the open and accepting atmosphere in which children felt free to contribute and the best groups were those which provided a feeling of belonging. Apart from the moral or social learning which was involved, the stimulation of language development with educationally sub-normal pupils was excellent.

Drama work is also closely related to the development of oracy but in addition there is the difficulty of social organisation, as most drama work requires collaboration between pupils. In some cases groups which had been together for a considerable time could not work cohesively and it required perseverance on the part of the teacher, though this was well rewarded. It helped particularly when another adult could assist and in some cases the teacher and a helper joined in the improvisation to control and prompt the other players. In one school a group of maladjusted boys used drama extensively to explore both their relationships with authority figures, in particular the police, and their personal experiences. One difficulty that some teachers found was that there could be frequent shifts in the focus of the children's attention and the theme of the improvisation could change very rapidly.

The period of the trial working was thought to be too short to produce positive changes in behaviour and the development of a more considerate life-style but the conclusion was that this was a valuable activity which was of direct relevance to the work of these special schools.

Appendix K

Publication and the future

The programme outlined in this book was published in the spring of 1978.

David Ingram has been funded by the Schools Council to direct the dissemination of the Project from September 1976 to August 1978, He is at present (1978) at:

Hughes Hall,
Cambridge CB1 2EW.
and his phone number is:

Cambridge (0223) 57492.

We are delighted that his continuing support is being provided and hope that the influence of the work will go on growing. It would be impossible to list here the implications of that work, but, for example, they include new evolving approaches in international education, race relations work, political education and health education.

It is our hope that future initial and in-service teacher education will be based increasingly on, and designed to meet, the needs of children, young people, parents and teachers, and will reject a limited, sterile professionalism devoted exclusively to intellectual attainment and subject teaching.